Rethinking Multilevel Governance

RETHINKING POLITICAL SCIENCE AND INTERNATIONAL STUDIES

This series is a forum for innovative scholarly writing from across all substantive fields of political science and international studies. The series aims to enrich the study of these fields by promoting a cutting-edge approach to thought and analysis. Academic scrutiny and challenge is an essential component in the development of political science and international studies as fields of study, and the act of re-thinking and re-examining principles and precepts that may have been long-held is imperative.

Rethinking Political Science and International Studies showcases authored books that address the field from a new angle, expose the weaknesses of existing concepts and arguments, or 're-frame' the topic in some way. This might be through the introduction of radical ideas, through the integration of perspectives from other fields or even disciplines, through challenging existing paradigms, or simply through a level of analysis that elevates or sharpens our understanding of a subject.

For a full list of Edward Elgar published titles, including the titles in this series, visit our website at www.e-elgar.com.

Rethinking Multilevel Governance

Arthur Benz

Professor Emeritus of Comparative Politics and German Government, Institute for Political Science, Technical University of Darmstadt, Germany

RETHINKING POLITICAL SCIENCE AND
INTERNATIONAL STUDIES

EE Edward **Elgar**
PUBLISHING

Cheltenham, UK • Northampton, MA, USA

Cover image: Bernd Dittrich on Unsplash

Published by
Edward Elgar Publishing Limited
The Lypiatts
15 Lansdown Road
Cheltenham
Glos GL50 2JA
UK

Edward Elgar Publishing, Inc.
William Pratt House
9 Dewey Court
Northampton
Massachusetts 01060
USA

A catalogue record for this book
is available from the British Library

Library of Congress Control Number: 2024939197

This book is available electronically in the **Elgar**online
Political Science and Public Policy subject collection
http://dx.doi.org/10.4337/9781035306299

ISBN 978 1 0353 0628 2 (cased)
ISBN 978 1 0353 0629 9 (eBook)

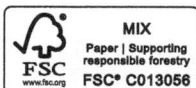

MIX
Paper | Supporting
responsible forestry
FSC
www.fsc.org   FSC® C013056

Printed and bound in Great Britain by
TJ Books Limited, Padstow, Cornwall

Contents

Preface

When working on this book, I was aware of standing on the "shoulders of giants" in political science. In rethinking multilevel governance, I reread ground-breaking books and articles that advanced research and theories. The necessary brushing up of my knowledge was an inspiring intellectual pleasure. The more I delved into the broad literature, the more I also realised how many scholars these eminent works have influenced and attracted to research on multilevel governance. A growing community of political scientists have contributed with qualitative and quantitative studies to empirical research, clarified concepts and extended the research field by including local governments, looking beyond Europe, applying the concept to federalism studies or focusing on private governance and the role of private actors. Quite a few among them introduced different analytical or normative perspectives on multilevel governance.

In this broad research field, this book also reflects a specific perspective. It might appear as government-centred, reduced to two levels, underestimating private actors and neglecting function-specific types of governance. Yet my intention was not to narrow the concept to these aspects. I have tried to explain my understanding of multilevel governance and why I focused on specific aspects. If my perspective appears government-centred, this has to do with the institutionalist approach and the fact that governments hold the power to make binding decisions and that the accountability of governmental actors to citizens legitimizes their power within a territorial jurisdiction. My concept of governance points to an actor-centred institutionalism and includes non-governmental actors. Emphasising economic disparities and identity politics as fundamental challenges of multilevel governance requires looking at the territorial structuring of these conflicts, but these topics open the perspective to society-centred approaches. I consider contemporary political polarization, divides and power asymmetries between parties, distinct communities and governments as the main reasons for rethinking multilevel governance, though I am aware of the historical evolution of these conditions.

My work on multilevel governance in general and this book in particular was inspired by many colleagues. My "governance turn" developed in cooperation with Roland Czada, Susanne Lütz, Georg Simonis and Uwe Schimank. Gerda Falkner, Adrienne Héritier, Liesbet Hooghe, Gary Marks, Renate Mayntz, Fritz W. Scharpf and Michael Zürn mostly influenced my thinking about multilevel governance, in different ways and on different occasions. My work on this book builds on rewarding cooperation with Jörg Broschek, Markus Lederer and Jared Sonnicksen in joint projects. Fritz W. Scharpf, Jared Sonnicksen and Klaus Dieter Wolf read drafts of chapters, and their comments helped me to clarify my arguments.

Finally, I thank Harry Fabian and the editorial team of Edward Elgar Publishing for their excellent support and enjoyable cooperation.

1. Introduction: reasons for rethinking multilevel governance

Considering the turbulence in politics and societies we have experienced during the last few years, there is obviously a lot to rethink for social scientists. However, is this the right time to rethink multilevel governance? When this concept surfaced in the literature on European integration about thirty years ago (Marks 1993) and later travelled to research on international relations and regionalization of unitary or federal states, it indicated a transformation of the state. It claimed that a state-centric view on politics was no longer appropriate since the state had lost its exclusive control over policies and policymaking (Hooghe and Marks 2001: 6–8). With multilevel governance, scholars drew attention to the dispersion of authority from national to regional or local governments and international organizations or supranational confederations of states. The concept has instigated research on the evolving division of power, policy coordination across levels and the restructuring of politics. These changes in polities, policymaking and politics responded to an increasing diversity and interdependence of societies, economies and governance in states. Economic crises, social inequality, poverty, pandemics or climate change revealed the challenge of complexity. They emerged in local contexts but have global effects, and their consequences at the global level have repercussions on local economies and societies. Multilevel governance aims to cope with this complexity.

Over the last years, however, refugee flows and immigration, which relate more to a persistent dependence of southern on northern countries rather than an interdependence between them, demonstrated that states have not lost the power to control their borders. After the outbreak of the COVID-19 pandemic, governments intensified border controls and temporarily closed borders. Brexit and secession movements within states have shown efforts to separate governing powers rather than to share and coordinate political authority. At the global level, endeavours to coordinate policies to prevent global warming continue, but at the same time so-called "systemic rivalry" between the US, China and Russia evolved, while "emergent powers" like Brazil, India, and Turkey increasingly contest the hegemony of the three "superpowers".

When Russia started the war in Ukraine on 24 February 2022, efforts to mitigate enduring and complicated conflicts resulting from the dissolution of the Soviet Union came to an end. All parties seemed to ignore the multilevel character of the conflict and instead played a power game between states and antagonist alliances of states. The compromise negotiated in the so-called Minsk format is now declared a failure. Nationalism has superseded the idea of a regionalization of Ukraine. Instead of developing an intermediary position, the country became the site of a confrontation between Russia and NATO. The interdependence of economies and trade relations between Russia and the EU suddenly appeared as dependence. Against the background of the war in Ukraine, the systemic rivalry between China and the US turned into a confrontation backed up by military posturing and in some cases overt threats. Antagonistic alliances of states more and more obstruct global cooperation among governments. Political power has shifted back to states. At the same time, the EU and NATO have gained collective power which is concentrated in the executive in response to exceptional challenges (Laffan 2023; Seybert and Katzenstein 2018; White 2019). Claiming to manage crises, central governments have extended their power against regional and local governments within states. In brief: Politics within and beyond states tends towards a separation of power instead of integration, autonomy instead of coordinated action, concentration instead of a division of power, and confrontation instead of cooperation.

Nonetheless, multilevel governance has not become irrelevant. Still, governments of states – local, regional as well as central – are confronted with the fact that jurisdictions are often incongruent with the scope of problems to be solved and tasks to be fulfilled. They are facing complex matters, caused by the diversity and interdependence of economies, societies and environments of territories, positive and negative effects of trans-border mobility of people, trade and communication, and changes in the global, regional and local natural environment and climate. All these challenges require coordinated action of local, regional and national governments as well as international authorities and private actors. Hence, recent developments have not at all reduced the need for multilevel governance, quite the contrary.

The multiple crises and changes in society and politics have not escaped the attention of scholars working on multilevel governance. On the one hand, they have drawn attention to the contestation of the multilevel international political order (Zürn 2018), to new territorial cleavages in national societies and the restructuring of party systems (Kriesi et al. 2006), to polarization in politics and societies (Pontusson and Rueda 2008; Somer and McCoy 2018; Winkler 2019) and to a legitimacy crisis in multilevel governance, for instance in the European Union (Scharpf 2009; Schmidt 2020) or in the divided US federation (Kettl 2020). On the other hand, research on the management of the fiscal crisis (Braun, Ruiz-Palermo and Schnabel 2017), the pandemic (Allain-Dupré et al. 2021; Vampa 2021) or the energy transition to renewable sources (Deters

2018; Balthasar, Schreurs and Varone 2020) has revealed positive effects but also various deficits of multilevel policy coordination. Nevertheless, there are still reasons to conclude that a concentration of power in a central government does not have any significant benefits compared to a division of power and coordination in multilevel systems. The latter provides better conditions for managing complex tasks, for adjusting structures in times of turbulence, for policy learning (Benz 2021) and resilience (VanNijnhatten 2021) than central-ized governments and uniform governance.

Yet the economic, societal and political conditions for policy coordination across levels have significantly changed. After the period of economic growth and stability which began in the 1990s had come to an end, social inequality fuelled the rise of nationalist parties and politics. Distributive conflicts among states pursuing their selfish interests undermine multilateral regulation of global markets. They have slowed down global cooperation and local imple-mentation of climate policy and energy transition. Digital media of communi-cation have proved to be more of a source of risks and divides than a means to promote knowledge transfer or dialogues among citizens and political actors from different countries. Instead of strengthening civil society within and across states, the Internet has turned into a tool of guidance and control. It is abused by populist and autocratic governments, which are challenging complex governance. Finally, failed revolts of citizens against autocratic rulers and military conflicts dashed the hope of a diffusion of liberalization and democracy to all parts of the world. Perceiving growing security risks, consolidated Western democratic governments have significantly increased their investment in defence, with unpredictable consequences for economic stability, social welfare and sustainability of democracy.

In response to these changes, recent research on national and supranational governance has focused on the complexity of governance systems, crisis man-agement and turbulence. Scholars have called for flexibility, adaptation and political leadership in governance within and beyond states (Ansell, Trondal and Øgård 2017; Bednar and Page 2016; Seybert and Katzenstein 2018). Yet recent or imminent economic, social and ecological crises and political con-flicts or instability have not only increased complexity and turbulence but have also laid bare disparities of resources and wealth among territories, diversity within societies and nations, and asymmetric power relations between govern-ments at the different levels. Hence, complexity has increased diversity while at the same time entailing deep-rooted divides. These divides obstruct crisis management which would require collaboration. Turbulence reduces political control due to uncertainty and pressure of time, but also comes with vicious cycles of self-reinforcing confrontation in politics and societies. What is perceived as interdependence between societies, economies and governments now often appears as imbalance or dependence. In brief: crises, turbulence and complexity have exposed inequality, divides and asymmetries in politics and policymaking linking local, regional, national and transnational levels.

These developments warrant shifting the focus of research and the analytical perspective on multilevel governance. In addition, the advancement in research inspired by the concept and the diffusion of the concept to different research fields calls for reviewing the definition and the analytical framing of multilevel governance. Evidently, there are reasons for rethinking multilevel governance, some of them concerning the concept, others the focus of empirical research.

REASONS FOR RETHINKING MULTILEVEL GOVERNANCE

The conceptualization of multilevel governance that Liesbet Hooghe and Gary Marks suggested (Hooghe and Marks 2001: 3) was undoubtedly a "breakthrough in political science" (Jeffery and Peterson 2020). Initially focused on European integration, it has inspired research on international politics, federalism, regionalization and public administration in political science, international law and economics. This research has analysed the shifts of authority and power from the state to supranational federations or associations of states (especially to the EU) and international organizations on the one hand, and to regional and local governments on the other hand. Inspired by studies on policymaking in federal systems and the EU (Scharpf 1988), political scientists discovered, compared and evaluated different modes of inter-jurisdictional and multilevel coordination among governments. The division of authority in multilevel polities has raised questions about the demarcation or sharing of responsibilities or the distribution of fiscal resources among levels of government and territories, as well as about the protection of spheres of authority against interference and authority migration. In addition, related changes in party systems, electoral behaviour, interest organizations and civil society gained attention in research. From a normative perspective, scholars also addressed the consequences of divided authority and conditions for effective and legitimate governance (for overviews see Bache and Flinders 2015; Benz, Broschek and Lederer 2021; Enderlein, Wälti and Zürn 2010).

Given the many aspects and varieties of multilevel governance, there is certainly a need for further research. A future research agenda would cover several topics and questions which have not been answered as yet, like the effects of digitalization, polarization, disintegration and redistributive conflicts on various forms of multilevel governance (Benz, Broschek and Lederer 2021). Nonetheless, the outcome of three decades of research is impressive, as the available data sets, case studies and advanced explanations about the causes and effects of multilevel governance reveal. Theoretical approaches like postfunctionalism (Hooghe and Marks 2009, 2016, 2020), actor-centred politics (Marks 1996), actor-centred institutionalism (Scharpf 1997, 2006) and concepts like rescaling (Brenner 2004; Keating 2013), network governance (Marcussen and Torfing 2007; Jordan and Schout 2006; Provan and Kenis 2008), political mobilization (Marks 1993) and decision traps (Scharpf 1988; Falkner 2011) have proved useful to structure research, formulate hypotheses and understand the evolution and operation of multilevel governance. They provide valuable frameworks for comparative research.

Despite these advancements in data collection, empirical analyses of structures, processes and outcomes and theorizing on multilevel governance, at least four reasons call for reviewing the concept and the approaches that are applied to analyse and compare cases or to explain their evolution, change and consequences for politics and policymaking: in brief, for rethinking multilevel governance.

First, there is still no agreement on the definition of multilevel governance. Scholars have not yet come to a common understanding of what they mean by "governance", "levels" or "multiple" when they address the "dispersion of authorities across scales" and the "coordination of jurisdictions at diverse scales" (Hooghe and Marks 2021: 19).

–   In mainstream research on multilevel governance, "governance" refers to the distribution of authority between different jurisdictions and the coordination of policies in executing divided authority. However, the interplay between policy coordination and changes in the division of authority remains to be clarified. In addition, scholars have emphasized that governance includes private actors or can even imply that private actors govern. Yet, the distinction between intergovernmental, public-private and private governance can conceal the complex relationship between governmental and non-governmental actors, not only concerning their authority or legitimacy to make policies but also the structures and interactions linking these actors. The concept of governance captures this complexity. Accordingly, the diverse institutional conditions of governments also deserve more attention in theory and empirical research.

–   The term "level" denotes a set of jurisdictions dividing larger (upper-tier) or encompassing smaller (lower-tier) jurisdictions. They can be demarcated according to territorial or functional criteria. In the first case, territorial boundaries are given and authority for a task is assigned to those jurisdictions which, according to their size, provide better conditions for fulfilling the task than smaller or larger territories. In the second case, the territory is adjusted to the scope of a particular task. In consequence, authorities in territorial jurisdictions fulfil multiple tasks, whereas those in functional jurisdictions are limited to single tasks. Accordingly, Liesbet Hooghe and Gary Marks distinguished two types of multilevel governance

(Hooghe and Marks 2003). However, territorial boundaries demarcate both kinds of jurisdictions. Functional jurisdictions are regularly embedded in territorially organized governments, and policies coordinated across levels of government concern special tasks. Yet, boundaries alone cannot characterize levels; they also constitute the institutional setting of governance and spatial conditions of economy and society.

–   "Multiple" indicates the number of levels, but scholars rarely specify whether this means more than one, several or many. Applied to European integration, multilevel implies that authority has shifted from the state to European institutions and, simultaneously, to regional or local governments. Thus, three levels seem to be covered by the concept. Yet studies on coordination in multilevel governance often focus on two levels, for the plausible reason that coordinated decisions or actions result from negotiations among representatives of upper- and lower-tier governments, while actors from third levels may participate in some way or another, but usually remain in the background. Therefore, the number of levels seems to depend on the roles and the responsibilities by which actors from different levels contribute to multilevel governance.

Second, given the many structures of governance spanning across jurisdictions and the different and changing conditions which impact the dispersal of authority and coordination of policies, theories and analytical concepts need to capture the variety and dynamics of multilevel governance. In consequence, scholars have introduced new approaches or have advanced their previous approaches. This demonstrates the relevance and theoretical substance of the concept (Piattoni 2010). However, it has also become fuzzier with the extension of the research field (Papadopoulos, Tortola and Geyer 2024; Stephenson 2013). Comparative research would significantly benefit from a typology of distinct patterns of multilevel governance. For instance, it makes a difference whether multilevel governance operates in the shadow of hierarchy of a unitary state or in federations or intergovernmental organizations, where the central authority is limited or non-existent. Besides, the variety of governments is usually low in multilevel governance within unitary states, whereas democratic and autocratic regimes have co-existed in emergent federal democracies (Gibson 2012), and such mixed configurations are more prevalent in instances of multilevel governance beyond the state.

Third, multilevel governance does not only deal with complex problems and tasks, it institutionalizes complexity. Beyond the division of power between levels, authority is divided between institutions and actors involved in policymaking within the different jurisdictions. As a rule, political leaders or heads of departments regularly represent governments or international organizations in multilevel governance, but they are supported by civil servants in public administration who interact in formalized committees, networks or issue-specific communication. Nongovernmental actors can be involved in different ways in policy coordination across levels. Like parliaments and parties, private interest organizations or corporations regularly address political or administrative actors of governments or international organizations. They may also participate in arenas of multilevel policymaking where, however, executives from governments or international organizations dominate.

The differentiation of institutions and actor constellations within and between levels significantly affects the effectiveness and legitimacy of multilevel governance. Deadlocks among political executives can often be dissolved by shifting policymaking to specialists in administration or by including private actors who are neither aligned to individual governments nor committed to parliaments or parties. Given their specialized responsibility, civil servants have limited power, which they can only extend by shifting policymaking back to political actors, but they provide the view of experts on problems and potential solutions. Institutional differentiation is also an important factor in dividing authority in multilevel governance. Although it aims at effectively coping with complex problems and collective action dilemmas in societies, it results in power structures which are always contested among political actors. Therefore, the division of authority needs to be protected by institutional safeguards (Bednar 2009; Filippov, Ordeshook and Shvetsova 2004; Thorlakson 2006). Parliaments, parties and civil society organizations which are not directly involved in multilevel policymaking can respond to a perceived imbalance of power and initiate processes to restore a balance.

Analytical concepts and theories need to reduce the complexity of reality. This certainly also applies to studies on multilevel governance. However, concepts should not mask the differentiation and dynamics of institutions and actor constellations which have essentially affected how multilevel governance evolves and operates.

Fourth, apart from these conceptual issues, recent crises and changes in international and national politics call for rethinking multilevel governance. They suggest considering the economic, social and institutional foundations of multilevel governance in empirical research. Observed shifts of authority to supranational federations or international organizations or to regions and cities and permanent conflicts over power demonstrate the dynamics of multilevel governance. However, they also reveal disparities and divides among jurisdictions and communities as well as asymmetries in authority patterns and effective power structures. During recent crises, economic disparities, social conflicts and institutional asymmetries have caused political polarization, contestation of patterns of authority or imbalances of power, and have sometimes set off turbulent developments.

All multilevel governance systems include diverse territories and communities, and most of them also reveal a more or less differentiated assignment of authorities to jurisdictions or various patterns of coordination. These constitutional designs and practices can compensate for economic imbalances and the distinctness of communities to a certain extent. The fact that "asymmetric decentralization" and "differentiated integration" have become widely used practices in national and supranational federations indicates the challenge caused by economic and societal conditions. Comparative studies on federations have described "constitutional asymmetry" (Popelier and Sahadžić 2019b; Watts 2005), in particular as a tool to accommodate diversity in multinational federations (Agranoff 1999; Kymlicka 2005). Empirical research on the rise of regional authority (Hooghe and Marks 2016: 100–21, 2023) or decentralization (Allain-Dupré, Chatry and Moisio 2020) discovered territorial variations in self-rule and shared rule. In a broader perspective, studies on "differentiated integration" in the EU (De Vries, Leuffen and Schimmelfennig 2023; Gänzle, Leruth, and Trondal 2020b; Leuffen, Rittberger and Schimmelfennig 2013) investigated the distribution of authority, European legislation and implementation of EU law that differ between member states in specific policies. The questions of whether these institutional asymmetries and differentiated patterns of governance can compensate for socio-economic disparities or whether they attenuate or intensify conflicts between distinct societies, deserve more attention in research on multilevel governance (Allain-Dupré 2020). Besides looking at institutions, participating actors and policy output, research has to consider the historical roots of economic and social diversity and the long-term consequences for multilevel governance. Distinct societies can be traced back to periods of nation-building. Fiscal capacities of governments changed with the transformations of spatial economies. A differentiated division of authority can fuel identity politics or distributive conflicts between governments and turn into asymmetric power structures. As short-term responses to political conflicts and policy deadlocks in times of crisis, it may have problematic effects if it entrenches disparities and divides in structures of multilevel governance. The flexibility of structures and processes of multilevel governance can elicit a vicious cycle of differentiation ending in disintegration.

Therefore, the tendency towards asymmetries in multilevel governance sheds new light on widely discussed questions: How can conflicts on the distribution of resources be solved and how can diverse communities be accommodated in multilevel governance? How can power and policy be legitimized in multilevel political systems under the condition of territorial diversity? And how can these systems be stabilized given the continuous contestation of authority and power? Justice, democratic legitimacy and balancing power in multilevel governance seem all the more essential under the conditions of economic disparities, societal diversity and institutional asymmetry.

These lines of rethinking suggest a reformulation of the concept of multi-level governance as an analytical framework which allows us to better consider the changes of the last decades. Moreover, they imply a critical perspective on current trends in national and international politics like the resurgence of nationalism, centralization and power concentration in politics, or the rise of populist revisions of democracy. These developments undermine efforts to cope with complex problems and obstruct coordination across the boundaries of political jurisdictions. Multilevel governance is polycentric, it is a complex system of governance providing necessary, though not sufficient conditions for dealing with complex problems of contemporary societies. If multilevel governance were in fact in decline in political practice, scholars would have every reason to argue against this trend.

PLAN OF THE BOOK

Against the background outlined above, this book contributes to rethinking the concept of multilevel governance. It emphasises the need for a new research perspective in the face of recent crises, turbulence and political changes in national and international contexts. The first three chapters propose a revised conceptualization of multilevel governance, starting with the common understanding of multilevel governance as a dispersion of authority and inter-jurisdictional coordination of policies across levels. Based on this analytical framework, the following chapters address economic disparities, societal diversity and justice, and they reconsider power in multilevel policymaking and discuss how powers and policies can be legitimized in multilevel governance.

To turn the mentioned definition of multilevel governance into an elaborated concept, *Chapter 2* addresses the three questions introduced above: What does governance mean? What characterizes a level of governance? And how many levels does the word multiple indicate? The answers to these three questions pave the way for developing an analytical model of multilevel governance. It encompasses the vertical (inter-level) and horizontal (intra-level) dimensions of the division of power and coordination as well as the linkage between politics inside and across jurisdictions. This model opens a perspective on the complexity and the varieties of multilevel governance. It implies that the dispersion of authority across levels does not only follow functions or demands of communities. Rather it essentially results from politics which aims at coordinating interdependent policies and at the same time has to cope with the distribution of authority between levels and the contestation of power among actors.

Focusing on this dual character of politics, *Chapter 3* advances the conceptualization by looking at the differentiation of levels, distribution of authority and different modes of coordination in multilevel governance.

Following Hooghe and Marks (2009, 2016), the rise of multilevel governance is explained as the integration and differentiation of states. How authority is divided between levels results from joint decisions of involved governments on constitutions, treaties or other kinds of intergovernmental accords. Therefore, the "Joint-Decision Trap" model (Scharpf 1988) appropriately captures the problem of dividing authority. The distribution of authority constitutes institutional conditions for coordinating policies across levels, but it does not determine modes of coordination. This chapter outlines the variety of these modes. They provide options for responsible actors to adapt multilevel governance to changing challenges from societies and disputes over power structures. Although constitutional rules, treaties or accords are difficult to amend, power structures in multilevel governance are highly dynamic and modes of coordination flexible. Yet this dynamism bears the risk of authority migration, power imbalances and arbitrary domination of actors.

Chapter 4 addresses the complexity of multilevel governance; that is, the differentiation and interdependence of actors and arenas. Actors represent governments, international organizations and private or non-governmental organizations. Institutions and processes established within these organizations shape, though they do not entirely determine, actors' preferences, action orientations and legitimacy. As generalists, political leaders, ministers and senior executives are responsible for coordinating policies across levels while specialized civil servants and private actors influence policymaking as specialists. Within governments or organizations, political executives are subject to institutional rules, have to consider policy preferences, mandates and expectations of political parties, and are accountable to assemblies which represent members or citizens. They must harmonize commitments resulting from "domestic" and multilevel politics. Thus, coordinating policies turns into a strategic game in two arenas, in which actors try to play off internal against external obligations or constraints (Putnam 1988). The outcome of this strategic interaction in "connected games" varies according to the institutional conditions and power structures in the "domestic" arena of governance. It makes a difference whether governmental actors represent democratic or autocratic governments, whether and how they are accountable to a parliament or depend on the support of a political or private elite. Processes linking multilevel governance to domestic politics are particularly relevant in democratic governments, but they also matter, though in a different way, in autocratic governments and international organizations.

The analytical framework elaborated in Chapters 2, 3 and 4 points to a theoretical approach which combines actor-centred and institutionalist explanations. The following two chapters turn to a society-centred approach. Looking at the horizontal dimension of multilevel governance, they address the causes and the manifestation of spatial diversity of economies and societies and how diversities are framed as political issues of distributive justice and identity of communities. They further discuss whether and how multilevel governance provides appropriate conditions and procedures to deal with distributive conflicts and conflicts about the rights and recognitions of distinct communities. The answers to these questions differ when we shift the focus from the national to the international context or consider instances of multilevel governance which include nondemocratic governments.

Chapter 5 starts with the economic causes of divisions between territories in multilevel governance. In politics these matter as fiscal disparity and distributive conflicts, but they are rooted in the spatial diversity of the economy, in particular the natural resources and the long-term development of economies within a territory. They change due to the mobility of people, goods and capital and political interventions in the market. Disparity refers to the fiscal capacities of governments to fulfil the tasks which derive from the division of authority. In multilevel governance, governments can mitigate unjustified disparities either by redistributing authority or by establishing procedures of fiscal equalization. Both policies of redistribution require coordinated action among governments with contrasting preferences (Beramendi 2012). The institutional conditions for solving these conflicts are more favourable in a state than in multilevel governance beyond the state.

The natural environment and economic conditions over time shape the living conditions of communities of people concentrated in specific territories. Their distinctness reflects their history, their religion or culture. In the first place, the language in which their members communicate and how they satisfy basic needs and gain wealth in a societal and institutional context characterizes communities. In politics, distinctness is constructed through social communication but mainly expressed through identity politics. Citizens or their political leaders use it as a strategy to demand recognition of their distinctness, to claim authority and autonomy and to achieve distributive justice. Identity politics reframes distributive conflicts into value conflicts, as a matter of recognition and social justice. The diversity of societies turns into divides in multilevel politics, if distinct communities feel discriminated against, if they request special rights and powers or call for secession. *Chapter 6* elaborates on the consequences in terms of differentiated integration and asymmetric distribution of authority in multilevel political systems. Particularly, it discusses constitutional asymmetries and flexible patterns of multilevel governance as ways to meet the demands of minority communities and accommodate societal diversity. Again, the context conditions need to be taken into consideration, in particular the type of governments involved (Hooghe and Marks 2016: 142–5).

Chapters 7 and 8 reflect on the consequences of complexity, diversity and asymmetry for governing multilevel systems. *Chapter 7* considers governance as policymaking spanning across levels and jurisdictions. Given the diversity of preferences of actors involved and the complications due to intersecting conflicts, the distribution of power seems to constitute the decisive conditions determining the outcome of policymaking. While authority is dispersed between levels, power to manage complex policies by multilevel coordination emerges in transboundary relations among authorized actors. The chapter introduces three types of power that appear particularly relevant in multilevel policymaking: bargaining power, epistemic power and power of the last resort. An appropriate balance of these three types of power can prevent policy coordination from running into decision traps. Therefore, modifying power structures, for instance through changing venues, actor constellations or modes of governance, appears essential for effective policy coordination in multilevel governance.

Chapter 8 turns to a normative perspective and addresses the problem of legitimacy of governance in multilevel political systems. The starting point is the well-known dilemma of effectiveness and democratic legitimacy in power sharing and coordination (Dahl 1994; Scharpf 2000). Democracy, in the modern sense of responsible and accountable governing according to the will of people, requires a congruence of a *demos* and political authority. This principle applies to governments at different levels of a state, but it cannot apply to a coordinated use of authority across the borders of jurisdictions. However, the principle of democracy speaks for multilevel governance because it allows for representing the people who are affected by the external effects of politics reaching across jurisdictions and levels. To resolve this dilemma, the chapter explicates complementary and democracy-conforming modes of legitimizing the distinct types of power, provided that multilevel governance is embedded in democratic governments. Accountability of executives to citizens and their elected representatives within jurisdictions legitimizes their bargaining power in multilevel governance, yet under specific conditions preventing information asymmetries and avoidable deadlocks. Deliberation among a plurality of free and equal experts can legitimize epistemic power. If authorized by a constitution, treaty or accord, power of the last resort or power to manage governance processes is acceptable, if permanent efforts to prevent imbalances counter the inherent risk of power concentration.

The *Conclusion* summarizes arguments for rethinking multilevel governance. Given the increasing polarization of national and international politics and the increasing divides between communities, territories, states and macro-regions of the world, political scientists should consider the risks of decay of multilevel governance, but also the chances for resilience. If we analyse multilevel governance from different analytical perspectives applied in this book – actor-centred, institutionalist, society-centred or policy-science approaches – we find reasons why multilevel governance can fuel political polarization. However, we also can explain why and under what conditions it can work despite polarization and, by appropriately dealing with complex problems, mitigate confrontations of actors or governments. Research should address this ambivalence of multilevel governance, without claiming to solve the dilemmas causing this ambivalence. Coping with the challenges of complex governance is the task of politics. Recent changes in national and international politics demonstrate the urgent need to face these challenges. Against all odds and despite its ambivalence, only multilevel governance can prevent further polarization, confrontation and deadlocks and the foreseeable catastrophic consequences. Scholars should therefore search for ways to make multilevel governance adaptable, sustainable and resilient.

Rethinking multilevel governance is a continuous task of political scientists. Yet this book also makes the case for multilevel governance to cope with the complexity of societal and political problems. It argues against political ideologies reducing complexity like libertarianism, populism, nationalism, identitarianism or authoritarianism. Instead, it suggests dealing with the dilemmas of multilevel governance from a pragmatic perspective.

2. Understanding multilevel governance

Whenever social scientists invent a new term, they should be aware that the facts or occurrences which they intend to describe by the term, are, in most cases, not new, or are new only in a particular context or a particular aspect. When Gary Marks introduced the term multilevel governance in a study on structural policy in the European Community, he accurately characterized the unique features of this policy, in which, for the first time, regions played an active role in European governance (Marks 1993). This mobilization of regional or local actors was indeed new in European Structural Policy. However, similar patterns of politics have existed in federal and regionalized states for a long time and have been studied under the label of intergovernmental or central-local relations. If governance here means the mobilization of private actors, the term multilevel governance also pointed to a new aspect in the reformed European regional policy, but similar practices of public-private cooperation emerged, for example, in the US during the 1960s, when the federal government started programmes to alleviate poverty in cities. In Germany, federal and *Länder* executives cooperated in the joint tasks of rural and regional development policy established in 1969, and they included representatives of local governments, unions and associations of farmers or industry in informal working groups. The dispersal of authority between levels of government, which later became the focus of research, advanced in modern states no less than with European integration and the internationalization of politics. The need to coordinate policies across levels has changed governance in federations and central-local relations in unitary states since the 19th century.

The elaboration of the concept of multilevel governance was nevertheless an innovation which paved the way for a research programme and significantly advanced the theory of European integration (Jeffery and Peterson 2020). Given the manifold instances of multilevel governance, it is not surprising that the term travelled towards studies on intergovernmental relations in federations, central-local relations in unitary states, and international politics. Accordingly, Hooghe and Marks extended their research on European governance to comparative studies, in which they described and explained the increasing dispersal of authority within and beyond states and the division of power between international organizations, regional associations of states and central, regional and local levels in state governments (Hooghe, Lenz and Marks 2019; Hooghe et al. 2016). Yet once the genie had been let out of the bottle, the term multilevel governance spread from the specific case of European integration to the broad field of comparative research. Accordingly, it had to cover "a diverse set of arrangements, a panoply of systems of coordination and negotiation among formerly independent but functionally interdependent entities that stand in complex relations to one another and that, through coordination and negotiation, keep redefining these relations" (Piattoni 2010: 26). In consequence, the concept became blurred, and many publications on multilevel governance started by defining the concept on their own terms (cf., Stephenson 2013; Tortola 2017; Trein 2022).[1]

If we address multilevel governance in comparative research, the diversity of the cases requires defining the term on an abstract conceptual level. Accordingly, Hooghe and Marks have reduced the definition of multilevel governance to the "dispersion of authority across scale" (Hooghe and Marks 2021: 19) and inter-jurisdictional coordination of interdependent policies of states and within states (ibid.: 24–9). What then remains to be clarified as the core of the concept are the three parts of the term: What does governance mean? What is a level of governance? How many levels does the prefix "multi" indicate? The answer to these questions leads to a revised concept and an analytical model of multilevel governance.

GOVERNANCE

The term "governance" particularly complicates the definition of multilevel governance. As "a popular but notoriously slippery term" (Ansell and Torfing 2022: 2), it has become a topic of much dispute (Bell and Hindmoore 2009; Kooiman 2003; Pierre 2000b; Zumbansen 2012). Social scientists apply it to describe ideas, rules, norms and established practices determined to solve collective action problems. They distinguish types of governance in the economy like markets and firms, or self-governance in society like associations, networks or organizations. All these forms of governing the economy and society can reveal different, interconnected levels. The term multilevel governance, however, has been used to describe political systems which institute power to solve collective action problems through authoritative decisions. Here, the word governance stands for a more specific concept, elaborated in political science.

Political scientists for a long time considered government in a state as the institution designed to regulate societies and provide for the public good. They introduced the concept of governance when they realized that collective action problems increasingly arise beyond the state. In addition, they had to come to terms with the fact that, on the one hand, varieties of governance in economy and society contribute to fulfilling governmental functions, while, on the other hand, governments constitute and regulate markets, corporations or associations to a large extent (Stoker 1998). On this background, political scientists differentiated their terminology. The term government describes institutions of a state which authorize actors to execute power over people in a specified jurisdiction. Governing means, simply put, what a government is doing. Governance, in a general sense, is defined as a mode, method or capacity of authoritative decision-making on societal problems, public goods or the distribution of goods and values, determined to generate compliance with decisions on the part of those persons to whom they are addressed (e.g., Fukuyama 2013: 350; Rosenau 2004: 32). In contrast to government and governing, the concept includes institutionalized and informal practices of governing within or outside the institutions and boundaries of a government. Governance can work with or without government (Rosenau 2004: 40–46).

Including forms like market and private network governance confuses the concept of levels, as defined below. Markets, firms, networks and civil society can solve specific coordination problems in societies and shape the lives of people, but they primarily serve private or particular interests. These forms of governance are not designed to solve social problems in the public interest in the first place. Their capacity to contribute to social welfare largely depends on regulation and support by political authorities and public governance. Therefore, as a characteristic feature of multilevel governance, the term governance means "regulations, including policies, programs and decisions designed to remedy a public problem via a collective course of action", with the participating actors claiming "to act in the name of a collective interest or common good (Zürn, Wälti and Enderlein 2010: 2).

In this sense, governance indicates that governmental actors are authorized to make binding decisions, but non-governmental actors participate in politics in some way or another. Accordingly, some scholars have suggested explicitly differentiating between multilevel governance and intergovernmental relations (Alcantara, Broschek and Nelles 2016; Peters and Pierre 2004: 82). It is correct that intergovernmental relations may not span across a level. Hence, there are good reasons to demarcate intergovernmental relations and multilevel governance. Whether the role of non-governmental or private actors makes the difference can be disputed. In their seminal 2001 book, Hooghe and Marks did not mention private or non-governmental actors in their definition of the multilevel governance approach (Hooghe and Marks 2001: 3–4) and rarely referred to them in the book. In a recent publication, they explained: "*Governance* became a general term for the act of governing in states, among states, above states, and by non-state actors. The authority-monopolizing state, which was in any case idealized, is no longer a plausible description of the contemporary world" (Hooghe and Marks 2020: 821). Hooghe and Marks do not spell out whether non-state actors are always included and what role they play when we speak of governance instead of government. Sharpening the concept of governance, as Alcantara, Broschek and Nelles propose, to policymaking by co-decision or co-production among governmental and non-governmental actors seems to specify the definition. In fact, this definition either narrows the scope of application in empirical research or remains imprecise. Some scholars run into the first trap even when they focus on the implementation of policies as an arena of co-production (e.g., Alcantara, Broschek and Nelles 2016: 39; Bache and Flinders 2004a: 3; Piattoni 2015: 326). In other definitions, the role of non-governmental or private actors can range from influencing policy to co-decision. Bartolini, for instance, agrees that governance is "a co-production mode of decision-making among different types of actors". However, he adds that "the type of actors involved, the extent of involvement of public authorities and partners, the outcome of the production, the decision procedures, as well as the institutional context and the type and role of sanctions all vary and define different kinds of governance mode" (Bartolini 2011: 11–12).

Without neglecting the importance of non-governmental actors, governance and governing or government cannot be distinguished with regard to actor constellations alone. More important is the analytical perspective that the concept implies. Governance is a "heuristic lens through which the reality of policy governance can be reconstructed" (Capano, Howlett and Ramesh 2015: 16), a reality characterized by polycentric and dynamic structures, interactions of multiple actors and policymaking addressing complex problems and distributive conflicts. The alternative concept of government indicates an analytical perspective focusing on rules and institutions that legitimize, constitute and limit the power of actors holding political offices. It presumes either that institutions determine politics or that a government operates as an agency of the people or a state. Governance, in contrast, shifts the focus of attention towards "the structure and process of interaction among many different groups or organizations engaged in governing" (Ansell 2023: 4), with interaction, more often than not, exceeding the boundaries of institutions. In this perspective, boundaries and structures of institutions are not a given; rather they emerge and fluctuate. Actors are subject to the rules and norms recognized in institutions, but they also shape these rules and norms in their relations with other actors (Mayntz and Scharpf 1995). Power structures are not determined by institutions, they result from the combined effects of institutions, the distribution of resources and strategic interactions.

As an analytical concept, governance refers to modes and mechanisms of governing, but it does not imply a theory. Though not meant to explain, it sheds light on the causal connection between institutions, power structures, processes of interaction among actors and outcomes (Levi-Faur 2012: 8–10). Modes of governance can be characterized by particular social mechanisms and institutional arrangements, like top-down regulation in hierarchy, competition in markets or market-like contests, trust and exchange in networks, loyalty and shared norms in communities, or negotiations or discourses in organizations or inter-organizational relations. In the complex governance which evolves in multilevel settings, various modes are often combined and processes of policymaking shift between specific modes.

In multilevel governance, non-governmental actors may participate and influence policymaking, but governmental actors, in particular political executives, who are legitimized as agents, hold pivotal positions. Their power is founded on two institutional contexts. One concerns the division of authority among governments (or organizations fulfilling functions of governments, like international organizations) and procedures of coordination between governments, the other the internal structure of the government or organization for which executives act. Inside governments or international organizations, institutions and emergent norms constitute a denser set of rules binding governmental and non-governmental actors, whereas multilevel interactions are, in general, more informal. Nonetheless, the functional need to coordinate policies in multilevel governance and the dynamics of multilevel coordination can be stronger compared to institutional rules. This is the reason why governance in multilevel systems is regularly affected by tensions between institutions and functions.

LEVELS OF GOVERNANCE

In research on multilevel governance, levels signify scales of integration or decentralization of political authority. Metaphorically speaking, they all combine into a "ladder of scale" (Hooghe and Marks 2016: 12–15). The word "ladder" points to the distinction of upper or lower tiers, without implying a hierarchical order or superiority or inferiority of power. Instead, it refers to a division of authority (Peters and Pierre 2004: 79). Each level consists of spatial or territorial units. Their borders demarcate jurisdictions of governments or organizations which are authorized to make binding decisions. In political systems, jurisdictions regularly encompass a territory, a land area delineating the power to rule.[2] Other criteria for determining boundaries, such as the spatial scope of tasks or the membership of people or corporate actors may be relevant as well (Hooghe and Marks 2003), but for practical reasons, territories evolved as a basic dimension of structuring political authority and of dividing power between jurisdictions. If communities, associations or agencies fulfil specific public tasks in a single-purpose jurisdiction designed to conform to the functional space, their boundaries regularly concur with the territorial delineation of some or all lower-tier general-purpose jurisdictions.[3] The congruence of task-specific and general-purpose jurisdictions reduces coordination costs between authorities in different policy sectors.

The distinction between general-purpose and special-purpose jurisdictions and accordingly, type I and type II multilevel governance, as suggested by Hooghe and Marks, nevertheless is relevant. Both interact in existing multilevel systems. Societies are mainly differentiated into "spaces" defined by functions, interactions or affiliations and demarcated by changing borders, as will be shown in the following Chapters 5 and 6. They may link governance in territorial jurisdictions by establishing overlapping arenas of politics. However, multilevel governance in general solidifies territorialized politics within boundaries that separate authority through precisely determined, mapped and acknowledged borderlines. At least three causes explain the preponderance of territories as units constituting levels: first, the reframing of special economic diversity into disparities in politics based on data that distinguish territories (cf. Chapter 5), second, the increasing relevance of identity politics that reconstructs the diversity of societies in a political competition between governments (cf. Chapter 6); third, the fact that a territorial organization constitutes a fundamental prerequisite to legitimize government for the people and by the people and to prevent conflicts between governments (cf. Chapter 8).

And yet, the rise of multilevel governance has changed both the territorial and spatial structure of politics. Levels of governance result from processes of integration or differentiation. Integration means that existing governments or governmental organizations constitute an upper-tier political authority in a jurisdiction comprising their territory. Typical examples are the coming together of states to form a federation or a confederation or the formation of associations of central, regional or local governments within states to fulfil certain tasks in order to benefit from economies of scale. Governments of the same level often coordinate their policies in processes of cooperation, but as long as they do not institute a kind of organization to which they shift authority, they do not constitute a level of governance. A level is characterized by institutional stability and formal assignment of authority (Zürn, Wälti and Enderlein 2010: 3–4). The division of jurisdictions to differentiate governance is another process of level formation, in this case the formation of a lower tier. The evolution of federations in Belgium or Spain are cases in point, but also processes of regionalization in France and Italy or devolution in the United Kingdom. In contrast, secession or the dissolution of a state or region subdivides the territory of a level. It does not constitute a new level, although it changes the institutional conditions for the relations among governments and other actors at the level concerned. Within the context of a multilevel political system, the structure of a level can be "differentiated", when these changes of territories and power structures do not involve all territories of an existing level (cf. Chapter 6). In all these cases of level formation, authority can be assigned by constitutional law or delegated by treaties or agreements among the participating partners.

Besides the territorial dimension, the term level designates an arena of governance and the location of political authority. Within a territorial jurisdiction, a government, an executive agency, an association of governments or an international organization holds the authority to make and implement binding decisions. These governments or organizations vary in their internal division of governmental functions. As a rule, general decisions are made by an assembly representing citizens or member state governments, these decisions are prepared and implemented by executive bodies, and conflicts among actors and the interpretation of rules are settled by an independent judiciary. In policymaking, public and private actors participate in shaping the agenda of governments, drafting proposals for decision-making in an assembly or executing these decisions. In contrast, multilevel governance is mainly executive politics. As a rule, members of the political executive or civil servants act for a government or international organization, and, in general, are accountable to the political assembly. The autonomy of executives in multilevel governance however varies significantly according to the type of governance system established within a jurisdiction. It can be more or less institutionalized, that is, based on rules or personal leadership; more or less democratic, autocratic or technocratic; and more or less open to private actors or civil society organizations. These conditions of internal governance of jurisdictions significantly influence political processes in multilevel governance (cf. Chapter 4).

Governance at the different levels and jurisdictions is based on distinct institutions and territories demarcating the scope of divided authority. Multilevel governance links politics and policymaking at different levels and in different jurisdictions. It divides authority and separates jurisdictions but creates interdependence between policies made in these contexts. Therefore, the division of power through centralization or decentralization entails coordination in interactions between actors affiliated to different levels.

MULTIPLE LEVELS OF GOVERNANCE

The last question concerns the number of levels characterizing multilevel governance. As an adjective, multiple means more than one; but usually, one would expect several, which is more than two.[4] Many scholars do not care about this question. In studies on European integration, multilevel governance encompasses the European Union, member states and regions of member states (Hooghe and Marks 2001), and meanwhile, the concept also includes cities (Heinelt and Niederhafner 2008; Kern 2019). Applied to federal states, scholars may focus on the federal and "sub-federal" levels, and the latter may or may not include both the regional and local levels. Considering multilevel governance as the result of a transformation of the nation-state, Piattoni proposed that the concept indicates relations among at least three levels of government (Piattoni 2015: 326). Hooghe and Marks pointed out that the number of "type I multilevel governance" consisting of general-purpose jurisdictions is limited by the territorial organization of politics, whereas the number of task-specific jurisdictions in "type II multilevel governance" is not limited by these territorial structures (Hooghe and Marks 2003: 236). This argument should distinguish the two types of jurisdictions and does not aim at defining the concept of multilevel governance. The article further insinuates that the authors would also apply the concept to federations or central-local relations in unitary states where authority in general is divided between two tiers of territorial jurisdictions.

Obviously, the question of quantity cannot be answered without considering the roles which actors play at different levels in multilevel politics. Therefore, the specification of numbers can remain in abeyance in a definition of multilevel governance, although it is not irrelevant. In the broadest sense, which seems an appropriate point of departure for comparative research, the concept of multilevel governance covers the basic territorial levels of governance: (1) the global level, which mainly consists of the UN system with its international organizations, (2) associations or federations of states (AU, EU) or international organizations in macro-regions of the world (Council of Europe, NATO, NAFTA),[5] (3) nation-states, (4) regions within states, and (5) the local level. A territorial level consists of one or multiple territories, which, as a political concept, define the "geographical domain of a political entity" (Moore 2015: 15). In a synopsis of these levels, the "ladder of scales" (Hooghe and Marks 2016: 13–14) describes the fundamental structure of the multilevel organization of politics and the essential arenas of governance. Intermediary special-purpose jurisdictions can be considered either when describing the actor constellations of a level or as units constituting additional levels in studies on specific policies. In general, the effective political power in multilevel governance rests in the basic territorial jurisdictions. For example, local governance includes municipalities which may be divided into districts, associations of municipalities and counties, but in multilevel governance, they are all represented by selected local actors. At the regional level, administrative districts exist in addition to regional governments, and in federations, the general-purpose regional governments may institute specialized sub-units (e.g. planning regions in Germany). Nonetheless, it is representatives of "states", "provinces", "*Länder*" or "cantons" who negotiate or co-decide with federal governmental actors on the division of authority and the coordination of policies. Beyond the state, multilevel governance is more segmented and state governments hold membership in various international organizations and associations or federations in macro-regions or at the global level. Still, the distinction between macro-regions and the global level is sufficient to elucidate the territorial differentiation of multilevel governance.

And yet, even if we take the five territorial levels as the basic structure of multilevel governance, not all of them are included in policy coordination with the same competences or are affected by governance in all instances. Irrespective of how many additional levels we include in this basic scheme of multi-levels, we can conclude that governance at upper tiers interferes with lower-level governance and the other way around. In many policy fields, this interdependence reaches across all or most levels. Many national or international policies, in one way or another, have effects on politics and policies at the local level, and local or regional decisions and actions can influence the global climate, the biodiversity in a world region or national territory, or the economic development within or beyond the territory of a state, thus causing problems to be dealt with at upper tiers. However, not all levels matter for determining the division of authority or are involved in coordination, at least not in the same way, and those levels that matter in the relevant processes of multilevel governance fulfil different functions. The institutional structures or patterns of interaction established to cope with interdependence are not necessarily congruent with the scope of problems or the external effects of decisions made at a level of governance.

As a rule, authority is divided between institutions of all or many levels, and decisions or actions at all levels may influence a policy. However, modes of active policy coordination regularly involve two or three levels. For example, the formal delegation of power to the EU requires that member states, via their central governments, ratify a joint decision, and intergovernmental agreements become binding by ratification. In the federations of Germany and Belgium, regional governments participate in the ratification of EU Treaty amendments. The federal governments of these countries therefore negotiate the position of the member state in European politics with regional governments, which thus indirectly take part in EU multilevel governance. In other member states, regions or local governments can promote their interests via the Committee of the Regions. Likewise, federal and regional governments negotiate amendments to federal constitutions affecting the distribution of authority between them, irrespective of formal amendment rules. Representatives of local governments or private actors pursuing special interests participate in deliberation or engage in lobbying. Yet having no right to co-decide, these actors communicate their opinions and interests in modes of interaction, which complement but do not change the two-level structure of multilevel constitutional policy (Behnke and Benz 2020; Benz 2016). The cohesion policy of the EU includes European, national and subnational actors, but governance is focused on two levels in a sequential process. Decisions on the financial framework are negotiated among the Commission, the EP and member state governments in a two-level game. Based on the outcome of these negotiations and final legislation, the Commission decides on the allocation of funds to regions in bilateral interactions with individual states or regions. Finally, the regional administration, in cooperation with local governments and private actors, implements the measures co-financed by EU funds (Piattoni and Polverari 2016). Climate policy, in particular, exemplifies the different scopes of inter-dependence, division of authority and policy coordination. At the global level, the United Nations Climate Regime evolved as the core structure of international governance. Binding agreements are passed in conferences by official representatives of national governments, following discussions and negotiations in multiple venues in the context of the "Conferences of the Parties" (CoP) and the reports issued by the "International Panel of Climate Change". In a different setting of multilevel governance, the EU engages in climate policy through regulations and co-financing of investments. International accords and European policies need to be transposed into legislation and implemented by national, regional and local governments, which requires them to coordinate their policies in intra-state multilevel governance. Regional governments and cities have formed networks to exchange experiences, identify best practices and gain support for their policies within their government. In the implementation of goals and measures, national and sub-national governments are subject to the supervision of the CoP and the European Commission and monitored by independent research institutes (Benz 2021: 86–119).

As these examples illustrate, governance often includes most, if not all, levels from the local to the global, but in multilevel politics, authorized actors from higher or lower tiers fulfil different functions and play varying roles in the course of policymaking. Accordingly, governance is organized in distinct processes of policy coordination which never include actors from all levels, even if the agenda concerns complex global problems or a distribution or redistribution of authority, that is, in matters that affect all levels. The functions and the corresponding modes of interaction in multilevel governance can be distinguished, in line with the policy cycle. The patterns and density of interactions emerging in multilevel politics vary accordingly. In most cases, negotiations and agreements include actors from two levels, while actors from other levels participate as observers and try to influence official representatives. In implementation, governments and their administration unilaterally adjust their policy to the outcome of multilevel governance or obstruct compliance, while higher-level authorities monitor compliance, organize best practice competitions, advise actors responsible for implementation, and launch infringement procedures in cases of non-compliance. As a rule, decisions on coordinated governance in a multilevel system result from a "two-level game" (Putnam 1988) which is embedded in a wider structure of upper-tier deliberation and monitoring and lower-tier implementation. These two-level relations of coordination can bypass intermediary levels. "Bypassing the states" became a practice in the US federal system when the Johnson Administration invented "creative federalism" and directly allocated conditional grants to local governments, private businesses and non-profit organizations (Robertson 2012: 132). Likewise, the European Commission tried to bypass member state governments in the implementation of Structural Funds, though with limited success (Keating, Hooghe and Tatham 2015: 456–9). By way of "paradiplomacy", regional governments circumvent their central government in international politics (Aldecoa and Keating 1999; Tavares 2016). In city networks, local governments bypass regional and national governance to coordinate policies at the European or global level (Acuto and Rayner 2016; Kern and Bulkeley 2009).

AN ANALYTICAL MODEL OF MULTILEVEL GOVERNANCE

The review of the concept of multilevel governance leads to an analytical model. It describes a three-dimensional space of governance consisting of a set of structures and arenas, where authorized actors provide public goods and regulate societal conflicts in the public interest. In general, the term dimension "implies direction, implies measurement, implies the more or less", as Edwin A. Abbott defined in his novel "Flatland" (Abbott [1884] 2006: 8). The model of multilevel governance focuses on the direction of interactions that are more or less intense, while it does not aim at measurement. The space of governance encompasses the vertical dimension of inter-level politics, the linkages between inter-level politics and "domestic" politics inside the jurisdictions concerned, and the horizontal dimension, that is the relations of governments at the same level.

The vertical and primary arena of governance concerns the division of authority or effective power and the coordination of policies between higher and lower tiers. How authority is divided between the different levels affects the patterns of coordination. Authority sharing requires that governments or responsible actors negotiate agreements, make joint decisions on a policy and pool resources. Self-rule is based on separate responsibility which allows the authorities at the different levels to finally decide and act if they do not reach an agreement. Under these institutional conditions, multilevel coordination is achieved through voluntary cooperation, by unilateral decisions requiring governments at other levels to adjust their policies, or by mechanisms inducing mutual adjustment. Governance in the vertical dimension can incorporate all jurisdictions of a lower tier or only a selected number of them. Accordingly, higher and lower-tier authorities interact in multilateral and inclusive or bilateral and differentiated relations in multilevel governance. Patterns of interaction emerge or are designed in processes of undifferentiated or differentiated integration and decentralization respectively.

As mentioned above, governmental and non-governmental actors are involved in multilevel governance. In interactions across the boundaries of the basic territorial levels, executives of governments or international organizations take the lead as agents, but they may be supported or influenced by private actors. Representing citizens of their jurisdiction and being responsible for the public interest within their territory, governmental actors are subject to institutional rules and supervision by parliaments, parties, interest groups and courts. Institutions of their government define their authority. They also constrain their power in multilevel governance, to an extent that differs between democratic and autocratic governments (cf. Chapter 4). Non-governmental actors enjoy a comparatively greater leeway, especially if they are not accountable for outcomes of multilevel policymaking within an organization. Under these conditions, they may contribute to coordinating public policies across levels. In contrast, governmental actors have to take into account the expectations of their parliaments, parties or public opinion within their jurisdiction, and their hands are tied by institutional rules and mandates. It is the institutions and politics of a government or an international organization that first and foremost influence politics and policymaking beyond jurisdictions. This linkage of multilevel governance to systems of government constitutes a second dimension of interaction and a second arena of politics. Variations of these systems and their institutional configurations need to be taken into consideration in studying multilevel governance.

In the horizontal dimension or the relations among governments on the same level, structures are characterized by the territorial organization of the basic levels as defined above. In theory, criteria of an effective size should determine the demarcation of territories, but in practice, implementing a rational design is hardly feasible. Most borders of territorial jurisdictions developed in history as the accidental result of occupation, secession, wars or other kinds of power politics (O'Leary 2001). Territorial reorganizations determined to correct historical legacies rarely achieved the aims of planners and experts. In the jurisdictions concerned by reorganization, holders of political offices and citizens usually defended the status quo, and at least in democracies, often succeeded in preventing significant change. Where they prefer a division of territories, they make their claims for political reasons of gaining autonomy rather than for functional reasons. As a consequence, the territorial structures of the levels of states, regions and local governments are in several respects characterized by diversity and asymmetries. Jurisdictions cover areas which differ according to the natural resources and economic structures or the language, values and ways of living shared by the community of people. This heterogeneity significantly affects multilevel policymaking (Holzinger 2008: 179–88). Moreover, if a higher authority like a central state government does not harmonize the institutions of lower-tier governments, they often reveal different patterns of government and hold different sets of authority.

In the horizontal dimension, boundaries of jurisdictions on the basic levels separate authority, but do not prevent interdependence of policies. Interdependence tends to increase with the size of jurisdictions and the decentralization of authority and economic diversity, and it varies with territorial distance and the capacity of governments to control the borders of their jurisdictions. In general, interdependence induces two kinds of inter-jurisdictional relations on a level of governance. On the one hand, governments or non-governmental actors contributing to providing public goods cooperate to fulfil joint tasks, either within a special-purpose jurisdiction or informally, in order to avoid a centralization of the policy concerned. On the other hand, governments of states, regions or municipalities compete for fiscal resources, either by trying to attract mobile tax-payers and businesses or by rivalling for grants from the upper-tier government.

This analytical model of multilevel governance rests on the following premises: Boundaries of jurisdictions demarcate authority in the vertical and horizontal directions. Yet authority to make and execute binding decisions in the public interest rests in a government, where institutions divide power to fulfil governance functions and different institutional actors participate in exercising these powers. In addition to considering structures and processes dividing power and coordinating policies between levels and jurisdictions, it is essential to understand how governance inside governments is linked to multilevel governance (Putnam 1988). Linkages can be generated through formal procedures of mandating executives and scrutinizing them, strategic interactions in the two-level game, or channels of communication. Furthermore, the horizontal dimension of multilevel governance affects the division of authority and coordination across levels, depending on whether governments cooperate or compete and depending on the symmetry or asymmetry of territorial structures, institutional conditions and capacities of governments. The implications of these premises will be discussed in greater detail in the following chapters.

THEORETICAL IMPLICATIONS

The model of multilevel governance outlined in this chapter draws on various proposals to elaborate the concept for comparative research. It provides an analytical framework for structuring research, which, depending on the research question, may focus on one of the dimensions without ignoring the impact of others. Beyond that, it points out five basic theoretical premises.

First, the concept of multilevel governance links two strands of research. The first advanced research on European integration and the transformation of the state (Hooghe and Marks 2001, 2003), the second emerged in policy studies and addressed politics and policy coordination in multilevel systems, or, as Scharpf put it, "multilevel governing" (Scharpf 2001). In fact, both research perspectives overlap. The division of power and authority between levels, which transforms political structures within and beyond states, results from policies of institutional change and politics driven by the contestation of power. Processes of policy coordination between levels and jurisdictions, by which governmental and non-governmental actors respond to the growing complexity of problems, tasks and policies, implicitly or explicitly revise the division of effective power. Therefore, multilevel governance should be understood as "dual politics" of constituting and changing a division of power and coordinating decisions under the condition of divided authority. Normal and constitutional politics are not separated, as implied in Ackerman's theory of "dualist democracy" (Ackerman 1991: 3–33), they rather coincide. Multilevel policymaking on particular issues like economic regulation and development, energy transition, greenhouse gas emissions, or migration not only concerns these problems but also provokes strategic power games. As authority is divided in these policy fields, actors defend or try to extend the scope of their power during the process of policymaking. When, in institutional or constitutional policy, a renegotiation and redistribution of authority is on the agenda, actors try not only to extend or defend their power but also to change the condition for coping with substantial policies in "normal politics". Conflicts on the redistribution of authority or fiscal resources also reflect conflicts on the substance of specific policies. Therefore, the dynamics of power structures in a multilevel political system and coordination processes in this system are closely connected. Chapter 3 discusses this dual character of politics in multilevel governance in greater detail.

Second, the concept of level not only indicates territorial, general- or special-purpose jurisdictions but also arenas of governance, where governmental actors make authoritative decisions and non-governmental actors try to influence these decisions. The "domestic" governance arenas at the basic levels, their institutions and the politics within these institutions are linked with multilevel politics. The division of power, actor constellations and modes of governance within domestic arenas influence those characterizing the vertical arena of multilevel governance, where we find, for instance, relations between parliaments, political executives, civil servants and courts. However, functional requirements for multilevel policy coordination explain why executives take the lead and may establish special agencies or administrative networks for continuous interactions. Domestic governance and governance spanning across jurisdictions and levels evolve according to distinct logics. Therefore, multilevel governance describes a complex governance arrangement characterized by difference and interdependence. Composed of two types of arenas, it is shaped by inherent tensions between multilevel and domestic politics. Both are connected through communicative and strategic interactions of political leaders or executives who engage, with dual commitments and capacities, in the "connected games" (Scharpf 1991) of politics in the two arenas.

The internal institutional differentiation of domestic arenas increases the complexity of multilevel governance. Levels are divided by boundaries of jurisdictions and the division of authority. They are linked by interconnected tasks and patterns of interaction and coordination. Interactions can include different actors like political executives (heads of governments, ministers), civil servants with general or special competences, independent experts, and non-governmental actors pursuing their special interests. These actors can participate in deliberation on relevant policies, negotiations, or the conclusion of agreements, they exchange experiences, search for best practices, engage in comparative evaluation of policies and set incentives by distributing grants or monitoring policy outcomes. Depending on their role in multilevel policymaking, actors must comply with different institutional rules, face expectations in accountability relations and are influenced by political or professional action orientation. Whereas the different structures of multilevel and domestic governance cause tension, the differentiation of patterns of coordination provides favourable conditions for coping with these tensions. When processes of politics and policymaking shift between linkage structures established by political and administrative executives, generalists and specialists, or governmental and non-governmental actors, these changes in actor constellations open ways to solve conflicts or dissolve gridlock. At the same time, it drives the structural dynamics of the division of power that can lead to imbalances and instability. Chapter 4 will explain these ambivalent consequences of complexity.

Third, the horizontal dimension of multilevel governance regularly reveals manifold divides and asymmetries. Territories of jurisdictions rarely concur with distinct geographic areas, economic spaces or communities of people who share a certain identity, but this does not make a level homogeneous. The diversity of the physical environment, economic conditions or identities of communities reflect specific problems to be coped with in jurisdictions, but also specific interests that affect multilevel governance. Diversity of territories translates into conflicts of interests among actors in multilevel governance, and economic disparities and identity conflicts cause antagonist action orientations that obstruct coordinated policies. To a certain extent, differentiated integration or differentiated decentralization compensate for economic or social diversity. Such asymmetric structures of multilevel governance increase the diversity of institutions and rarely prevent individual actors involved in multilevel governance from participating with unequal governance capacities. In consequence, policy coordination across levels not only has to cope with economic disparities and demands for justice and recognition of distinct communities, but it also proceeds under the condition of asymmetric structures. Chapters 5 and 6 elaborate on these important aspects of multilevel governance.

Fourth, multilevel governance encompasses multiple levels of territorial jurisdictions and special purpose jurisdictions. In governance processes, the functions fulfilled at a level differ and they change throughout the policy process. At upper tiers of global politics and macro-regions, multilevel governance mostly focuses on regulation, standard setting and monitoring, whereas in states, it serves to coordinate public goods and services and implement regulation and standards. Accordingly, the number of relevant levels varies and is more or less limited. In general, actors from the basic territorial levels predominate the division of authority and coordination of a policy in multilevel governance while actors affiliated with special-purpose jurisdictions participate. Levels may be directly linked in governance or constitute a context for policy coordination in specific policy fields.

Considering the relevance of basic levels, we have reasons to distinguish multilevel governance within and beyond the state. A state establishes institutional conditions that do not exist in macro-regional or global international politics. This affects the distribution of authority which in a state is a matter of central legislation or constitutional amendment, whereas beyond the state, national governments decide on the delegation or pooling of power (Hooghe, Lenz and Marks 2019: 32–3). Coordination of policies across levels of a state is facilitated, but sometimes also constrained by a stable institutional framework, whereas in international multilevel governance, structures emerge more on an ad hoc basis, in reaction to specific situations or problems to be solved. The constitution of a state regulates the basic institutional features of national, regional and local governments and reduces their variety within levels. This is not the case in international multilevel governance which regularly involves democratic and autocratic governments of various kinds. The institutions of a state constitute a shadow of hierarchy for horizontal policy coordination at regional or local levels. International organizations and even macro-regional associations of states lack this power, with the exception of the EU, where it has evolved through Treaty amendments and jurisprudence of the Court of Justice of the European Union, but is still contested.

Accordingly, empirical studies mapping the division of authority and explaining the evolution of multilevel governance include basic levels of either state or macro-regional and global governance. Studies on multilevel politics and policymaking often focus on two or three levels, for the reasons mentioned above. However, they should not neglect the context of other levels or the effects of multilevel coordination beyond those involved in policy coordination. Likewise, a change in the division of authority between two levels regularly affects the effective power structures in the ladder of scales, although not the formal authority assigned to other levels.

Finally, the asymmetry in the horizontal dimension and the differentiation of levels in the vertical dimension raise fundamental challenges for governing multilevel political systems and legitimacy. Governance is confronted with distributive conflicts concerning the distribution of authority, resources and public goods or the consequence of regulation. Distributive conflicts and institutional asymmetries provoke contestation of power. They call for justifying or revising imbalances. Hence multilevel governance is always about balancing powers between levels and jurisdictions, all the more in times of crisis or during and after institutional or constitutional reforms. These aspects will be considered in Chapters 7 and 8.

NOTES

1. A few examples must suffice here: Bache and Flinders identified four "common strands" in the definitions of multilevel governance, which refer to structural features: "First, that decision making at various territorial levels is characterized by the increased participation of non-state actors. Second, that the identification of discrete or nested territorial levels of decision making is becoming more difficult in the context of complex overlapping networks. Third, that in this changing context the role of the state is being transformed as state actors develop new strategies of coordination, steering, and networking to protect and, in some cases, enhance state autonomy. Fourth, that in this changing context, the nature of democratic accountability has been challenged and need[s] to be rethought or at least reviewed" (Bache and Flinders 2004b: 197). Piattoni (2010: 26–30) designed a conceptual space which should cover the dynamics of multilevel governance in terms of politics, policy and polity along the centre-periphery dimension, the domestic-international dimension and the state-society-dimension. Zürn, Wälti and Enderlein take into consideration the process dimension and define multilevel governance as "a set of general-purpose or functional jurisdictions that enjoy some degree of autonomy within a common governance arrangement and whose actors claim to engage in enduring interaction in pursuit of a common good" (2010: 4). Schmitter emphasizes actors and their interaction, defining multilevel governance "as an arrangement for making binding decisions that engages a multiplicity of politically independent but otherwise interdependent actors – private and public – at different levels of territorial aggregation in more-or-less continuous negotiation/deliberation/ implementation, and that does not assign exclusive policy competence or assert a stable hierarchy of political authority to any of these levels" (Schmitter 2004: 49).
2. The corresponding German term *"Gebiet"* refers to the word *"gebieten"*, which means to command or to rule.

3.   Indigenous people may exist as tribal communities, but in multilevel political systems, their political authority has been more and more demarcated by a territory.

4.   See for example the definitions of "multiple" in the Merriam-Webster Dictionary (https://www.merriam-webster.com/dictionary/multiple); or Cambridge Dictionary (https://dictionary.cambridge.org/dictionary/english/multiple).

5.   International organizations are defined as bodies created by treaties among nation-states which delegate authority to the organization. Delegation assigns "the autonomous capacity of international actors to govern" (Hooghe, Lenz and Marks 2019: 33) and usually concerns specific purposes. Associations of states serve to pool power and resources for joint policies. Governments decide with unanimity or near unanimity on policies which each member state implements on its own. In federations of states, member state representatives not only decide with a majority, but they also delegate, to a certain extent, the implementation of their decisions to supranational executive bodies.

3. Dual politics: division of authority and coordination

In the realm of politics, multilevel governance is based on a division of authority and power within and beyond. Hooghe and Marks focused their research on the question of how this division of authority between governments and governmental organizations beyond the states evolved over time. In 2016, they published the elaborated, book-length version of their "postfunctionalist" theory of multilevel governance. Their book begins with a concise presentation of the basic premise of their theory. The authors explain

> ...that governance is not one thing. It is at least two things: it is a means to realize ends and it is an end in itself. The first conception conceives governance, binding collective decision making in the public sphere, as a functional adaptation to the provision of public goods. The second conceives governance as an expression of human sociality. It stresses that humans are social beings who value self-rule for what it is as well as for what it does. (Hooghe and Marks 2016: 1)

The postfunctionalist theory provides a parsimonious explanation of the rise of levels of governance and changes in the division of authority between levels. Hooghe and Marks, together with their research teams, confirmed this transformation of governance through their data sets and data analysis. Interested in long-term development, they identified two logics of politics as the main causal mechanisms of the observed transformation. The functionalist logic explains institutional reforms reacting to externalities and economies of scale. It presumes that actors drive a change in the division of authority if they are interested in effectively and efficiently providing public goods and reducing inter-jurisdictional conflicts. In practice, this rationality does not aim at an optimal congruence of tasks and jurisdictions, but at balancing costs and benefits of centralization or decentralization and of separated or shared authority. Besides a rational cost-benefit calculation, the selfish interests of officeholders in maintaining their power and resources influence the choice for a certain structure of multilevel governance. The social logic explains the responses of communities to a functionally justified redistribution of authority. It complements, but also contrasts the functional logic. As social beings, people are interested in collective self-determination of the common affairs of their community. Therefore, they defend their right to self-rule in politics of institutional or constitutional change.

The term logics indicates mechanisms of collective action and processes of decision-making on the design and change of multilevel governance. Actors, who, following the functional logic, argue for transferring or delegating authority, encounter actors interested in preserving or extending their autonomy according to the social logic. As long as the transformation of governance reacts to the complexity of public tasks and increases governance capacities by dividing power, this process turns into a path-dependent evolution driven by both logics. With the consolidation of levels, however, dividing power entails the distribution, demarcation and, from time to time, redistribution of authority assigned to the different levels. These processes concern the right of institutional actors to use power for specified purposes and the right of communities to determine how they are ruled in different policy fields. Changing these rights regularly sparks intense conflicts which are difficult to solve in negotiations. However, only negotiating an agreement guarantees that the outcome of a redistribution of authority is acceptable for the affected actors. The division of authority can also be changed by unilateral decisions, but in this case, the conflict is likely to endure. In a multilevel political system, the non-hierarchical institutional structure usually prevents this proceeding anyway.

In consequence, the political processes in which the functional and social logic of multilevel governance materialize seem to bear a high risk of ending in a deadlock. This is exactly what Fritz W. Scharpf has described as the "Joint-Decision Trap" (Scharpf 1988). Scharpf discovered this trap in his research on multilevel policy coordination in the German federal system and the European Economic Community (EEC), the precursor organization of the EU, during the 1970s and early 1980s. At that time, a minority of *Länder* governments in Germany and individual member states in the EEC obstructed policy reforms by using their veto power, although they realized the ineffectiveness or inefficiency of existing programmes and implementation deficits and, in principle, acknowledged the need for reform. In both political systems, the power of individual governments or political parties to prevent a decision rested in authority sharing. Decisions required unanimity or a double majority in bicameral legislative bodies. Under these institutional conditions, changes of joint policies in areas of regional economy, agriculture, urban development or education in Germany and European agriculture policy ended with compromises on incremental amendments that the common denominator of opposing policy preferences allowed. In both cases, policy specialists defended joint policymaking for functional reasons. They opposed the proposal for institutional reforms advocated by generalists and representatives of the people who preferred either centralization or decentralization of authority (Scharpf 1988: 250, 256).

Though arguing from different theoretical angles, Hooghe and Marks as well as Scharpf suggest that decisions on the distribution of power are closely connected with policymaking. Political actors arguing from a functionalist viewpoint and policy specialists call for adjusting the multilevel system to eliminate structural constraints that obstruct decisions on specific matters. Communities call for extended autonomy in order to control political decisions concerning their values or identity, and political leaders or generalists from central governments respond to these claims to attenuate conflicts. The post-functionalist approach emphasises the logic of functionalism and community to explain the dynamics of structures and the change in the division of power. Scharpf's actor-centred approach to "multilevel governing" focuses on the constraining effects of institutions requiring joint decisions and draws attention to the reasons why existing patterns of governance persist and constrain policy change.

Upon closer inspection, the evolution of multilevel governance is more policy-driven than Hooghe and Marks seem to assume, and existing structures of multilevel policymaking are less rigid than Scharpf observed in his initial studies. To substantiate this conjecture, the following sections will distinguish three developments. The first is the emergence of multilevel governance through processes of layering of governance through the formation of levels inside and beyond the state. The second process concerns the distribution and redistribution of authority between existing or evolving levels. The third results from the multilevel coordination of policies, which, more often than not, is associated with an adjustment of structures and a migration of authority by stealth. All these processes reveal the dual politics which characterizes multilevel governance.

LAYERING OF GOVERNANCE

Hooghe and Marks introduced multilevel governance to explain European integration. Their ensuing research on the rise of regional authority and the development of macro-regional and global international organizations remained within the conceptual framework of state transformation through integration and regionalization (Hooghe, Marks and Schakel 2010; Hooghe et al. 2016; Hooghe, Lenz and Marks 2019). Yet the basic structure of multilevel governance results from processes of level formation that create a path-dependent development. "Unravelling the central state" (Hooghe and Marks 2003) requires looking at the layering of the territorial structure of politics. Integration sets off with the coming together of governments to establish and develop higher levels of governance, which are meant to endure. It evolves through the deepening institutionalization of intergovernmental relations with the establishment of decision-making bodies and administrative organizations.

Starting with a network of governmental actors, it can end with a supranational federation or an international organization. The internal layering of state governance indicates the formation and development of lower levels by a reorganization of regional or local jurisdictions, the empowering of existing administrative agencies or communities with governmental functions, the creation of political institutions and the emergence of party politics in a new territorial arena of politics. Layering transforms the politics of the central state. Supported by parties and non-governmental actors, governments of states – first and foremost the executives of these governments – have been the main drivers of this change (Marks 1996).

The formation of levels is part of the process of integration. Yet this is not the place to discuss different theories of integration. What is important to demonstrate is that the evolution of multilevel governance does not entail a dispersion of power at the cost of central governments of states. As a logical consequence of integration or differentiation, these governments delegate or transfer authority; that is, the right to decide and act on public policies. In contrast to the distribution of authority, the layering of governance is not necessarily a zero-sum game in terms of power: that is, the capacity to effectively regulate conflicts in society or to provide and allocate public goods. Governments engage in multilevel governance to pursue substantive policy goals (Marks 1996: 24) in matters that either extend beyond the borders of states or require responses in regional or local territories. This way, they gain the power to deal with these matters.

Integration of states into supranational federations, associations of states or international organizations significantly expanded during the three decades after World War II, as the rising number of international organizations indicates (Eilstrup-Sangiovanni 2020: 352). First, maintaining peace was the primary motivation. Yet during the post-war era, the interdependence of national economies and societies dramatically intensified with the evolution of transportation and communication technologies. The need for transnational coordination to foster the positive effects of cooperation and the negative effects of unregulated and unfair competition increased accordingly. The economic growth stimulated by the international division of labour and trade required coordinated action in security, social policy, health and environmental policy – since the 1980s with a growing focus on the global problem of climate change. Governments of states, but also regional and local governments, all had reasons to engage in efforts to cope with these interdependences by internationally coordinating their policy.

Aside from functional considerations and interests in solving political conflicts and problems, executives from national governments supported the organization of international authority at the global and macro-regional levels for selfish motives. They voluntarily constrained their autonomy to rule in matters that they could no longer control within their jurisdiction, while they at the same time increased their capacities to fulfil their tasks in multilevel governance and gained power against parliaments and interest organizations (Grande 1996; Wolf 1999). In consequence, the overall structure of political power changed with the rise of multilevel governance, but this was not a transformation at the expense of the state in general. Rather, national parliaments lost their sovereignty in legislation and faced information asymmetries in relations with the executive, people depending on the welfare state suffered from international tax competition, and state-related interest organizations lost influence compared to internationally organized associations and NGOs. On balance, benefits and costs of internationalization or globalization of markets and politics are unevenly distributed within national societies (Milanocvić 2011; Piketty 2020). For this reason, the legitimacy of international governance is increasingly contested and conflicts in multilevel governance are rising (Hooghe and Marks 2018; Zürn 2018).

The rise of regional and local governance with the vertical differentiation of the central state reveals different power dynamics. Governments established regions and local governments and formed new associations of cities in response to the spatial restructuring of the economy and pressure from regional communities (Keating 2013). Both the functional reasons and the rise of societal regionalism can be traced back to the history of countries and regions. In general, however, they reveal another side of the globalization of the economy. In competition on deregulated international markets, private firms gained comparative advantages mainly from favourable local and regional production conditions. To improve these conditions, public and private actors cooperate in decentralized policies to develop specific local production systems (Crouch et al. 2001). Likewise, people discovered the benefits of social relations in regional and local communities, the more internationalized communication weakened their social ties in a "society of singularities" (Reckwitz 2020) and the more they realized the impersonal functionalism of globalization (Castells 2009b).

These processes affected regions and local territories in different ways and with different intensities. Central governments supported the formation of regions or the upgrading of regional or local administrations for functional reasons, but they also faced regionalist movements that called for autonomy. As a way to settle conflicts between both logics of level formation and to prevent disintegration, differentiated patterns of sub-national governance have become the "new normal" in multilevel structures of states (Hooghe and Marks 2016: 18, 100–14). Nonetheless, scholars observed an overall trend of "rescaling the state", at least in Europe and other OECD countries with democratic governments (Keating 2013; cf. also Hooghe and Marks 2016: 49). The increasing relevance of regional politics and the disintegration of centralized states towards multilevel governance changed party politics. State-wide or mainstream parties that are organized across the state territory and seek electoral success at all or most levels of a government adopted decentralist reform proposals. They responded to a paradigm shift from centralization to decentralization as well as to the rising challenges of regionalist parties. Accordingly, they modified their ideology and demands in constitutional policy, and they revised their organization by strengthening their regional and local subdivisions (Detterbeck and Hepburn 2018; Swenden and Toubeau 2013). Interjurisdictional competition reinforced the general trend towards regionalization. Regions which did not gain power in a policy of status differentiation tried to "catch up" in the ensuing reform processes. In Spain, where the constitution distinguishes Nationalities and Regions and allows an Autonomous Community to claim authority provided that the central government agrees, regional governments' competition for power developed in a cycle of differentiation and convergence (Hombrado 2011). In Canada, the claim for distinctness and autonomy of the province of Quebec was countered by calls for "Western independence" in the Prairie and Pacific provinces (Hueglin 2021: 184).

Compared to integration, which has been primarily driven by functional logic, the politics of regionalization of the state have manifested a stronger influence from the social logic of governance. To get political clout, communities had to draw attention to their claims, organize collective action and change the predominating politics. Primarily, however, they had to be accepted as a community. In contrast to a *demos* which is defined by the national law of citizenship, a community is socially constructed. It exists as an "imagined community" to which people feel attached (Anderson 1998: 141), and this imagination is created or fostered by identity politics (cf. Chapter 6). The evolution of identity politics challenging the state resonates with a wide diffusion of the idea of regionalism, which explains the rise of regional or regionalist parties and the adjustments of mainstream parties in many democracies (Massetti and Schakel 2020).

If we consider the evolution of structures of multilevel governance as a process of state transformation, layering describes the process in a double sense. It means the differentiation of levels of politics, which had been previously concentrated in the central state. In terms of historical institutionalism, the establishment of a level reveals a mechanism of "layering" (Mahoney and Thelen 2010). Level formation adds an arena of governance to existing ones, which over time consolidates through institution building and the expansion of authorities and capacities to govern. While the increasing complexity of problems or tasks challenging governments and the demands of communities for recognition or autonomy – the functional and social logics of governance, as Hooghe and Marks put it – drive the formation and evolution of levels, the division of authority between levels is a matter of constitutional policy.

DISTRIBUTION AND REDISTRIBUTION OF AUTHORITY

Politics shapes the basic structures of a multilevel governance system through a layering of institutions, but over time these structures evolve in a path-dependent process. The up-grading of regional or local jurisdictions and the consolidation of supranational federations, associations of states or international organizations continues through the establishment of institutions and the assignment of authority; that is, the right to decide and act on specific issues, by constitutions, intergovernmental treaties or agreements. In contrast to the formation of levels and institutions, the distribution and demarcation of authority must be frequently renegotiated because problems to be addressed and tasks to be fulfilled change. In other words, the division of authority is a matter of regular redistributive politics in multilevel governance. Unlike the differentiation of levels as arenas of governance, the distribution of authority is likely to bring about winners and losers. In general, assigning authority to one level constrains governance at other levels, regardless of whether it is defined as an exclusive, concurrent or shared competence. Actors negotiating on the distribution often combine different matters of competence, but still, the balance of proposed package deals can be disputed, not the least as the evaluations within the different jurisdictions at lower tiers regularly diverge.

According to a widely acknowledged principle, the authority to make and execute binding decisions which demand the compliance of individual or corporate actors should be precisely delineated and thus limited. In multilevel systems, the separation of authority follows from this principle and appears as a condition of effective and accountable governance. Nevertheless, authority may be shared between levels, in federations more than in regionalized states and in international multilevel governance more than in states (Hooghe et al. 2016; Hooghe et al. 2017; Hooghe, Lenz and Marks 2019). This sharing applies if authorized actors representing an upper-tier government or organization co-decide in lower-tier governance. Shared authority also results from the pooling of power, if governmental actors from lower tiers co-decide on policies at an upper tier in intergovernmental councils, committees or conferences. In general, these joint decisions commit all participating governments to comply with them (in this sense see Hooghe, Marks and Schakel 2010: 22–9).[1] They increase the risk of gridlock in policymaking and of a diffusion of responsibility among actors. However, authority sharing permits all participating governments to have a say in decisions and to prevent outcomes of coordinated policymaking that cause negative consequences on their own jurisdictions or meet opposition in accountability fora such as parliaments, interest groups, civil society associations or the public. Separation of authority empowers responsible governments to self-rule within the frame defined by constitutional law, treaties or organizational statutes. In contrast to shared authority, it reduces the "decision costs", but it raises problems of demarcation. Instead of ruling out coordination between levels, separation alters the institutional conditions for coordination compared to authority sharing.

In the constitutional politics of determining the division of authority, separation appears as a zero-sum game, whereas governments conceive sharing either as a positive-sum outcome or a compromise which is preferable to losing in authority separation. Still, both alternatives are highly disputed as they affect the power of a government. Nonetheless, governments cannot avoid these disputes as they are permanently confronted with the issue of the division of authority, for several reasons. First, irrespective of the policies concerned, there are always arguments speaking for centralization and other arguments speaking for decentralization (Treisman 2007). Like separation of authority, sharing has its benefits and its costs. In both cases, the assessments of the cost-benefit ratio depend on policy preferences, and these preferences change. Education, for instance, is in many states an exclusive competence of regional or local governments, but central governments began to intervene when they considered the quality of education as a crucial factor in international economic competition. Second, societal, environmental and technological developments affect the appropriateness of levels for policymaking (Dardanelli and Kincaid 2019) and make the division of authority more and more complicated. The regulation of international trade needs to be harmonized among states, while the competitiveness of firms in the global market depends on regional or local production conditions. The evolution of information technologies has accelerated information exchange across territories to the benefit of decentralized administration, but it also has caused new problems of regulation at the national and international levels. Efforts to reduce global warming and climate change require central regulation and joint actions among states, while adaptation to climate change largely requires decentralized policies.

The third reason is that the division of authority in a constitution or treaty never covers all possible matters. It can neither anticipate new issues appearing on the agenda of politics nor follow the constant changes in the economy, society and politics that affect the cost-benefit ratio of centralization and decentralization. Pandemics, for example, are not a new problem, but with the invention of vaccines, the management of a pandemic changed and brought about new challenges in regulation, distribution and administration. Finally, the division of authority is a regular matter of court proceedings. Courts change a constitution by interpreting the law, and they thus have a significant impact on multilevel governance in national and supranational federations

(Aroney and Kincaid 2017). The power of courts increases if requirements of qualified majorities or a consensus among governments make amendments to the constitutional law difficult. In the US, for example, the procedure for amendment was invented to protect the US Constitution against party politics. In consequence the courts, in particular the Supreme Court, gained decisive power in shaping constitutional change (Tushnet 2015). In a similar vein, the integration through law in the EU was to a considerable extent driven by court decisions (Cappelletti, Seccombe and Weiler 1986; Schmidt 2018).

While the division of authority in multilevel systems is always in flux, within states as well as beyond states,[2] revising the legal basis of this division is difficult. De facto, if not according to rules, many participants in constitutional legislation or treaty politics hold veto power and can thwart a redistribution of authority. In negotiations on amendment proposals, representatives in constitutional conventions, intergovernmental councils or committees need to find agreement or at least broad support for a proposal. To change the constitution of a state, a qualified majority of members of legislatures or voters in a referendum must approve an amendment proposal, while international treaties need to be ratified by all parliaments in participating states. Revising the distribution for authority constitutes a particular challenge of multilevel governance.

With his theoretical model of a "Joint-Decision Trap", Fritz W. Scharpf proposed an adequate analytical model to capture the challenges of dividing authority in multilevel governance (Scharpf 1988). The dilemma of joint policymaking, which Scharpf explains, results from the dual nature of politics in multilevel governance. In normal policymaking, actors are compelled to negotiate agreements on a policy issue because they share authority or because mutual dependence rules out unilateral decisions. The veto power of each participating government significantly constrains the power of all, and strategies to prevent vetoes often cause ineffective or inefficient policy outcomes. However, though actors are aware of the institutional constraints and their effects, they are not able to change institutions which would require either centralizing or decentralizing authority. To achieve centralization, all or most of the lower-tier governments (regions in a federal system, member states of the EEC/EU) have to consent. Decentralization meets resistance from the central-level government, and it is usually not the preferred solution of lower-tier governments with limited governance capacities, whereas others seek to expand their power. Actors are also not willing to change authority sharing because they would abandon their veto power. Consequently, they are caught in what Fritz Scharpf designated as the Joint-Decision Trap.

As Scharpf made clear, it is mainly policy specialists who prefer shared authority. In contrast, "generalists" – that is, heads of governments, ministers and members of parliaments – could profit from the right to self-rule (Scharpf

1988). Yet they are also not immune from the hazard of running into the Joint-Decision Trap. If authority is separated, actors realize the negative effects of unilateral decisions. Centralizing policies can overburden responsible agencies in highly diversified matters and increase conflicts instead of solving them, whereas decentralization reaches its limits with increasing externalities. Furthermore, even if representatives of upper- and lower-tier governments agree on the need to redistribute authority, the interests of actors to influence policies in the matters concerned raise disputes on how to change the division of authority, which cannot be revised unilaterally.

As Scharpf and others have shown in empirical research, the Joint-Decision Trap model does not justify the conclusion that multilevel governance is doomed to failure. Research has identified "escape routes" from the negotiation dilemma in normal policymaking and from gridlock in constitutional policy or treaty amendment (Benz 2016, 2021; Falkner 2011; Héritier 1999, 2007). Concerning the redistribution of authority in constitutions or treaties that reflect "incomplete contracts", Adrienne Héritier has drawn attention to sequences of informal "interstitial change" and reforms formalizing the informal practice (Héritier 2007). Research on constitutional change in multilevel governments, that is, federations and regionalized states, has revealed similar sequential processes between what Stefan Voigt labelled implicit and explicit constitutional change (Voigt 1999). In addition, it has drawn attention to the differentiation of arenas in which different actors are involved in either initiating, negotiating or ratifying an amendment of constitutional law. Processes regularly pass intergovernmental politics, constitutional courts, committees of experts, hearings of actors representing civil society, conventions of elected representatives, and legislative chambers. The multiple proposals and perspectives emerging from these arenas can increase the chance for successful reform (Benz 2016). Nonetheless, a significant redistribution of authority is rather the exception than the rule. The path-dependent evolution of multilevel governance mostly results from an incremental development of the division of authority. What is more, policymakers often avoid the dilemma of the Joint-Decision Trap by adjusting modes of coordination in multilevel governance. These adjustments change power structures without a redistribution of authority.

MODES OF COORDINATION AND DYNAMICS OF POWER STRUCTURE

The dual nature of politics in multilevel governance also appears in policy coordination, with considerable practical consequences. Rules dividing authority between institutions abstract from the real policy which a matter of competence subsumes. Therefore, responsible actors must specify the exact demarcation of who has the right to decide or act on an issue in "normal" policymaking. The problem of demarcation arises whenever political power is divided. The delineation of executive, legislative and judiciary power can be defined by distinguishing functions of a government, nonetheless, it regularly raises disputes in specific cases. To prevent or settle these conflicts, constitutions of democratic governments enshrine special rules and procedures. They designate the right to initiate a bill in the legislature to selected actors or institutions, they specify parliamentary control over the executive, define conditions for initiating legal proceedings and require courts to explicitly justify that they are responsible for a case. In the division of authority in multilevel systems, comparable procedures exist in federations, where constitutional courts can be called to decide on competence conflicts. The EU has introduced a unique subsidiarity control procedure which includes national parliaments. In the hierarchical structure of unitary states, the central government can make a final decision on competence conflicts. In contrast, the authority of international organizations depends on the compliance of member state governments and private actors, and those contesting the authority for a particular decision do not comply with a policy.

Whereas research on democracy has inquired into the causes and consequences of executive domination over parliaments, scholars working on federalism have extensively discussed the problem of "authority migration" (Gerber and Kollman 2004) and the resulting imbalance or instability of federal systems. Assuming that holders of political offices in federal and regional governments try to extend their power and exploit the scope of interpretation of constitutional law in pursuing their own interests, they discussed balancing mechanisms (cf. Chapter 7). However, not only the division of authority but also the mode of policy coordination between levels influences power relations. Separating or sharing of authority constitutes essential institutional conditions for coordination. Within this institutional context, actors can select among different governance modes and change them whenever they deem it appropriate.

If authority is shared, actors have to coordinate their policies in negotiations and joint decisions. As Scharpf convincingly explained, this is an appropriate mode of governance when new policies are to be established in a "single shot" decision (Scharpf 1988: 257). A new programme to advance renewable energies could be a case in point because the regional and local authorities should coordinate their decisions on wind turbines and solar plants with central agencies responsible for the grid transformation and energy market regulation. Yet coordinated policies on renewable energy must be adjusted during the transition process. Joint decisions, however, constrain governance when existing policies should be changed or terminated. As authority sharing discloses the fall-back option of unilateral decision-making, negotiations are more likely to

end with a continuation or incremental modification of a policy than a significant revision. Still, agreements can be achieved within a joint-decision system,
as Scharpf himself has pointed out. On the one hand, actors can redefine the
policy agenda to avoid impending vetoes, for instance by linking different
issues to package deals, by compensating losses in redistributive policies, or by
excluding matters of dissent. On the other hand, they can incrementally reduce
conflicts in a sequence of bilateral negotiations ("negative coordination"),
separate decisions on norms of distribution from the ensuing application of
the accepted norms, conclude agreements with a selected group of actors,
allow dissenting actors to opt out from an agreement, or delegate controversial
decisions to experts (Scharpf 1976: 54–66, 1988: 261–4, 1997: 125–35). The
second set of strategies changes the actor constellation and power structure
among the participants in governance. Thus, an informal modification of joint
policymaking is feasible even if authority is shared.

Nonetheless, shared authority constrains the options for modifying joint
policymaking. Separation of authority provides more elasticity of power
structures and more alternatives for varying coordination modes. Neither does
authority centralization necessarily entail governing from the top nor does the
decentralized authority to self-rule mean that lower-tier governments decide
and act independently. Under the condition of separate authority, the autonomy to make policies first and foremost requires determining how to cope with
the complexity of policies in multilevel coordination.

Centralization allows the upper-tier government to decide on the methods
of coordination and the way of top-down governing. This power is limited if
authority is divided according to functions; that is, if central governments hold
the authority to legislate on a policy issue and implementation is a matter of
lower-tier governance. Under these institutional conditions, which we find in
unitary states, in federations designed according to the principle of "administrative federalism" (Hueglin and Fenna 2015: 148–55), in the EU (Schütze
2009) and in international multilevel governance, patterns of informal communication across levels allow responsible actors to adjust central regulation
to foreseeable problems of implementation or to come to terms with these
problems through interpretation of legal rules.

A second mode of top-down governance operates by incentives instead of
law. Central governments regularly grant earmarked funds to influence decentralized policies. In practice, negotiations between central authorities providing grants and governments or administrations receiving them help to improve
the effectiveness and efficiency of the incentives (Shah 2007). Third, central
governments can also allow experimental governance by waiving regulations
for selected jurisdictions (Sabel and Zeitlin 2008). In this case, a central policy
can be adjusted in consideration of successful experiments and thus increase
the chance of compliance in decentralized implementation. Fourth, under the

condition of concurrent competences, central authorities can motivate decentralized intergovernmental cooperation in the "shadow of hierarchy", thus significantly extending the power of lower-tier governance and using central authority only if cooperation fails to meet expectations (Bakvis 2013). In this mode, the threat of losing power and the uncertainty about how a central decision will turn out motivate actors at lower tiers to find an agreement (Scharpf 1997: 198–200).

Decentralized self-rule seems to rule out multilevel coordination. Yet without central authority to regulate, the need to cope with interdependence has given rise to new modes of "soft" governance. Upper-tier public agencies, international organizations and private organizations started to govern by standards (Biermann, Hickmann and Sénit 2022, Büthe and Mattli 2010). In negotiations with actors responsible for applying standards in governments or private organizations – itself a multilevel process – they define policy objectives and indicators for measuring the performance of decentralized governance in the policy field concerned. Monitoring the performance and blaming and shaming inappropriate or ineffective policies motivates actors at lower tiers to comply with objectives and standards. This motivation can be reinforced by a yardstick competition, a contest for best practices organized in multilevel governance. Inside democratic governments participating in such a process, the comparative evaluation of policy performance can instigate public debates within jurisdictions and initiate policy adaptation to a best practice model (Salmon 2019). Alternatively, upper-tier authorities can use soft power by communicating ideas or recommendations for policies and by providing expertise and assistance to responsible actors in lower-tier jurisdictions with the intention of coordinating decentralized policies. In this case, coordination is achieved through policy transfer and diffusion in processes of communication and persuasion (Karch 2010; Volden and Shipan 2008). Based on their right to self-rule, governmental actors also engage in voluntary negotiations with representatives from neighbouring jurisdictions or cooperate across the whole territory of a multilevel polity, either to cope with externalities or to safeguard power against central intrusion. This horizontal coordination is not only embedded in the multilevel system but also affects the vertical dimension of multilevel governance through the dual character of politics. The coordination of a policy remains within one level, but it changes the power structure between levels, above all if it is organized in "intergovernmental councils" (Behnke and Mueller 2017).

Decentralized self-rule may generate coordinating effects in another way. In a market economy, governments compete for tax-payers or firms. As an – often unintended – consequence of mutual adaptation, decentralized policies assimilate in a "race to the bottom" or "race to the top", for instance by reducing taxes or regulations or providing special goods or services. Although traditional economic theories of federalism evaluate such outcomes as positive (Tiebout 1956; Oates 1972), tax competition can generate more problems than benefits and call for central regulation. Only if a central authority intervenes should this pattern of inter-jurisdictional competition be discussed under the concept of multilevel governance.

In reality, these typical modes of coordination are often combined. They are linked in the stages of the policy cycle which often proceed at different scales of a multilevel system. For example, goals and standards are often defined by international organizations or private corporations, and their implementation turns into a matter of coordination between central, regional and local governments within states (Büthe and Mattli 2010; Ordóñez and Raven 2022). Banking regulation after the 2008 global crisis was up-loaded to international bodies and conferences of governments which negotiated agreements on the principles of the necessary reforms, but in the Eurozone, the revised regulations had to be negotiated and passed in the EU joint-decision system (Mayntz 2015). Covering the combined modes of multilevel governance in all their varieties would lead too far in this context. It is sufficient to outline the basic modes of coordination and the social mechanisms explaining how they work, which are summarized in Table 3.1.

Given the division of authority, responsible actors select the mode of governance in consideration of the institutional conditions and the issues on the policy agenda. Even though they aim at solving policy problems, actors prefer coordination modes which extend their power. Therefore, strategic actions and reactions of actors shape the development of multilevel governance over time, and these strategies reflect the dual politics aiming at policymaking and the division of authority. The following examples illustrate the resulting dynamics of power structures.

The first case illustrates the emergence of a joint-decision system under the condition of shared and concurrent authority in the Australian federation, as well as the change of governance put into effect within this system. In the Australian mainland, which is divided into six states and two territories and where the population is concentrated in cities on the western and southern coast, policy interdependence between jurisdictions resulted less from cross-border externalities. It was rather caused by economic disparities and calls for distributive justice among states and territories. Cooperative federalism aimed at equalizing public services and welfare in all parts of the federation, mainly by fiscal equalization and federal grants. However, the Australian constitution does not provide for "mechanisms for pooling governments' law-making or executive authority to deal with these shared functions" (Painter 1998: 6–7). This was the reason for the rise of intergovernmental coordination and authority sharing without constitutional change. In 1992, governments established the Council of Australian Governments (COAG) to institutionalize intergov-

Table 3.1   Modes of multilevel coordination

Division of authority		Mode of coordination	Mechanism of coordination
shared authority		• joint decision	negotiation, compliance with an agreement
		• joint decision allowing opting out or opting in	negotiation, compliance of those signing an agreement
Separate authority	centralized	• central regulation of decentralized policy	mutual adjustment, supported by informal communication
		• conditional grants	incentives to adopt central objectives in decentralized policies, supported by informal negotiations
	concurrent	• experimental governance	central policy adjustment to successful decentralized policies
		• cooperation in the shadow of hierarchy	negotiation at lower tiers under the threat of a central decision in case of disagreement
		• governance by standards	guidance and monitoring (blaming and shaming)
		• yardstick competition	contest for best practice, policy adjustment motivated by citizens' demands
		• policy transfer	communication, persuasion
	decentralized	• horizontal cooperation	voluntary negotiations to prevent centralization

ernmental coordination (Anderson 2008). Hence important decisions in the Australian federal system became a matter of joint decisions of the Australian Prime Minister, the premiers of the states and territories, and the president of the Australian Local Governments Association. Consensual decisions should include all states and territories (Towmey and Withers 2007: 29). Although all governments could in principle act autonomously, the acknowledged norm of cooperation ruled out this option in the key areas of intergovernmental policymaking.

Among other issues of economic reform (Painter 1998), fiscal equalization was negotiated in the COAG, before the federal parliament transposed the agreement into law. Governments jointly decided on general principles for distributing the equalization fund and left the application of these principles to an expert commission. By joint decision, they also revised the distribution of federal grants. Previously allocated for specific purposes, they have been allocated to states according to performance indicators since 2007. Centralized governance by incentives thus turned into governance by standards. The

COAG set up a Reform Council whose task was to evaluate the performance of selected decentralized policies on a comparative basis. Later, the task of "performance reporting" was transferred to the Productivity Commission, an independent expert commission affiliated with the federal government. It should be noted that agreements on joint policies came about under the leadership of the Australian Prime Minister, notably after a further institutional reform responding to the COVID-19 pandemic. However, the power of the federal government has its limits. Though the Prime Minister and the federal cabinet can rely on a majority in the House of Commons, they need to consider the opinions of small parties in the Senate which usually advocate the interests of states and territories. The institutional context of a bicameral parliamentary system motivated the federal executive to cooperate with state and territorial governments in a joint-decision system.

A second instructive case is the rise and decline of the Open Method of Coordination (OMC) in the European Union, a policy approach covering different varieties of governance by standard (e.g., Barcevi, Weishaupt and Zeitlin 2014; Büchs 2007). This mode had already evolved during the 1990s before the European Council at its Lisbon meeting in 2000 officially introduced it to implement the "Lisbon Strategy". This programme aimed at making the European economy competitive in the global market, dynamic, knowledge-based, sustainable, and stabilized by better jobs and social cohesion. In social and labour market policy, which remained largely under the authority of member state governments,[3] the new mode of multilevel coordination should serve as an innovative, informal and experimental procedure to harmonize decentralized governance. Based on guidelines defined by the Council of Ministers, member state governments elaborate national and regional policies, which are evaluated according to indicators and benchmarks of best practice. The delegation of coordination to the Council and Commission occurred without changes to the EU Treaties because it appeared as a kind of soft governance. Over time, the OMC became a template for coordination in several policy fields and more and more variegated (Shaw 2011; Tholoniat 2010).

When the Commission used the results of performance evaluation to "name and shame" individual member states, national governments realized the potential political consequences, such as pressure from opposition parties or interest organizations and debates in public. Attenuating the emerging policy competition among member state governments and avoiding blaming those governments which had missed the policy targets was one of the modifications that resulted from the 2005 revision of the OMC. After the revision, the Commission intensified bilateral cooperation with responsible governmental actors in member states (Borràs 2009). This change was a response to complaints from national governments against the intrusion of the Commission and the bureaucratic burden of reporting and evaluation. Moreover, the Commission started to use the OMC to shape European policy by setting goals in informal cooperation with member state governments. With this turn from coordination by comparative performance evaluation – stimulating yardstick competition – towards a "deliberative mode" based on common objectives, information exchange, persuasion and partnerships (Benz 2007: 511–13), the OMC lost effectiveness as a tool to translate European goals into national policies. Still, it remained an issue in the power struggle between the European Council, the Commission and the European Parliament, as well as between national parliaments and departments of member state governments. Moreover, the "peer pressure" and the effects of disclosing deficits in national policies (Tholoniat 2010: 113) influenced social policy and education and fuelled party competition. The OMC not only inspired national policies but also political debates and was "likely to contribute to a further politicization of the European arena" (ibid.: 113).

The Euro-Crisis significantly changed coordination in EU economic and social policy. In 2011, the "Six-Pack Regulation 1175/2011" introduced the "European Semester" and integrated various sector-specific OMC procedures that emerged in economic and social policy into a streamlined annual cycle of coordination. In substantial terms, the Regulation focused economic policy on macroeconomic growth, budget consolidation and fiscal stability. In institutional terms, it strengthened the power of the Commission. The EU still uses the label of the OMC, and the deliberative version of the method survived, for instance in education and cultural policy (Gornitzka 2018; Psychogiopoulou 2018). However, in economic and social policy, the mode of governance significantly changed and the power shifted to the European level of governance (Dermine 2018).

The third exemplary case, multilevel governance in the Canadian federation, differs from the previous case in several respects, with the division of power being the most relevant. In the EU, authority is shared in many policy fields and the functions of regulation and implementation of law are divided between levels. The Canadian constitution separates the authorities and assigns policies either to the federal government or the ten provincial governments. During the 20th century, the original division of authority proved inadequate for a modern welfare state. The federal government used its "spending power" to expand its impact on provincial policies, but also sought to cooperate with the provinces. In consequence, intergovernmental relations evolved (Webber 2015: 146–71). The typical mode has been conferences of first ministers or ministers who negotiate and decide on intergovernmental agreements (Adam, Bergeron and Bonnard 2015). However, the separation of power, antagonistic position of governments in the divided federation and political constraints due to parliamentary sovereignty have prevented an institutionalization of multilevel governance, which explains the instability of coordination (Bolleyer 2009: 61–91).

In the intergovernmental negotiations among members of the cabinet, power conflicts between the federal and provincial governments regularly interfere with policy conflicts. Disagreements on policies often reflect identity conflicts and economic interests. In the French-speaking province of Quebec, regionalist and secessionist movements have influenced politics since the 1960s, with varying intensity over time. Other provinces like Alberta reject federal interference in policies which affect the local oil and gas industry. To avoid deadlocks in multilevel governance or compliance problems in implementation, the federal and provincial governments conceded that a disagreeing provincial government could opt out of an agreement (Painter 1991). This way, a government could participate in federal funds without signing an accord, provided that its policy addresses the joint objectives. Nevertheless, the relations between the federal government and the provinces has remained contentious, especially when the federal government alienated the provinces by unilaterally cutting its share in co-financing social policy programmes in 1983 and 1995. Moreover, the stalemate in constitutional amendments has put a strain on intergovernmental negotiations since the 1980s.

Two developments have moderated the political confrontation. First, intergovernmental relations shifted to administration as is indicated by the rising frequency of meetings headed by deputy ministers (Gauvin and Papillon 2017). Second, provinces turned towards interprovincial coordination in different formats. Since the turn of the 21st century, they have intensified their bilateral and multilateral horizontal relations. Interprovincial cooperation was institutionalized with the "Council of the Federation". Activities of this Council aimed both at protecting areas of jurisdiction against federal government encroachment and joining forces in cooperation with the federal government (Simmons 2017). Beyond trans-Canadian cooperation, regional forums of interprovincial coordination emerged, and in several policies, this cooperation materialized in intergovernmental agreements (Adam, Bergeron, and Bonnard 2015: 156).

As these cases illustrate, multilevel policymaking not only operates in various modes of coordination, but the varieties also open ways to change power without a revision of the division of authority. Separation of authority does not institutionalize negotiation systems and thus opens more flexibility to modify modes of coordination. And yet, shared authorities also allow shifting between different patterns of negotiations and agreements which may comprise all jurisdictions or exclude some of them. Politics of coordination therefore always shape the effective power structures in multilevel governance.

CONCLUSION

The dual politics of multilevel governance manifests itself in the dynamics of structures of authority and patterns of policymaking. Considering the basic structures of multilevel governance, Hooghe and Marks convincingly identified the general forces driving the rise and evolution of multilevel governance; that is, politics responding to the complexity of public policies by adjusting governance on the one hand, and the pressure of communities and their governments for autonomy on the other hand. These driving forces materialize in the dispersion of authority across levels of governance which demarcate territorial and functional jurisdictions. A second source of dynamics appears in political processes which aim at dividing authority, as well as in the ongoing contestation of the scope of authority and effective power. This contestation demonstrates that functional logic never brings about an optimal scale for policies. Arguments for distributing authority balance the different costs and benefits of centralization and decentralization. However, they also reflect political processes of balancing the powers of governments and governmental or nongovernmental actors, all of whom claim either competences to decide or rights to participate. Compromises on the division of power often lead to authority sharing, a functional division of responsibilities for legislation and implementation of the law, or concurrent competences. All these varieties of authority division increase the need for coordination in multilevel governance.

In the context of these structures, various modes of multilevel coordination evolve, and the selection of specific modes shapes power relations in policymaking. As Peter Leslie observed in the Canadian Federation: "Shifts in the working relations among governments, and consequently in the power that each order of government can effectively exercise, occur as part of everyday politics, not ostensible concerned with constitutional questions" (Leslie 1987: 85). This flexibility within the division of authority, which is enshrined in constitutions or treaties, has ambivalent consequences. On the one hand, it enables actors to find ways out of the decision traps in a complex structure of governance. On the other hand, rational actors exploit opportunities for authority migration by stealth (Bednar 2009: 66–77) and engage in discourses on the interpretation of authority (Schmidt 2010). The adaptability of multilevel governance to changing challenges for policymaking is essential for governing modern societies, but flexible structures increase the risk of instability or arbitrary predominance of central governments, executives, experts, party leaders, business people, etc. Both aspects will be discussed in Chapters 7 and 8.

NOTES

1. The terms shared-rule and self-rule originated in the literature on federalism (e.g. Elazar 1987: 5). In this literature, self-rule usually means autonomy of lower-tier governments against the central state. We find different meanings of the term "shared rule" (for an overview cf. Mueller 2024: Ch. 1). However, to rule means to exercise authority and regularly requires coordination between levels, whereas authority means the right to rule. Considering the division of authority, we should speak of separation of authority, which refers to the autonomy of both upper- and lower-tier governance, and sharing of authority in the sense defined above.

2. Empirical studies have proved these dynamics, based on different indexes of decentralization, among them the RAI (Regional Authority Index; Hooghe and Marks 2016; Hooghe, Marks and Schakel 2010; data set available at https:// www.arjanschakel.nl/ index .php/ regional -authority -index); the Measure of International Authority (MIA; Hooghe et al. 2017, data available at https:// garymarks.web.unc.edu/data/international-authority/) and the Local Authority Index (LAI; Ladner, Keuffer and Bastianen 2021; data set available at http:// local-autonomy.andreasladner.ch/). For an extensive comparative review of indexes of decentralization see Harguindéguy, Cole and Pasquier (2021).

3. The Treaty of the Functioning of the European Union (TFEU) provides a legal basis for this kind of multilevel coordination. Accordingly, "the European Union shall support and complement activities of the Member States" to achieve the objectives of social policy (Article 153 TFEU, section 1). This includes "measures designed to encourage cooperation between Member States through initiatives aimed at improving knowledge, developing exchanges of information and best practices, promoting innovative approaches and evaluating experiences, excluding any harmonization of the laws and regulations of the Member States" (Article 153 TFEU, section 2a). The Treaty also mentions "means of directives, minimum requirements for gradual implementation, having regard to the conditions and technical rules obtaining in each of the Member States" (Article 153 TFEU, section 2b). Article 156 of the TFEU states, that "...the Commission shall encourage cooperation between the Member States and facilitate the coordination of their action in all social policy fields...".

4. Complex governance: actors, institutions and linkages

As mentioned in the Introduction, research on multilevel governance draws inspiration from different theoretical approaches. Recently, scholars have introduced complexity theory – or at least emphasized the complexity of governance as an important aspect (Bednar and Page 2016; Thiel, Blomquist and Garrick 2019; Trondal et al. 2022). Compared to governance in general, multilevel governance is obviously more complex, as the three-dimensional model presented in Chapter 2 indicates. Complexity characterizes a system consisting of distinct, diverse, interdependent and connected entities whose interaction is determined by institutional or emergent rules (Page 2011: 6). In theory, these conditions make a system turbulent but at the same time adaptable (Bednar and Page 2016; Page 2011).

Diversity and interdependence characterize all dimensions of multilevel governance. In the vertical dimension, the division of authority and policy coordination across levels corresponds to the complication of problems in contemporary societies and constitutes political systems with the "requisite variety" of possible actions in order to select appropriate outcomes (Ashby 1956: 202–13). In the horizontal dimension, governance can profit from a plurality of governments provided that decentralization of authority stimulates policy innovation and diffusion of innovation, although the diversity of territories and political communities can also cause distributive conflicts and political polarization, as will be outlined in Chapters 5 and 6. This chapter addresses the institutional complexity of the governance system that results from the relations of politics inside governments and multilevel politics. It addresses the diversity of actor constellations, institutions and prevailing logics of interaction of both "arenas" of politics.

Extending the analysis to varieties of governments reveals a dimension of variety that research on multilevel governance has so far rarely addressed systematically. In the relevant literature, the processes inside governments are considered, implicitly or explicitly, from different analytical perspectives. Scholars have applied the principal-agent theory to understand the relation between intra- and intergovernmental processes (e.g., Dür and Elsig 2012, da Conceição-Heldt 2017). Looking at agenda setting, others have focused on preference formation of governments and how they affect and are affected by intergovernmental negotiations (Kassim, Saurugger and Puetter 2020). The functional and social logic that Hooghe and Marks highlight in their theory of multilevel governance can be interpreted as emphasizing orientations of actors towards either policy interdependence or the interests of people in their jurisdiction. An actor-centred institutional framework can integrate these approaches (Scharpf 1997). It suggests that the preferences of actors evolve in "domestic" politics inside governments and in multilevel politics. Institutions shape the action orientations and strategies of actors. In multilevel governance, actors' affiliation to governments, their mandates or expectations resulting from domestic politics and their commitment to rules and responsibilities constrain policy options in the short term, while these conditions can increase the dynamics of structures in the longer term.

The following reflections on institutional complexity caused by the interplay of governance inside governments and across multiple levels and jurisdictions start with characterizing actors, their roles, positions and power in multilevel governance from an institutionalist perspective. They continue by considering arenas of intragovernmental and multilevel governance as spaces of collective action that are enabled and guided by institutional rules and emergent informal practices. This section draws attention to the variety of institutions of governments and their consequences for multilevel politics. The third section turns to the linkages between arenas. As will be explained, these are essential to making multilevel governance work. The fourth section discusses how linkages affect the dynamics of authority allocation and shifting power.

ACTORS IN MULTILEVEL GOVERNANCE

As explained in Chapter 3, the concept of government implies the distinction between public and private actors while governance often presumes the participation and interaction of both types of actors. The model of multilevel governance outlined in that chapter suggests discerning, in the first place, actors who directly participate in processes of multilevel governance and those who are indirectly involved. The former includes those actors that a government authorizes to coordinate policies across jurisdictions. For this purpose, they engage in intergovernmental communication, consultations or negotiations with the capacity to prepare coordinated policies, allocate funds, sign agreements or make joint decisions with other governments. Indirectly involved actors supervise and influence policymaking in multilevel governance or ratify agreements and implement coordinated policies.

The first group of actors includes executives representing governments. Members of parliaments or courts rarely participate directly in policy coordination across levels. The increasing interparliamentary relations in federations, the EU and international politics (Benz 2017; Bolleyer 2010; Crum and Fossum 2013) or dialogues of courts (Law and Tushnet 2023; Sandholtz 2021) constitute communicative linkages between levels but are not meant to intervene in policy coordination of executives. In contrast, private actors representing NGOs or interest organizations may participate in intergovernmental consultations or negotiations, with different functions. Usually, they contribute expertise and communicate opinions without the right to co-decide. They have a significant bearing on policy coordination when they organize yardstick competitions among governments. In market regulation and the setting of technical standards in special areas, private governance may replace governmental power in multilevel governance (Cutler and Dietz 2017; Wolf 2006). This substitution has led to the modern version of the "lex mercatoria". However, in contrast to the merchant law of the medieval period in Europe that emerged from contracts among traders it has evolved and been stabilized in the shadow of hierarchy established by the authority of states and international organizations.

In multilevel governance, the directly involved actors represent governments or non-governmental organizations and are accountable to their organization. In legal terms, it is corporate actors who are involved in multilevel governance, while in reality, representatives act in a boundary-spanning position. In this position, the interests of the corporate actor and the need to coordinate policies in multilevel governance shape their preferences and action orientations. Scholars have identified two types of boundary-spanning executives, who differ in how they balance the conflicting expectations concerning the multilevel coordination and the interests of their government or organization. Generalists, like heads of a government, ministers or senior civil servants, act for their government. Considering their territorially demarcated authority, Samuel Beer called them "topocrats" (Beer 1978: 18). Specialists provide specific competencies in a policy. The alternative term "technocrats" insinuates that they profit from their advanced knowledge and information asymmetries in relations with generalists. Besides civil servants, experts from non-governmental organizations or scientists belong to this type of actor.

Generalists claim to act in the interest of the citizens of their jurisdiction and pursue policy preferences defined inside their government. At the same time, they are responsible for the outcome of multilevel policy coordination and accountable to citizens. They face the challenge of balancing domestic and multilevel politics in strategic interactions (Putnam 1988; Moravcsik 1993), with institutions and policies of their governments constraining their set of available strategies (cf. second section of this chapter). Policy specialists, on the other hand, are responsible for solving problems. Their expertise on specific issues makes them relatively immune from being influenced by parties or the general public. They usually cooperate in administrative networks in the horizontal and vertical dimensions of multilevel governance. In multilevel administration beyond the state, civil servants tend to communicate with their partners from other governments or international organizations and seek common ground on appropriate policies by deliberation (Benz 2023).

The division of labour between specialists and generalists in multilevel governance can cause tensions in governments. Both groups of actors perceive the dual nature of multilevel politics, described in Chapter 3, from a different perspective. Dealing with policy issues, interactions of specialists follow the functionalist logic of governance and drive the evolution of multilevel policymaking through voluntary cooperation or authority sharing. In contrast, generalists who represent the interests of a citizenry put more emphasis on the autonomy of their government, although they accept power sharing in matters extending beyond the jurisdiction of their government. Other things being equal, they are torn between the functionalist and the social logics of governance (Scharpf 1988: 250, 256). A second cause of tension relates to power structures in governments. Multilevel policy coordination can turn into technocratic governance if the functionalist logic of specialists prevails. Otherwise, it may be burdened by politicization if generalists define policy issues. Nonetheless, the division of labour between generalists and specialists is an essential condition for the effective coordination of policies among governments because it reflects the distinct, but overlapping, preferences and facilitates reconciling them in governance processes.

Processes of policy coordination are influenced by actors who do not directly participate but are indirectly involved in multilevel governance. Three groups appear particularly relevant:

– First, parliaments, parliamentary committees or parties in parliament holding executives accountable for their decisions and actions monitor multilevel policymaking. Majority parties in parliament may instruct the executive to pursue a certain policy, request information, ratify intergovernmental agreements or transpose legislation of an upper-tier government into decree-law, as is the case, e.g., with EU directives and federal law in Switzerland. Executives in multilevel governance have to take into account these actors' right to decide and in particular anticipate potential vetoes. In general, accountability to and monitoring by parliaments induces executives to communicate their policy to members of the responsible parliamentary committee and deliberate with them. It is up to opposition parties to scrutinize multilevel governance through public debates in parliaments, and their capacity to influence public opinion must be considered by generalists in multilevel policymaking.
– Second, in matters affecting the constitutional law of a government, courts can be called to check the legality of decisions resulting from multilevel

governance. Given the incompleteness of constitutions or intergovernmental treaties regarding a division of authority, parties or interest groups
opposing decisions in multilevel systems often argue that the responsible
policymakers transgressed their competence. Apart from the recognition
of human rights and the rule of law, market liberalization through harmonized regulation, or the delegation of wicked problems by political actors
(Hirschl 2008), the contestation of authority has increased the power of
courts in multilevel governance, as has been widely discussed in federalism studies (cf. Aroney and Kincaid 2017). The shadow of hierarchy cast
by court judgements has gained more and more influence on politics in
multilevel governance.
- Third, non-governmental organizations usually send specialists to participate in multilevel policymaking. In contrast to independent experts, they
  speak for the members of their organization who can threaten with exit if
  they feel not appropriately represented. Their power to pursue interests,
  however, has its limits. The challenges of multilevel governance require
  policymakers to focus on the preferences of their government and seek
  the support of their counterparts in other governments. While expertise
  is invited in processes of consultation and negotiation, the dispersion of
  authority and power-sharing weakens the effects of interest intermediation (Grande 1996). However, powerful private interest organizations
  constitute multilevel structures on their own. By addressing executives on
  different levels, they can extend their influence in matters of multilevel
  governance (Mende 2021: 182).

Despite their limited power, we should not underestimate the influence of
indirectly involved actors on multilevel governance. Governmental actors
stand out in this respect. Irrespective of whether they can veto decisions in
multilevel politics or prevent or obstruct the implementation of such decisions, they de facto tie the hands of executives who engage in policy coordination across levels. This power to constrain strategic action of the executive
varies according to institutions of government, as will be explained in the
ensuing section. In general, it results from the accountability of executives to
forums within a government. While accountability is necessary to legitimize
authority and policy outcomes, the power of scrutiny can have unintended
effects in multilevel governance (Benz 2004). Actors holding executives to
account may lack information on alternative options to cope with the imminent governance problems and, by narrowly defining policy preferences of
the government from an idiosyncratic point of view, reduce the "win set" of
feasible alternatives (Tsebelis 2002: 21–6; Putnam 1988: 442–8). Information
asymmetries between directly and indirectly involved actors cause the
widely discussed unintended defection and predominance of executives or

"technocrats". The risk of these effects can be diminished by appropriate linkages between multilevel policy coordination and politics in governments. Before we turn to linkages, we have to consider the institutional conditions of "domestic politics".

INSTITUTIONS: MULTILEVEL GOVERNANCE WITH DEMOCRATIC AND AUTOCRATIC GOVERNMENTS

In terms of game theory, the complexity of multilevel governance crystallizes in governmental actors' interaction in connected games, in which their strategic moves in one game impact another game. Actors play these games in arenas of policymaking which, depending on the tasks to be dealt with, develop "a characteristic political structure, political process, elites and group relations" (Lowi 1964: 689–90). Institutions and policies demarcate the circle of participants and shape the patterns of interaction and modes of politics (Timmermans 2001).

In multilevel governance, policies generally have a stronger impact on the arena of policy coordination in the vertical and horizontal dimensions, whereas in the arenas of domestic politics, institutional constraints prevail, though they vary according to policies. In most instances, relations between governments in the vertical or horizontal dimension are weakly institutionalized, apart from the division of authority. The need to permanently manage interdependence has strengthened the institutionalization of multilevel governance in national and international contexts, for example in the form of policy-specific associations of governments, regular conferences or permanent councils, most of them having a secretariat and statutes defining functions and proceedings of these bodies. Majority rule and internal differentiation into committees and administrative staff indicate a further advanced institutionalization (Bolleyer 2009: 23–6). Still, the joint-decision systems that exist in the EU and the German federal system are exceptional forms of strongly institutionalized multilevel governance, and even they reveal policy-specific variations and adaptation of structures over time (Benz, Detemple and Heinz 2016; Scharpf 1988). The overall flexibility of multilevel governance is a necessary condition of effective policy coordination given the constraints established by institutions of and politics inside governments. Hence, to understand how multilevel governance develops and works, we must take into consideration the systems of governments, the authorization of executives to act in multilevel politics and policymaking and the politics of holding executives to account.

Scholars have so far studied the impact of systems of governments on multilevel governance mainly for democratic states, including the EU as a federation of democratic states. Regarding the global context, they have discussed the general predicament of policymaking across levels and generating democratic legitimacy (Dahl 1994; Scharpf 2000). More detailed studies have compared intergovernmental relations in federations with various patterns of democracy (Benz and Sonnicksen 2021; Bolleyer 2009) or analysed the evolution of the division of power, policy coordination and democracy for specific countries (Lehmbruch 1978; Schmidt 2006; Sharman 1990). How non-democratic governments affect multilevel governance has not appeared as a significant topic of empirical research so far. Several reasons speak for including these cases in an extended research agenda.

First, at the global and macro-regional level, we find more non-democratic than democratic governments outside the "OECD world". To solve global problems like violence and terrorism, supply of sufficient food, water, energy and medicine, unfair trade, climate change, the decline of biodiversity, etc., governments have to cooperate or participate in international organizations, regimes or conferences regardless of whether they meet executives from democratic or non-democratic governments. Presuming a "system competition" between democratic and non-democratic states in world politics distracts attention from joint responsibility to meet the mentioned challenges. Second, existing federations do not per se conform to standards of democracy as has often been assumed. Robert Inman and Daniel Rubinfeld recently character-ized nine of 26 federations as "dictatorships"; that is, governments in which a change of power through competitive elections was not possible at the time of research and had not been possible in more than half the time since 1970 (Inman and Rubinfeld 2020: 12; cf. also Keil and Kropp 2022a: 23). Besides, the division of authority and multilevel governance is also a matter of con-tention in unitary states, in those ruled by authoritarian regimes no less than those governed democratically, with China and France representing exem-plary cases. Third, not only transnational multilevel governance, but federal or regionalized states as well may include both democratic and authoritarian governments, even though constitutions require conformity. Studies on com-parative federalism have uncovered several cases of sub-national authoritar-ianism in democratized federations (Behrend and Whitehead 2016; Gibson 2004, 2012; Giraudy 2015). Finally, local governments seem to be either democratic or provide good conditions for democratization, because citizens are in closer contact with holders of public offices and in a better position to control political power than at upper tiers of government. Yet the causal relationship between size and democracy is not as straightforward as it seems to be (for a detailed reasoning and empirical study cf. Denters et al. 2014). It is true that "participatory democracy is easier to practice at the local level than at other levels including the regional" (Hendriks, Loughlin and Lidström 2011: 729), and this applies not only to Europe. Moreover, many local governments have combined different patterns of representative and direct democracy and often experiment with new forms of democracy. However, elites including public and private actors often dominate local politics, not only in states where principles of democracy and the rule of law are weakly developed and recognized, and mayors can govern in an autocratic manner.

For these reasons, studies on multilevel governance should consider the institutional context of governments, and in doing so, take into account both democratic and autocratic forms of governments. Certainly, the dilemma of democracy and multilevel governance does not appear under autocratic rule, but we should not jump to the conclusion that autocratic governments do not constrain governance in multilevel systems, just as we should not presume that executive dominance in multilevel governance supports autocratic leaders. That actors in multilevel arenas represent autocratic governments does not significantly reduce the complexity of multilevel governance, as a closer analysis comparing the institutional constraints in democracy and autocracy demonstrates.

The challenge of such an extended comparative study, however, is obvious. Besides the variety of institutional forms and emergent patterns of democracy, research has to cover an even larger variety of autocratic regimes which is reflected in different typologies of non-democratic governments (e.g. Brooker 2009; Kailitz 2013; Schlumberger 2017). For rethinking multilevel governance, it is, however, sufficient to elaborate the basic theoretical reasoning and to indicate avenues for further research. Therefore, the following comparative view on democratic and autocratic governments focuses on the fundamental institutional features and logic of politics in democracies and autocracies that affect the division or redistribution of authority and policy coordination in multilevel governance.

Democratic Governments

Democratic governments combine institutions for legislation, execution and judiciary. The arena of democratic politics is embedded in this set of institutions which constitute, divide and limit power to rule over people (Merkel 2004). The basic mechanisms legitimizing executive power in multilevel governance are competitive elections with the probability of voting representatives out of their office and procedures requiring officeholders to justify their decisions and actions. They ensure the accountability of actors in power, with citizens having regular opportunities to change the majority forming a government and parliaments holding the power to control policymaking of the executive. For executives acting for a government in multilevel governance, these institutionalized mechanisms curtail their strategies and the range of feasible policies. Regardless of the type of democracy, which makes a difference (Benz and Sonnicksen 2021), this can occur in various ways.

First, national parliaments have a say on whether and to what extent executives participate in multilevel governance and in which institutional form
and mode of governance they should coordinate policies. They decide on the
division of authority between central, regional and local governments or the
delegation of authority to macro-regional federations or international organizations. In general, this power is held by national parliaments regardless of
whether multilevel governance inside or beyond states is concerned. In both
instances, regional parliaments and citizens may have the right to vote, but
decision-making in national parliaments and their final vote are essential.
The requirement of a unanimous agreement of all national parliaments in
delegating power to the EU in particular demonstrates the constraining effect
of democratic procedures on the division of authority in multilevel systems.

Second, the accountability of members of a cabinet to parliaments and
parties, the influence of interest groups or public discussions in the media
commit these political executives to pursue policies which are in line with the
interests of their government and citizens. Even if parliaments do not explicitly decide on mandates, ex-post scrutiny reduces the choice of alternative
policies and the range of strategies that executives can apply. In intergovernmental negotiations, it may prevent package deals if concessions concern
salient issues of a government. It may also induce the executive to soften
standards in implementation or impede the government from participating
in yardstick competition or from adopting policies which have proved successful in other jurisdictions. Possible scrutiny of parliament obviously has
demotivated executives of EU member-state governments to engage in the
Open Method of Coordination initiated by the European Commission when
parties in national parliaments have used the outcomes of comparative evaluation as "tools for criticizing government officials for their policies" (Duina
and Raunio 2007: 501). It also explains the reluctance of ministers of German
Länder to participate in the comparative performance evaluation of public
administration that a 2009 constitutional amendment intended (Seckelmann
2011). For executives, governance through contests for best practices or monitoring always bears the risk of being blamed for ineffective policies in party
competition and public debates.

Third, party competition in democratic governments requires executives
to demonstrate that they prioritize the interests of their citizens in multilevel
governance. In consequence, they emphasize the distributive consequences
of policies instead of the overall contribution towards solving complex
problems. To deal with distributive conflict, they turn towards joint policymaking as a mode of coordination and bargaining as a style of negotiation,
with the consequence that the scope of achievable policy change significantly
decreases (Scharpf 1988).

Fourth, elections can lead to a change in government. In consequence, executives have to revise their policy preferences and strategies in intergovernmental relations. Such developments can have significant consequences in multilevel policymaking. If a new government shifts from cooperation to confrontation and, by leaning towards populism, raises claims against other governments, negotiations can be blocked, the central government may withhold promised funds, and monitoring results or comparative performance evaluation can become a matter of controversy instead of promoting mutual adjustments. Regardless of such drastic effects, elections and changes in government always cause uncertainty in multilevel governance and destabilize the personal relations of executives representing governments.

Autocratic Governments

Compared to democracies, autocratic governments establish different institutional constraints on multilevel governance. Institutions of these states usually resemble those in presidential democracies, and an autocratic ruler cannot neglect the division of authority outright (Gandhi and Przeworski 2007). The power structures evolving in this institutional framework reveal, however, patterns which significantly differ from the checks and balances in a democratic presidential system. In a simplified conceptualization, they can be characterized as follows (Brooker 2009; Frantz 2018; Frye 2021; Linz 2000: 159–261): As stipulated in a constitution, power is, to a certain extent, divided between the executive led by the president, a parliament or congress of party members responsible for legislation and courts, whose members are selected by the executive and appointed by the president. De facto, the president controls decision-making in the legislature and the judiciary. To this avail, the president's power needs to be formally legitimized, either by a military coup justified to establish order, by ideology or by election. Since the constitutions of many autocracies adopt rules of democracy, elections of a president are not uncommon. However, irrespective of whether members of a legislature or citizens can vote, in neither mode do elections offer a real choice or give candidates challenging the autocratic ruler a fair chance to win. In contrast to a totalitarian government, autocracies allow a limited pluralism of parties and civil society. Citizens can express their opinions and enjoy individual rights granted in a constitution, but manifestations of opposition to the government are more or less suppressed, public opinion restricted and media controlled by the government. Autocratic governments do not lack institutions, they lack a guaranteed rule of law that prevents arbitrary power.

Despite the concentration of power, the president neither rules with unlimited competences nor is he or she fully autonomous in making decisions. To a certain extent, autocrats share power, but the effective division of power and legitimization of authority diverges from the institutional design. In reality, the president depends on the support of the army leaders, the secret service with paramilitary power and owners of large corporations dominating the economy (an elite of "oligarchs"). To stabilize the regime, he or she must cooperate with these different groups and maintain a balance of power among them. At the same time, an autocratic president needs the tacit acceptance of the larger society to prevent the rise of opposition or revolts and to prove his legitimacy to the inner elites. Therefore, he or she needs to shrewdly combine manipulation, suppression and output legitimacy by providing benefits to the people (Higashijima 2022). Finding the right balance between these strategies is essential since autocratic power depends on the de-politicization and demobilization of society (Linz 2000). Regardless of their legitimacy claims, which may include ideology or personal leadership (Tannenberg et al. 2021), output-legitimacy constitutes a decisive condition for de-politicization, which rulers can achieve through the co-optation of elites who promise to guarantee security and business people who enable the government to provide goods and services to people (Gerschewski 2013).

Autocratic presidents are neither subject to institutional constraints to the extent created in democratic institutions nor are they accountable in formal procedures. However, to maintain the support of co-opted elites and to appease mass society, they have to satisfy the particular interests of elites and avoid policies that raise resentment in society. Ministers representing the government in multilevel governance, follow the instructions of an autocratic leader to avoid the risk of losing their office. Lacking the protection of the rule of law, civil servants in specialized administration tend to avoid contradicting a president even when the solution to a problem would suggest this. "Typically, authoritarian leaders do not want to hear the truth that bureaucrats or other advisors might want to share with them, and only the bravest advisors may hazard going against the policies of those leaders" (Peters 2023: 8–9; cf. also Dylan, Gioe and Grossfeld 2022). Hence autocratic regimes no less constrain the strategic options and policy alternatives in multilevel governance than institutions of democratic governments. They even more strictly tie the hands of delegates by mandates of autocratic rulers. Such regimes lack mechanisms to learn and therefore rely on control. Therefore, governance by standards and monitoring, yardstick competition and policy adjustment by transferring best practices hardly work as modes of multilevel policy coordination inside these governments or including them.

Governance in the shadow of hierarchy or by incentives seems to be more promising. Under these conditions, negotiations can end in agreements committing autocratic as well as democratic governments. Intergovernmental negotiations presume the rationality of the participating actors. Each negotiator should, for good reasons, rely on all counterparts to pursue interests which are in principle reasonable and acceptable, are authorized by their government and can make credible commitments in negotiations. This rationality derives from the institutions of government that individual negotiators represent. Institutions of democracy define responsibilities, include procedures of decision-making and guarantee that politics stick to the rules. They facilitate negotiations although they constrain the discretion of negotiators. Autocratic institutions assign authority to governments, but they neither prevent arbitrary rule nor do they signify the credibility of commitments that negotiators representing such governments make. Based on her study on Uganda under President Musenevi, Rebecca Tapscott convincingly characterizes autocratic rule as "institutionalized arbitrariness"; that is, "a state that is illegible, unpredictable, and capricious for those inside as well as outside the system" (Tapscott 2021: 27). Opacity, volatility and capricious behaviour of political actors cause serious problems for negotiations and multilevel governance in general.

Interaction of Democratic and Autocratic Governments

To blame autocracies for governance failure would be too simple, however. As indicated above, the reality is more heterogeneous and the distinction between democracy and autocracy is not meant as a framework for comparative research but to shed light on the different conditions within governments that affect multilevel governance. With the rise of populist leaders in democracies, multilevel governance might change in the direction outlined here for autocracies. Moreover, policies may also make a difference. To stabilize their economy, autocratic rulers often cooperate with international organizations and adopt intergovernmental treaties. Besides, institutional constraints and rules do not determine politics in multilevel governance. It is the process of interaction among collective actors, that is, the communication, mutual adjustments and negotiations among governments and private organizations, and the evolution of politics within governments that reveals the effects of governmental institutions. In the interaction between autocratic and democratic governments, the different institutional logics influence each other and change accordingly. As a result, conflicts can attenuate or escalate. Typical causes of escalation are conflicts on human rights and the rule of law, mutual distrust in the credibility of proposals or the reliability of the implementation of agreements, strategies of self-commitment and actions of heads of government to demonstrate leadership through confrontation.

First, tensions burden the relations between democratic and autocratic governments in general. On the one hand, democratic governments dispute the legitimacy of autocratic rulers, openly criticize the suppression of opposition and point a finger at infringements of civil and human rights. On the other hand, autocratic leaders counter by reproaching the interference of foreign governments in their domestic affairs. When they declare opposition as subversion or terrorism against which they had to fight, they assert that democratic governments do likewise. These general disputes may be left in abeyance for pragmatic reasons, such as to come to agreements on pressing issues like climate change or to make deals from which all participating governments profit. They nevertheless maintain the potential to politicize intergovernmental relations and to increase confrontation.

Second, it is not unlikely that executives representing democratic governments in relations with autocracies take strategic actions that stir up conflicts. They perceive themselves in a confrontation with governments that are "illegible, unpredictable, and capricious" (Tapscott 2021: 27). One reason for this perception is corruption, which is more prevalent in autocracies than in mature democracies, as the index of Transparency International indicates.[1] Again, corruption in a country does not prevent intergovernmental cooperation, but it raises suspicion regarding the reliability of a government and its ability to appropriately implement agreements or regulations. In consequence, efforts to contain corruption appear on the agenda of multilevel governance with control mechanisms, which conflict with the autonomy of a government. Such issues are not conducive to reducing tensions. They can ignite conflicts through punishments which indirectly affect public services for citizens.

Third, confrontation can be caused by executives' strategies of self-commitment in bargaining by applying the "power to bind oneself" (Schelling 1960: 22). In intergovernmental or international negotiations, representatives of governments regularly use this strategy to compel their counterparts to make concessions. Yet this strategy bears the risk of running negotiations into a stalemate. In democracies, this risk is controllable because the opinions of majority parties in parliaments are a good indicator of the outcome that a negotiating executive can accept. As Thomas Schelling pointed out, "the ability of a democratic government to get itself tied by public opinion may be different from the ability of a totalitarian government to incur such a commitment" (ibid.: 29). He also presumed that coordination games, in which all parties would be better off by an agreement than the status quo, are more likely to end with a positive outcome if the stability of institutions and an esprit de corps among participating diplomats prevent or overcome polarization (ibid.: 91–2). Institutional stability is lacking in autocracies. Mutual understanding and trust can develop among professional civil servants in international administrative networks, but whether this can be expected to occur in administrative relations between democracies and autocracies is uncertain.

Fourth, heads of government or parties may use confrontation in multilevel governance as a strategy to demonstrate leadership. Leadership is relevant when generalists and highly-ranking members of the political executive negotiate on salient issues. Demonstration of strength and perseverance in intergovernmental relations is particularly relevant for autocratic rulers. Populist presidents or premier ministers in democratic governments who prefer authoritarian methods of governance tend also to confrontation in order to indicate leadership. Political leaders in stable democracies seem to profit from cooperative coordination, but they cannot succeed with this strategy in relations with autocrats or populist rulers.

To conclude: If these hypotheses can be confirmed by empirical research, the interaction of democratic and autocratic governments significantly impacts multilevel governance. Presumably, institutional diversity is a constant risk for the integration of a governance system. Policy coordination across levels is difficult under these conditions. The variety of democratic and autocratic governments in multilevel governance may prompt dynamics but can cause more instability than adaptability and more stalemate than flexibility. Research on multilevel governance has so far underestimated this problem.

STATE GOVERNMENTS AND INTERNATIONAL ORGANIZATIONS

The confrontation of democratic and autocratic governments in multilevel governance first and foremost appears in the macro-regional and global context. Besides, international or global multilevel governance reveals another institutional divergence. In states, the central government holds constitutional supremacy. Intra-state multilevel governance operates in the shadow of hierarchy created by central legislation, fiscal power and arbitration in case of escalating conflicts among governments. Nevertheless, confrontation arises between the central, regional or local governments, whenever the latter perceive an imbalance of power and contest the intrusion from the top into their jurisdiction. In a federation, this confrontation often turns policy issues into matters of authority distribution and the interpretation or amendment of constitutional law. Institutional interests justified by functionalist reasoning and claims referring to the rights of national or regional communities intensify these discords in policy coordination and constitutional policy (Hooghe and Marks 2009, 2016). The existence of autocratic governments at the centre usually overwhelms demands from sub-federal governments, but conflicts regularly surface in processes of democratization which often end in heterogeneous governmental structures and instability of the federal system (Filippov and Shvetsova 2013; Keil and Kropp 2022b).

In the global context, it is not a government but an international (or intergovernmental) organization which constitutes the enduring institutional setting at the upper tier of multilevel governance. Having neither the supreme authority nor the resources and capacity of a government, the characterization as autocracy or democracy does not fit them. Unlike autocratic governments, the power of international organizations does not depend on the support of private sponsors, although such sponsors exist and might pursue a specific mission. Unlike democratic governments, international authority is not based on accountability to a community of citizens. Instead, it is defined by acknowledged institutional rules dividing authority and establishing multiple veto points. In general, an assembly of delegates from member state governments makes decisions which are prepared by a secretariat and its administrative staff. Committees representing non-governmental associations play a consultative role in policymaking. As a rule, implementation of decisions remains the responsibility of member state governments (Rittberger and Zangl 2007: 63–77).

International organizations gain the power to decide and act either through the delegation or pooling of authority by national governments. An act of delegation transfers the capacity to govern autonomously in specified matters to international organizations; pooling means that member state governments collectively exercise power in institutions of international organizations and decide by unanimity. In the first case, international organizations constitute a shadow of hierarchy in a multilevel system, in the second case they establish a joint-decision system. As Hooghe, Lenz and Marks point out, national governments face a dilemma when deciding on the division of power:

> The strategic problem in delegation is the trade-off between the benefit of international governance and the cost of shirking when an international agent pursues its own agenda. The strategic problem in pooling is the trade-off between the benefit of eliding the national veto and the cost imposed on a government when it is on the losing end of a decision. (Hooghe, Lenz and Marks 2019: 33)

Considering the coordinated exercise of authority, pooling significantly constrains the power of international organizations because member state governments can use their veto to prevent joint decisions. Delegation, on the other hand, can increase the problems of implementation of decisions.

For this reason, and given their limited political legitimacy and administrative capacities, international organizations seem to increasingly shift the focus of their activity from exerting power to decide on policy issues towards orchestrating international governance by governmental and non-governmental actors (Abbott et al. 2015). They fulfil policies through intermediaries, for instance by organizing networks of governmental actors to design and implement regulation, by cooperating with private organizations to provide goods and services to people in need, by organizing partnerships with governments or public-private partnerships to achieve policy goals, or by coordinating specialized international organizations to solve complex problems. By adopting the function of orchestrating governance, international organizations gain influence in multilevel governance beyond the jurisdiction defined by the delegation of authority and independent from joint decisions of member state governments, but in line with their basic mission. For practical reasons, the general secretary and the administrative staff of the secretariat fulfil the relevant tasks. Nevertheless, it would be misleading to assess orchestration as executive or technocratic governance. There is no doubt that administrations of international organizations are quite successful in isolating themselves from political control, for instance by initiating new organizations and preparing institutional designs for these organizations with the intention to weaken the control by member state governments (Johnson 2014). Thus, they play a decisive role in advancing the functional logic to expand the authority of international organizations. However, when exerting their authority, they have to closely cooperate with national administrations or private actors. The influence of the international administration, therefore, largely depends on the persuasive power of a general secretary and the management skills and policy expertise of staff members that are relevant in nurturing the cooperation of governments and maintaining networks of multiple actors. Hence, the trend towards orchestration in global or international multilevel governance goes together with a change of international administration. Instead of bureaucracies (Barnett and Finnemore 2004: 16–34; Biermann and Siebenhüner 2009; Trondal 2013), we observe the evolution of a transnational multilevel administration (Stone and Ladi 2015; Stone and Moloney 2019).

The unique institutional structure of international organizations has advantages and disadvantages for multilevel governance. Deadlocks in intergovernmental policies requiring joint decisions of member state governments cannot be prevented by orchestration. In a situation of confrontation, which often arises among representatives of autocratic and democratic governments or between the great powers competing for economic or military supremacy, the diplomacy of the secretariat or deliberation in multilevel administration reaches its limits. The Security Council of the UN exemplifies a joint decision system that eludes orchestration by the UN secretariat. In general, however, the particular institutional structure of international organizations allows the executive to participate in multilevel policy coordination without getting involved in authority conflicts or rivalries for power among national governments. Considering the dual character of multilevel politics, the strategy of orchestration stands out for its emphasis on problem-solving instead of authority. International executives contribute through their expertise, entrepreneurial styles of fulfilling tasks, their experience in mobilizing resources, their established networks and their communicative interactions with national administrations or actors from non-governmental organizations (Knill and Steinebach 2023).

Given this combination of an intergovernmental venue with a policy-oriented professional administration, international multilevel governance significantly differs from instances in states. They have facilitated diverse patterns of interaction, those linking national and transnational politics within an intergovernmental organization and those linking civil servants and non-governmental experts in multilevel administrative relations. Such multiple linkages are essential for effective governance.

INSTITUTIONAL CONSTRAINTS AND REDUNDANT LINKAGES

As explained above, the rules and procedures institutionalized or emerging in the inter- and intragovernmental arenas of multilevel governance entail often conflicting commitments or incentives which executives in boundary-spanning positions have to accommodate. The resulting tensions vary according to the systems of government, the position of actors in their government on the one hand, and the institutionalization of multilevel governance and modes of multilevel policy coordination on the other hand. Other things being equal, the institutions of states limit the power of chief negotiators in multilevel governance more than inter-level institutions or standard operation procedures of policy coordination. However, commitments resulting from multilevel politics can significantly constrain the discretion and strategies of these actors and their ability to meet the expectations of parties, parliaments, interest organizations or in general the citizens they represent. Their room for manoeuvre is shaped in different dimensions of a multilevel policy. It may be constrained by institutions of a government or international organization ("domestic institutions"), by institutions of multilevel politics, or by both. For the purpose of analysis, we can distinguish four typical constellations. Depending on the strength of constraints, they increase the hazard of governance stalemate in policymaking, ineffective policy coordination between levels and governments, executive predominance or instability of multilevel governance. Reality is certainly more diversified, but the bounded rationality of real actors suggests that they perceive the complex patterns of multilevel governance in accordance with the model of two connected games (Scharpf 1991).

In the first, obviously most challenging constellation, actors face strong institutional constraints within their government or organization and in multilevel politics. For example, if a minister representing a coalition government in a parliamentary democracy or an executive delegated by an autocratic regime negotiates in a joint-decision system, both have limited scope to make concessions to their counterparts in negotiations. The hands of the first executive are tied by their accountability to parliament, but more so the coalition agreement or the need to consider the positions of the different parties forming the coalition. The executive acting for an autocratic government is bound to a strict mandate and has to demonstrate a strong commitment to the political leader. Such representatives of governments are likely to prevent a joint decision by their veto or abstain from agreeing to a proposed accord. If, against all odds, negotiations end with an agreement, a joint decision concluded under these conditions hardly changes the status quo of an existing policy. The heads of governments can accept package deals in intergovernmental negotiations, but the transaction costs in negotiations and the barriers to ratification or implementation within governments rise with the number of states concerned (Scharpf 1997: 128–30, 143–5).

Intragovernmental institutional constraints presumably also constitute hurdles for multilevel governance if policy coordination across levels follows informal procedures, that is, without the pressure to negotiate agreements. If a strong central government can motivate regional or local governments to cooperate by either threatening with central regulation or promising fiscal grants, effectively coordinated policies are likely to crop up. Modes of "soft" governance by standards or best practice contests can also work. And yet, institutional constraints in governments, like ratification requirements, the power of a second legislative chamber or the incongruence of central and regional party systems in a federation or regionalized state, can significantly reduce the effectiveness of negotiated coordination. Changing the distribution of authority is even more difficult in such a constellation, as limited effects or failure of constitutional amendments in multilevel governments demonstrate (Benz 2016).

If institutional constraints of domestic arenas are weak but governmental actors coordinate policies in established joint-decision systems, the chances for agreements and a policy change which meets the challenges at hand are better than in the first two constellations of multilevel governance. For example, international market regulation mostly reveals a highly "technical" nature and, for that reason, is delegated to specialists. When cooperation in regulatory networks becomes institutionalized in transnational agencies, as can be observed in the EU, the effectiveness and stability of coordination may increase. However, in democratic governments, the advantage of policy coordination is dearly bought with a legitimacy deficit, because political scrutiny over specialists is regularly limited due to lacking capacity and expertise in parliaments. These deficits surface in matters of technical regulations that have significant implications for politics, if they touch, for instance, upon sustainable food production, dual-use goods or pharmaceutical products.

If both intragovernmental and intergovernmental institutions are weak, policy coordination in multilevel governance seems to be feasible, but there is no guarantee that problems will be solved. Such a system of multilevel governance suffers from a lack of stability, which is a precondition for reliable interactions and the acceptance of policy outcomes. From a theoretical point of view, a fluctuation between competition among autonomous governments pursuing their fiscal or institutional interests and cooperation under the pressure of problems can be expected under these conditions. Such dynamics can be observed, for example, in emerging forms of multilevel governance that include democratizing governments where constitutions or party systems go through a process of consolidation.

There is no need to elaborate on this theoretical reasoning in detail. Its purpose was to highlight, in an abstract manner, the basic challenge of multilevel governance if we consider its institutional complexity. The categorization in a two-by-to-table should not conceal the fact that institutional constraints vary on a scale between weak and strong and their effects shift in a range between rigidity and instability of policies and power structures. Researchers have observed many cases of policy failure and democratic deficits, but also effective management of interdependence between levels and jurisdictions and significant changes in the distribution of authority. Explaining the different dynamics and policy outcomes requires considering the institutional constraints, but also the ways in which actors cope with these conditions. Without claiming to suggest a comprehensive explanation, one important aspect of multilevel governance should be pointed out. It relates to the complex interplay of intra- and intergovernmental structures and processes.

The question to be answered can be put in this way: How could actors confronted with strong institutional constraints in intra- and intergovernmental relations or facing the instability of weakly institutionalized multilevel governance cope with these challenges of complexity? One fundamental condition was mentioned by Martin Landau a long time ago. Applying system theory to analysing federalism in the US, he observed various linkages between levels of government that create overlapping responsibilities and provide redundant patterns of interaction, channels of information exchange and power relations (Landau 1969). Adopting knowledge from technical and natural systems, Landau argues that the purpose of redundancy "is to guard against extreme mutability and extreme rigidity" (Landau 1973: 184). He hypothesized that redundancies "allow for the delicate process of mutual adjustment, of self-regulation, by means of which the whole system can sustain severe local injuries and still function creditably" (Landau 1969: 351). In complex systems like federations or multilevel polities, redundant linkages create loosely coupled structures (Landau 1973: 190, note 17). They prevent institutional constraints, rigidity or blocked processes appearing in one part from spreading across the whole system. In addition, they allow actors to shift from one to another pattern of interaction to circumvent stalemate, seek alternatives to coordinate policies, gain legitimacy or prevent instability.

Redundant relations between levels of government reflect the internal differentiation of governments as well as the differentiation of governments and society. They establish venues that can become relevant during the process of policy coordination across the boundaries of jurisdictions. The following can be distinguished:

- Intergovernmental relations: Policy coordination is mainly shaped by decisions of members of cabinets or senior executives who negotiate on the division of authority or intergovernmental agreements on policies. They also decide on the use of grants-in-aid programs if parliaments appropriate the necessary funds, or on standards or benchmarks. Beyond that, they usually engage in informal bilateral or multilateral relations with their counterparts from other governments.
- Inter-administrative relations: Official intergovernmental negotiations, governance by incentives or standards, yardstick competition or policy transfers regularly are prepared and assisted by specialists in public administration, who for this purpose often communicate and cooperate in inter-administrative networks or ad-hoc relations. The interplay of intergovernmental and inter-administrative relations, of political executives accountable to parliament and specialists in the civil service, characterizes multilevel governance in general. They fulfil essential and complementary functions.
- Inter-parliamentary relations: Many parliaments organize regular official meetings of selected groups of their members. Such venues exist between national parliaments of two countries, between representatives in inter-parliamentary assemblies, between the European Parliament and parliaments of member states and between national and regional parliaments in federations (Benz 2017; Bolleyer 2010; Costa, Dri and Stavridis 2013; Crum and Fossum 2013). Consultations rarely affect specific policies of multilevel governance but can influence parliamentary scrutiny over executive multilevel governance and stabilize cooperative relations.
- Multilevel parties: In federations or regionalized states, meetings of members of parliaments inside their party constitute additional venues to cope with conflicts in intergovernmental relations. Integrated parties, who compete at different levels of government for votes and divide their organizations according to levels of government, provide favourable conditions to link politics at different levels, whereas regionalized parties advocate the interests of distinct communities (Thorlakson 2020).

- Dialogues among courts: Courts may come into play to decide on authority conflicts. Within governments, a hierarchy of high and low courts prevents conflicting judgements and serves to maintain the consistency of the legal order. In the EU and the international context, this hierarchy is not as clear as in states. In consequence, judgements of courts can diverge, and they can intensify conflicts and cause a stalemate in multilevel governance. A case in point was the confrontation between the European Court of Justice and the Constitutional Tribunal of Poland on the Polish reforms of the court system in 2021. However, such a clash of court judgements is unusual. In case of disagreement, courts try to avoid contradicting decisions, leave the conflict in abeyance and pave the way for political solutions by outlining the legal principles. The competence conflict between the European Court of Justice and the Federal Constitutional Court of Germany exemplifies this interaction of courts (Mayer 2020), which has evolved in the background of an informal "constitutional dialogue" (Groussot 2012; Vosskuhle 2010).
- Consultative expert bodies: In special cases, non-governmental actors representing interest organizations or independent experts participate in multilevel politics. These actors are in no way subject to the institutional constraints of governments. They thus can contribute to moderating an imminent confrontation, improving information, extending the set of policy options and thus increasing the chance for solving conflicts.
- Networks of regional and local governmental actors: Like inter-parliamentary relations, horizontal relations between lower-tier governments can constitute important channels of communication. In policies aiming at an energy transition or adaptation of societies to climate change, city networks have proved essential to initiate policy change in multilevel governance and to implement standards or regulations (Bouteligier 2012; Kern and Bulkeley 2009; Kern 2019). Often, responsible departments of central governments, the EU Commission or international organizations have initiated and orchestrated these special venues in multilevel governance, in contrast to networks of private actors that try to influence policy agendas and coordinate the lobbying of intergovernmental conferences (Andonova, Betsill and Bulkeley 2009).

These venues of multilevel governance vary according to their institutionalization, from formal intergovernmental organizations to informal meetings or networks. They also include actors who are more or less constrained by rules or commitments to their government. Therefore, they reveal different modes of interaction, from rule-based or strategic interaction to deliberation or communication. Transferals of policymaking between these redundant venues allow actors to circumvent institutional constraints, although institutions remain in place and have effects. The consequences of moving between different venues to communicate, deliberate or negotiate across boundaries of jurisdictions turn strong or weak linkages into patterns of "loose coupling" between levels and governments. They mitigate information asymmetries, broaden the range of policy alternatives, provide additional options for strategic action, open ways to prevent or dissolve gridlock and nonetheless maintain commitments of responsible actors to their government and accountability of these actors.

CONCLUSION: THE AMBIVALENCE OF COMPLEXITY

Scientific analyses generate knowledge by reducing the complexity of the observed reality, in particular, if they aim at generalized knowledge that is valid beyond an observed object or individual cases. Research on multilevel governance reveals the challenge of finding an appropriate level of analytical complexity in the face of a highly complex reality. The model designed in Chapter 2 should pave the way to finding the right balance. Yet the challenge of complexity reappears when we consider the diversity of collective or corporate actors and the institutional or social contexts that determine their actorness. The discussion of this aspect of multilevel governance can be concluded with a paradoxical observation: The complex interplay of multilevel politics and politics inside governments entails deficits in the effectiveness or legitimacy of policymaking and jeopardizes the coherence of multilevel governance systems due to stalemate or instability. However, these consequences cannot be avoided by either turning politics back to "sovereign" governments or separating authority. Rather it is the increased complexity through redundancy that makes multilevel governance work.

As we can observe in various instances of multilevel governance, redundant patterns of interaction can complement strongly institutionalized hierarchies or joint-decision systems by highly informal communicative linkages among levels. Likewise, weakly institutionalized intergovernmental relations like governance by standards, yardstick competition or policy transfer following comparative performance evaluations can be embedded in stable institutional frameworks like intergovernmental councils or international organizations. Political executives representing governments still act in multilevel governance with their hands tied by institutions and their commitments to political leaders, parliaments, parties and citizens. Yet they can reduce the risk of policy deadlock by relying on input from independent actors, intensify information exchange via different channels, and generate output-legitimacy by policy proposals that result from deliberative processes.

Thus, redundancy (or increased complexity) promises dynamics in policymaking and innovative solutions to complex problems arising in contemporary societies. It also improves chances to cope with dilemmas of politics inherent in distinct but connected institutions. Institutions can maintain their stabilizing function while actors strategically switch interactions between the different venues. Whether and to what extent these conclusions apply depends on particular conditions, the most relevant being the homogeneity or diversity of territories and the intensity of conflicts among lower-tier governments or communities. These are the topic of the following Chapters 5 and 6 considering the horizontal dimension of multilevel governance.

NOTE

1.   https://www.transparency.org/en/cpi/2023.

5. Economic disparities and fiscal equalization

Research on multilevel governance, which over time focused on the division of authority, party politics, inter-parliamentary relations and various modes of coordination between levels, started with studies on policies that dealt with economic disparities between countries, regions or cities. Central-local or federal-regional relations mostly emerged when a central government allocated financial grants to support decentralized policies or to reduce a fiscal imbalance between regions or local governments. Fritz W. Scharpf derived his theory of joint policymaking from empirical research addressing, inter alia, German regional policy and agricultural policy in Europe. Gary Marks introduced the concept of "multilevel governance" in his research on regional structural policy of the European Economic Community. Complementing the liberalization of the common market, this policy dealt with economic disparities among member states and their regions (Marks 1993). The Community established a "Regional Development Fund" in 1975, which in 1988 was significantly reformed after the accession of Greece (1981), Spain and Portugal (1986), three countries which had not profited from the post-war economic growth and which suffered from an extreme inequality between urban and rural regions. To spend the budget for regional development more efficiently, the European Commission now concentrated funding on the poorest regions, addressed regional authorities in the member states directly, and allocated grants to projects that had been selected in partnerships between public and private actors in the regions concerned. Thus, the former top-down approach of regional policy turned into a process of multilevel policymaking. This reform initiated the rise of regional authority in Europe.

It is important to recall these origins of the research field. In fact, economic disparity characterizes the horizontal dimension of most instances of multilevel governance. It signifies a political framing of the spatial diversity of economies, which materializes in a specialization of production and trade in particular places. The concept of disparity measures the wealth generated in different territories according to specific indicators and evaluates the differences according to societal norms or political ideologies. These evaluations determine whether policies take advantage of economic diversity or deal with disparity.

How economic diversity is framed in politics depends on the scale of multilevel governance. Regional and local economies are embedded in the national and international market, the institutions and politics of a state and the international relations of states and societies. In this societal and political context, representatives of regional or local governments, parties or interest groups raise their voices against disparities and injustice. They address the central government which holds in principle the power to regulate markets and redistribute fiscal resources. Beyond the state, the gap between rich and poor people and territories is much wider than in states and there is no central authority capable of mobilizing and distributing resources to deal with unacceptable inequality. The only option to cope with conflicts is to negotiate and implement intergovernmental agreements, without a shadow of hierarchy stimulating agreement and compliance of participating governments.

This chapter analyses how territorial diversity and disparities affect multi-level governance in terms of distributive conflicts and redistributive policy. It turns to a political-economic approach. As a society-centred theory, this approach emphasizes the interplay of economic structures and politics. Accordingly, the position of actors in the economy influences their interests in politics, and the resulting cleavages in society correspond with different ideological discourses. In his research on the politics of fiscal federalism, Harmes (2019: 30–85) identified political ideas which shape discourses: a "neoliberal" and a "social-democratic" approach to fiscal federalism. These labels do not indicate party programmes. Rather, they characterize two normative positions in territorial politics and political debates on multilevel governance. They imply different explanations and evaluations of economic diversity. Accordingly, they justify different policies for dealing with dispar-ities, especially for the assignment of authority or fiscal capacities to levels of government and for redistributive policies. As Harmes demonstrates in his study on global, European and national politics in selected federations, these normative projects "can help to explain and predict the multilevel policies advocated by right/left economic actors and interest groups on a wide range of issues related to federal, regional, and global governance" (Harmes 2019: 210). In the first place, these policies differ in their definition of the spatial variations of economies as diversity or disparity.

In line with this approach, the first two sections outline the causes and institutional consequences of territorial economic diversity. The following two sections explain how economic disparities shape the ideas and interests of governments and how distributive conflicts can be solved in multilevel gov-ernance, either by changing the division of authority or by fiscal equalization or intergovernmental financial transfers inside and beyond the state.

DIVERSITY OF NATIONAL, REGIONAL AND LOCAL ECONOMIES

Over the last decades, several studies on the transformation of societies and politics in the so-called "OECD world" have drawn attention to changes in spatial structures (cf., e.g., Béland and Lecours 2007; Brenner 2004; Castells 2009a, 2009b; Keating 1998, 2013). They highlight the territorial differentiation of societies which either replaces or adds to the division into classes, social strata, segments or functions. The studies primarily focus on the spatial differentiation of regional or local economies, the rise of regionalism based on a social construction of identities, and the regionalization of party politics (Keating 1998, 2013). An influential strand of reasoning explains the re-scaling of governance as a reaction to crises of the capitalist state or the Keynesian welfare state (Brenner 2004; Jessop 2002; Peck 2002). Sociological studies call attention to new technologies of the "information society" that have increased opportunities to interact globally while local communication and cooperation have remained relevant to compensate for the threatening loss of social relations (Castells 2009a, 2009b). New spatial economics explains territorial differentiation as the clustering of production in industrial districts, where public-private cooperation should improve the competitiveness of firms in the global market (Crouch et al. 2001; Fujita 2010; Krugman 1991).

These theoretical and empirical works on the regionalization of economies and the consequences for politics complement comparative research on varieties of capitalism which focuses on the diversity of states. Assuming that "each national economy constitutes a system or model of capitalism" (Deeg 2006: 57), comparative studies show how institutional conditions of markets and politics influence the performance of firms and governments in international competition. They explain distinct mechanisms of corporate governance, industrial relations and modes of political regulation as a result of a path-dependent historical development (for a good overview cf. Deeg 2006). In the original version of the theory of varieties of capitalism, Hall and Soskice (2001) shed light on specific ways in which firms solve coordination problems, their methods to exploit institutional complementarities in inter-firm relations, the organization of vocational training, the regulation of corporate governance and the procedures to deal with conflicts between employers and employees. They characterized economies as centred on coordination via market mechanisms or regulation by a government. As critics of this binary classification pointed out, models of capitalism vary also according to production systems, the institutionalization of corporatism or the engagement of government in production (e.g., Gould, Barry and Wilkinson 2015: 591–5).

Based on this literature, and neglecting for the moment the differences between scales, we can explain the distinctness of economies in territorial jurisdictions as an interplay of the following material, social and political conditions:

First, natural resources, the quality of soil, the climate and technology determine the substantial conditions under which actors produce and trade goods and services. Water, soil and climate have been essential for people in agrarian societies and are still relevant for contemporary agriculture and the development of rural areas. Industrial societies depend on energy to the benefit of regions or countries where coal, oil, gas and uranium can be extracted. The transition from fossil-based to renewable energy will significantly change the territorial structures of the economy during the 21st century, while historical legacies entrenched in settlement patterns and locations of industries prevail and shape distinct economies.

Second, as spatial economics and new economic geography (Fujita, Krugman and Venables 1999) explain and as has been confirmed by empirical research, regional economies vary according to specific agglomerations of firms which provide complementary products and services. Labelled as "industrial districts" (Becattini 2004), "business clusters" (Porter 1998) or "local production systems" (Crouch et al. 2001), industries competing in a global market profit from reducing costs by specialization, division of labour and cooperation in a territorial context. The concentration of specific industries generates a labour market supplying employees who are appropriately trained. Governments arrange for necessary public utilities and services. The distinct spatial networks of production and trade are embedded in the social relations of public and private actors (Granovetter 1985).

The clustering of business in countries, regions or localities has evolved in a self-reinforcing dynamic. As the British economist Alfred Marshall discovered in the late 19th century, locations of industries persist due to the positive externalities of supplementary businesses and skilled labour force. Marshall also mentioned the effect of international trade on the territorial structure of the industry (Marshall 1890: 328–34). Since states have concluded free trade agreements to liberalize global markets and thus limited their ability to protect their industry against competitors from abroad, specialization and division of labour at places of production has remained a strategy to increase efficiency and stimulate innovation (Becattini 2004). The harmonizing effects of globalization on consumers' demands come along with the territorial diversity of economies.

Third, innovation requires an appropriate social and institutional context in places of production, but also dense trans-local, trans-regional and transnational interactions among firms. Therefore, business people engage in real or virtual networks of communication and cooperation over greater distances.

These relations link attractive urban regions, whereas other locations remain peripheral, are more difficult to access and often suffer economic disadvantages as a result. This spatial structure of centres and periphery characterizes the materiality of contemporary network societies (Castells 2009a: 407–59). Urban centres and peripheral regions provide unequal living conditions, but at the same time, they are connected by a division of labour between the diverse economies.

Fourth, the mobility of people and firms increases diversity in spatial economies. In search of attractive jobs, people commute or move to those places where they find work that conforms to their skills and interests. Others remain at the places where they were trained in local firms and thus contribute to the continuity of a distinct economy. Larger corporations, on the other hand, diversify their production at different places and concentrate their headquarters and research and development divisions in urban centres.

Fifth, specific policy regimes in territorial jurisdictions of governments support and stabilize distinct economies. They combine ideas and goals, power structures, institutions and rules of policymaking related to a specific issue (Wilson 2000: 257–8). They establish patterns of interactions among public and private actors through interest intermediation and the co-production of public services. For national economies, scholars have categorized regulation regimes (e.g., liberal or coordinated market economies; Hall and Soskice 2001), welfare regimes (liberal, corporatist or social-democratic; Esping-Andersen 1990) or urban regimes (maintenance and development regimes, middle-class progressive and lower-class opportunity expansion regimes; Stone 1993). These policy regimes contribute to preserving existing clusters of industry or fostering innovation and structural change. They stabilize a government's cooperation with industry and labour organizations, regardless of the specific aims of the parties in power.

Theories of spatial economics and empirical research on regional diversity influenced regional development policies since the 1990s in Western states and the EU. The new approach focused on promoting specific development potentials in regions, thus shifting the focus of policymaking from the central allocation of grants towards decentralized public-private cooperation (Amin 1999; Wannop 1997). While policies of distributing grants made regions dependent on central decisions, they gained power to determine their development with the changes in regional and multilevel governance. However, not all regions profited from this change. Strategies of mobilizing "endogenous potentials" aims at flexible specialization in global competition, but only urban regions and industrialized regions could profit. The problem of territorial disparities remained on the agenda of politics.

ECONOMIC DISPARITIES BETWEEN TERRITORIES

Economic diversity characterizes substantial conditions of production, special-ization, organization of business, political institutions, the structure of society and the environment. When scholars speak of economic inequality, they compare outcomes in terms of profit, income or accumulated wealth. These are typically evaluated by comparing the Gross National Income of countries or regions and measured by the "Gini coefficient", although scholars have developed and discussed other indices for welfare or sustainable development (Stilwell 2019: 16–34). The term disparity qualifies inequality as not justified according to normative standards. It indicates a mismatch between prevalent social norms of distributive justice and the real distribution of benefits and burdens. The reframing of diversity into disparity occurs in processes of agenda-setting in public policies, when political parties, business associations or civil society organizations raise the issue as a matter of politics. Ideas expressed in debates justify different preferences for policies and universalize particular interests, be it the institutional interest of governmental actors or the interests of groups in society (Harmes 2019: 20–23). Accordingly, the framing of diversity is a matter of dispute in politics.

Proponents of liberal ideas consider the diversity of economies in different spaces as an inevitable consequence of specific natural and environmental circumstances and the advancement of technologies, but also as a precondition of specialization, division of labour, trade and competition. Consequently, it appears essential for increasing wealth, as Adam Smith evoked in the late 18th century. In the fourth book of his "Inquiry into the Nature and Causes of the Wealth of Nations", Smith explained that international division of labour and trade is beneficial to nations, just as the division of labour within a country augments the overall wealth of the national society (Smith [1776] 1993: 278–301). These ideas prevailed in Western governments and left their mark on what researchers on international relations called the "liberal international order" (Lake, Martin and Risse 2021: 227–31). Neoliberal economists, who gained the lead in public debates during the 1970s, revitalized this theory and revised it by recommending the privatization of public utilities and services.

Twenty-four years after the publication of Smith's "Inquiry", the German philosopher Johann Gottlieb Fichte proposed to close state borders for inter-national trade (Fichte [1800] 1979). In contrast to Smith, who did not neglect the inequality of wealth but argued that all towns and countries would be enriched by free trade (Smith [1776] 1993: 310–1), Fichte assumed that the flow of goods, money and, finally, the exit of people would cause increasing disparities between countries. He elaborated his theory at a time when the political order in central Europe had disintegrated into autonomous states and governments promoted economic growth with mercantilist policies at the cost of other states. Lacking a superior government to balance the advantages and disadvantages of the spatial diversity of the economy, Fichte expected that trade between rich and poor nations must inevitably end in discrimination, power imbalance and political turmoil.

Social democrats adopted this critical analysis of trade but drew different conclusions. They acknowledge that differentiation of territories and spatial division of labour is beneficial for all, provided that two conditions apply: First, that territories are connected by fair trade, in which the price of a commodity or service covers all costs, including appropriate salaries for workers and social or environmental costs, and that the price reflects a voluntary agreement among actors on an equal, non-discriminating basis. Second, that terms of trade between territorial economies must aim at balancing exports and imports to prevent resource dependence. Realizing that markets cannot bring about these conditions, Social democrats stipulate that governments ensure the fairness of business and correct imbalanced trade between territories (e.g., Jörke 2019: 178–221). These ideas emerged during the 19th century when states consolidated in industrialized societies and governments used their power to regulate industry and trade.

With the opening of state borders during the 20th century and in particular after the Second World War, a division of functions evolved, with central governments providing for distributive justice among their citizens, regions and local governments, whereas the regulation of trade turned into a matter of multilevel governance beyond the state. Trade agreements concluded by national governments, regulation by intergovernmental organizations in macro-regions (European Union; EFTA; NAFTA) and global regulatory regimes established by the WTO have sought to guarantee free and fair trade. Besides, international organizations like the FAO or the IEA have taken action and organized global dialogues on quality standards of production, products and trade so that all people gain access to sufficient food, water and energy. The ILO was tasked with preventing the exploitation of employees or unhealthy production conditions. The United Nations Environment Programme was founded in 1972 to fight damage to the environment and to make sure that business people consider the ecological and social harms when they invest in foreign countries and calculate their costs or prices. According to a social-democratic perspective, global dialogues, intergovernmental agreements, arbitration by international organizations and regulation by transnational federations are necessary complements of the redistributive social policies in states. However, these approaches to international governance have proven more effective in curbing national market regulation in line with the ideas of liberals than in accomplishing fair trade.

Actual disparities characterizing the spatial economy of the world, continents, countries and their regions question Adam Smith's optimistic forecast, which he derived from his theory of division of labour and free trade, as well as the hopes of liberals adopting his ideas. As Branco Milanović demonstrates, inequality of individual income is meanwhile primarily determined by location, that is, the coincidence of where someone was born and lives (Milanović 2012: 127–30). Fate, however, is not an acceptable justification for inequality in modern societies. In addition, the framing of inequality as disparity reflects two aspects that directly refer to territorial conditions of multilevel governance: enduring power relations among governments and unequal mobility of private actors, goods and capital.

Besides the conditions mentioned above, the unequal distribution of wealth can be traced back to a long history of power politics and political domination in the relations between governments, nations and social classes. Colonialism was the most extreme form of this domination. With the emergence of the liberal global order after the Second World War, these historical legacies did not disappear. Inequality between distinct territories endures due to power relations among governmental actors and private interest organizations in multilevel governance (Hassel 2010; Mende 2021). Negotiations on tax agreements between low-income countries of the Global South and Northern industrialized countries exemplify how persistent power imbalances translate into unequal bargaining power, biased deliberation, lopsided lobbying and, in consequence, unfair treaties among governments. Meant to avoid double taxation, withholding taxation or tax fraud, these agreements constrain the fiscal power of governments in capital-importing low-income countries more than is necessary and contrary to their economic interests (Hearson 2021). They "are not negotiated in a vacuum but within an institutional framework built up over a century. It is clear … that, as historical institutionalism argues, institutions built in the past condition states' options for cooperation in the present day" (ibid.: 24; for details: 31–49).

Historical legacies of power structures might fade away with the diffusion of social-democratic ideas. However, unequal mobility counters such a development. In the liberal view of the world, mobility appears as a chance to mitigate disparities by advancing individual and collective welfare. Liberals presume that mobility stimulates competition among private actors and governments in diverse territories. Whereas competition motivates private firms to increase productivity and innovation, inter-jurisdictional competition instigated by exit options of private actors should motivate governments to provide public goods (Buchanan 1995; Tiebout 1956; Wellisch 2000).

As a matter of fact, the extension of mobility advanced economic growth in industrialized countries and regions, but it did not reduce inequality. Empirical research of recent decades has shown that disparities between states have changed to the benefit of those which have profited from the extraction of natural resources, in particular coal, oil and gas, and that economic development in Asian and Latin American countries has been catching up with the leading industrialized states. However, studies have also drawn attention to the widened inequality between owners of capital and employees in national societies (e.g., Milanović 2011, Piketty 2020; Stilwell 2019; Tridico 2017). As regards income and wealth, the gap between the 10 richest percent of people and the rest of the population has increased in most advanced national economies.[1]

For understanding multilevel governance, the interdependence of territorial and social inequality is essential. Social inequality counters the equalizing effect of mobility as expected by liberals. Mobility with a chance to benefit is more realistic for rich than poor people, like entrepreneurs who relocate their production to places where they realize higher profits, owners of capital who search for attractive investments, wealthy people or corporations exiting states or regions where they have to pay comparatively higher taxes than elsewhere. Labour mobility has increased, but economically developed states, regions and cities provide chances for highly educated and trained, rather than for poorly educated, immigrants (d'Aiglepierre et al. 2020). Governments indeed may compete with other governments for firms, investments and skilled labour force, but to succeed in this competition they need to privilege investors by reducing taxes, adjusting regulations or providing the expected production conditions. Instead of diminishing territorial disparities, mobility and competition empower mobile private actors to interfere in politics without any legitimacy to do so. In inter-jurisdictional competition, people who profit from the opportunity of exit and entry in pursuance of their private interests have more influence in politics than those who must raise their voices in political processes to defend their interests, provided that they live in democracies (Streeck 2014: 79–90; data for the EU: Wellisch 2000: 3–7).

The rise of financial capitalism and the digitalization of the financial sector have intensified the discriminating effects of mobility on spatial economies. This process achieved its climax around the turn of the 21st century (Peet 2011: 391) and was hardly disrupted by the financial crisis after 2008. It has created a new mechanism of exit and entry. Financial capital can be moved around the globe in no time via electronic transactions, without significant costs and, despite all efforts of governments, without being effectively controlled by boundary rules of states. Investment companies and banks provide capital and credit for firms. Indirectly by their capital deployment and directly by supervising the management, they influence the policy of corporations. They press for reorganization, cost reduction and profit maximization, always by threatening with exit – that is, the withdrawal of capital. Thus, they undermine the power of governments, unions and NGOs, actors who can raise their voice but cannot effectively counter the exit threats of private investors. Financialization is also a driving force for the commodification of land, data, knowledge and genetically manipulated natural products. This process has been advanced by big companies, private law firms and courts in the US, the United Kingdom and other liberal states where private actors have good chances to gain property rights (Pistor 2019). In defining these rights, courts often refer to constitutional principles protecting individual rights and thus constrain the power of governments to qualify these rights through legislation. The consequence of this process of commodification is a further concentration of financial capital and private wealth. In the territorial dimension, financial capitalism has boosted the rise of "global cities" and prosperous economic regions, with the consequence that economic and social inequality increases, not only between different states but also between urban centres and their peripheries (Milanović 2011; Sassen 2018). The concentration of public and private wealth in global cities at the cost of the periphery reflects the power hierarchies in governments and the social stratification in contemporary societies (Sassen 2018: 118–33).

This interplay of discriminating mobility of people, corporations or capital and politics causes another vicious cycle which concerns institutional conditions of multilevel governance, at least at the international level. According to a widely shared conjecture, countries with inclusive economic and political institutions that guarantee secure property rights, freedom to contract and trade, rule of law, division of power and the provision of public services by an authoritative, but accountable government constitute essential conditions for the prosperity of nations (Acemoglu and Robinson 2012). To put it in another way: A market economy and democratic government make nations prosper, whereas the absence of these institutions explains why nations fail and poverty persists. In a similar vein, Robert Putnam highlighted social networks of trust and cooperation in a vivid civil society; that is, a society of equal people engaging in the provision of public goods and services. As he concluded from his study on Italian regions, civil society and democracy facilitate good governance and make the regional economy flourish, in contrast to regions dominated by autocrats, oligarchies or exclusive clientelist networks (Putnam 1993). However, the transborder mobility of firms and capital inhibits the virtuous cycle of democratization, equality and prosperity, as long as autocratic rulers benefit from attracting firms and financial capital in liberalized markets. Autocratic regimes may be unattractive for investors as they do not guarantee property rights. However, their political elites depend on economic success and, therefore, provide for those conditions that benefit investors from foreign countries, such as low taxes, poor payment and limited rights of workers or deficient social and environmental regulation. When autocratic rulers and the economic elite supporting them accumulate wealth, for instance from extracting fossil energy and mineral resources, they seek further profit by investing their financial capital in foreign businesses, preferably in Western states, to the advantage of private corporations, but not of democracy.

Taken as a whole, territorial economic diversity entails economic and, in consequence, fiscal disparities between jurisdictions at the national, regional and local levels. These disparities result from a long history of power politics, unfair trade and discriminating mobility. Despite all the changes in the economic geography of the world, in macro-regions and at the regional and local level in states, the fact of territorial disparities persists. Therefore, they need to be considered as an essential condition in studies on multilevel governance. The following sections can only give a rough sketch of the necessary implications.

ECONOMIC DISPARITIES AND DIVISION OF AUTHORITY

In developed countries, a majority of citizens underestimate social inequality and poverty, thus reducing the electoral pressure on their government. Policies aiming at equality have redistributive effects and run contrary to the interests of the most powerful political actors (Stilwell 2019: 219–45). Researchers, governments and political parties diverge in their diagnosis of the causes of disparities and, accordingly, in their recommendations for policies. Nevertheless, territorial disparities matter in multilevel governance in terms of fiscal imbalance between governments. They burden coordination with distributive conflicts in many policy fields. The argument of liberals justifying fiscal imbalance as a result of differing performance and policy choices does not convince office-holders in governments if they lack the necessary resources to provide public goods and services in an appropriate quantity and quality.

As outlined in the following section, central grants and fiscal equalization may attenuate these conflicts. Nonetheless, they obstruct intergovernmental agreements on policies that affect the budgets of governments. They complicate coordination by standards, yardstick competition, experimental governance and policy transfer. As they divide governments of the same level, horizontal cooperation is hardly a favoured option. Centralization of authority promises to cope with distributive conflicts in the shadow of hierarchy. However, governments' preferences for such a change to the constitution or treaties diverge due to economic disparities. Apart from the functional and social logic of multilevel governance that influences deliberations of policy specialists and generalists or elected members of the executive, institutional interests, ideologies and economic disparities shape the preferences of governments. A redistribution of authority therefore raises three basic conflicts among actors involved in institutional change.

First, actors holding offices in government typically endeavour to extend
their power or autonomy. This is the reason why rational choice theories of
federal systems presume a continuous contest between federal and regional
governments that causes instability (Riker 1964; Filippov, Ordeshook and
Shvetsova 2004). Yet governments might also be inclined to shift the blame
for policy failure to other governments and therefore prefer to delegate authority to upper-tier agencies, to centralize legislation and decentralize implementation of a policy, or to share authority (Heinkelmann-Wild et al. 2023;
Weaver 1986). In politics of authority distribution, the interests of upper- and
lower-tier governments are typically at odds and may also clash in negotiations on how powers should be divided or shared. For international multilevel
governance, there is no upper-tier "government" with specific institutional
interests. However, executives of international organizations make efforts to
extend their power (Johnson 2014), for instance by cooperating with international NGOs or by joining administrative networks with civil servants from
member states. Though not institutionally entrenched and therefore volatile,
the power of international administration fosters the migration of authority but
also provokes the contestation of international authority.

Second, opposing ideologies of political parties, majorities in parliaments
or political elites cause conflicts over the distribution of authority, as Adam
Harmes has convincingly demonstrated. Ideas frame the perception of diversity. Besides, they also imply different conclusions for an institutional design
of multilevel governance and modes of coordination (Harmes 2019). In
a nutshell: liberals argue for decentralization to limit the power of a central
government and to induce lower-tier governments to make market-conforming
policies, in line with economic theories of competitive federalism. They claim
that governments holding the same authority, that is governments at the same
level, should attract mobile firms and individuals by providing public goods
and services and by raising taxes that outbid comparable policies of other
governments. Provided that a higher-level government establishes a common
market, guarantees fair institutional competition and commits governments
to balancing their budgets (Weingast 1995: 4), private actors' exit option or
"voting with their feet" should safeguard "market-preserving" governance in
decentralized multilevel polities (Tiebout 1956; Oates 1972; Weingast 1995).
Social democrats, in contrast, call for a welfare state and fiscal equalization to
mitigate the social and territorial disparities. They demand centralized social
policies and market regulation to rule out a "race to the bottom" of competing
regional or local governments. A central government should guarantee a high
quality of welfare policies and use its tax authority to align the fiscal capacities
of regions and local governments.

The conflict over ideas on the institutional design of multilevel governance
seems to have attenuated over the last decades. Scholars advancing the eco-

nomic theory of federalism recognize the limits and discriminating effects of inter-jurisdictional mobility. Besides, they draw attention to information asymmetries between governments and citizens or corporations entailing that exit options appear as reactions to the low performance of a government rather than as a way to influence policymaking (Breton 1996: 228–76). The "second generation" of the economic theory of federalism and decentralization (Oates 2005) therefore introduced the model of yardstick competition, a process in which governments compete with policies to attract voters rather than mobile taxpayers. In this process, citizens gain information about the policies of their government and can evaluate their government's performance in comparison to other governments (Salmon 2019). Liberal and social democratic governments have introduced benchmarking, contests for best practices, monitoring and evaluation as "new modes of governance". For liberals, it appeals as a "soft mode" of governance that could substitute central regulation. Social democrats advocate governance by standards, performance contests and evaluation as a method to guide and supervise decentralized governance since economists draw attention to "endogenous development potentials" in distinct regional economies (Stimson, Stough and Nijkamp 2011). Mobilizing these potentials seems a promising strategy to enable underperforming regional economies to catch up with prospering regions.

Judged from observations of Europe, what appears as a convergence of ideas for designing multilevel governance at a closer look exposes a functional differentiation between levels. While European integration and international trade treaties have perpetuated liberal policy at the national and transnational level, regions have adopted neo-corporatist modes of governance and engaged in economic development and social services for their citizens. However, there was no agreement on the institutional design. Notably, social democrats in economically well-off regions have campaigned for regional autonomy in a "Europe of the Regions" to gain power against the predominating economic liberalism. Governments of poorer regions hoped to get access to EU institutions and make their voice heard in a "Europe with the Regions" (Abels and Battke 2019; Moore 2008).

Third, economic disparities translate into fiscal disparities. They supersede institutional interests and ideological claims in power conflicts. In rich states, regions or cities, governments prefer autonomy and self-rule to determine the affairs of their citizens on their own. Governments in economically disadvantaged jurisdictions lack the necessary financial resources to fulfil the demands of their citizens. Instead of autonomy, they favour the sharing of authority with an upper-tier government. Alternatively, they may seek to share the fiscal and administrative burden of tasks in cooperation with governments of neighbouring jurisdictions. In contrast to governments of rich regions, they prefer centralization of taxation, tax sharing with the central government and fiscal equalization.

As Pablo Beramendi (2012) argues in a detailed approach, poor citizens in rich regions support decentralization because they expect to partake in the regions' wealth but call for centralization if they live in poor regions. Rich citizens in poor regions might not advocate for centralization, but they support fiscal equalization expecting that this reduces the pressure on governments to levy progressive taxes on people with high income and wealth. For lower-tier governments, social inequality matters only if the interests of poor people are advocated by parties representing these people. In democracies, this is probable, but unlikely in autocracies, and even in democracies, economic elites can de facto exert influence in negotiations with executives and threaten with exit. Therefore, it is likely that private actors and civil society support the rational interest of officeholders to gain authority and autonomy. Whether they push governments of poor regions to engage in fiscal equalization is not certain. However, these governments seek to share power and fiscal equalization for other reasons. In states and in the EU, legislative power has been centralized to regulate external effects and interdependence between jurisdictions, whereas the power to implement laws is decentralized because implementing a general rule or providing services requires knowledge of specific local conditions. Governments in poor regions with lower revenues per capita than those in rich regions are disadvantaged by the costs of administration and therefore dependent on fiscal assistance.

To conclude: Institutional interests, ideologies and economic disparities between territories result in divergent preferences of governments concerning the distribution of authority in multilevel governance. The overlap of different conflicts, changes in government and developments of ideas and ideologies make these preferences less predictable than theories of multilevel governance have assumed. As the distribution of authority is negotiated between representatives of upper- and lower-tier governments, notwithstanding the authority to decide on the constitution, the outcome of politics expresses a compromise resulting from negotiations. Obviously, economic disparities characterizing the horizontal dimension of multilevel governance matter in these processes. Distributive conflicts make agreements difficult, but participating actors cannot avoid addressing these conflicts and the problem of disparities. Given the dual nature of politics in multilevel governance (Chapter 3), bargaining on authority in multilevel governance is not only about power but also about fiscal capacities to fulfil the responsibilities that follow from authority. However, a redistribution of authority cannot solve disparities between territories in a multilevel system. Any division of authority between levels likely entails pressure for fiscal equalization among governments at the lower tiers. This situation raises the question of how this kind of redistributive policy is feasible in multilevel governance.

THE MULTILEVEL GOVERNANCE OF FISCAL EQUALIZATION

Economic theories of fiscal federalism distinguish between vertical and horizontal fiscal imbalances that call for equalization. The former results from a mismatch between the division of authority and the distribution of financial resources between levels of government. It can be solved by adjusting the division of authority or by redistributing revenues. In most cases, a vertical imbalance does not affect all lower-tier governments equally. Its consequences hinge on horizontal imbalance caused by disparities in spatial economy. This fiscal imbalance between governments on the same level is the topic of this chapter. It indicates a mismatch between equal authority of governments and inequality of expenditures, revenues, or both. To reduce this discrepancy, governments must agree on fiscal equalization to the benefit of governments in economically disadvantaged territories.

In principle, equalization can be achieved by revenue sharing or by general or special purpose grants. The funds for distribution can be provided by a central government or by contributions of individual governments participating in equalization. They can serve to close the gap between the revenue-raising capacities of governments or to downgrade differences in costs of required public services (for details, Blöchliger et al. 2007; Boadway and Shah 2007; Dougherty and Forman 2021). Regardless of the method, equalization has redistributive effects in the horizontal dimension of multilevel governance. Grants provided by the central budget create a positive-sum situation, whereas intergovernmental revenue-sharing or transfers confront governments with a zero-sum problem. Provided that a central government is willing to provide resources for equalization, grants are the preferred solution. However, they shift power to the centre and make governments in need dependent on fiscal aid.

Economists criticize fiscal equalization through transfers or revenue because of their market-distorting incentives (Smart 2007; Wibbels 2005). In politics, controversies over an appropriate solution to fiscal disparities reveal different ideological approaches. Liberals disapprove of equalization as contradicting the principle of fiscal equivalence. According to this principle, a government should bear from its own revenues the expenditures for tasks which it is responsible for. Otherwise, it would lack incentives to improve the efficiency of public governance. Social democrats prefer a policy that enables all governments to provide citizens with the necessary public goods and services at an equal amount and quality. Both arguments neglect practical problems. Fiscal equivalence is not applicable if the scope of a government's tasks or the effects of its policies exceed the boundaries of a jurisdiction in which a government collects revenues. This is obviously the case in a multilevel government where fiscally autonomous governments are integrated into a common market (Buchanan 1950: 590). Therefore, the call for equalization in line with the social democratic approach seems necessary to balance the costs and benefits of externalities that differ between individual governments. However, this call leaves open the norm of distributive justice that is appropriate. Disparities that require fiscal equalization concern the relation between necessary tasks and the fiscal capacities of a government, yet the necessity of tasks, the expenditures needed to fulfil them and the appropriate fiscal capacities are difficult to define or estimate. Pragmatically, the average revenues per capita which a government can collect within its jurisdiction indicate capacities. The average costs for special goods or services, or particular needs due to conditions that a government cannot influence specify the required expenditures. Both criteria can be combined in various ways (Dougherty and Forman 2021). In unitary states and federations, the central government holds the authority to decide on this norm; in practice, central and regional or local governments must negotiate an agreement to mitigate fiscal imbalances.

Thus, a dilemma characterizes multilevel politics of fiscal equalization: On the one hand, it requires governments to solve a problem of distribution or redistribution without finding guidance in a socially accepted norm of distributive justice. Such a norm may be discovered if rational actors deliberated without knowing their position in the actual distribution and the distributive consequences of applying a specific norm (Rawls 1999: 118–23). However, under the scrutiny of parliaments, parties and the media, the idea of a "veil of ignorance" is difficult to implement in fiscal policy. On the other hand, executives negotiating on fiscal equalization are expected to seek the best possible outcome for their government. Given the different options for defining distributive justice, democratically elected executives, and likewise delegates of autocratic governments, prefer a rule that optimizes the outcome for their constituency and increases their chance to stay in power. They consider fiscal equalization as a redistributive policy, a matter of winning or losing, and pursue bargaining strategies to maximize the benefits for their government. This unfavourable set-up of policymakers who tend to bargaining behaviour and lack a norm of distributive justice impedes an agreement on fiscal equalization in multilevel governance.

The chances for coping with this wicked problem are not very good in intergovernmental negotiations in a state. However, they are far better than in multilevel governance beyond the state, for the following reasons. First, state constitutions often assign the authority to decide on fiscal equalization to the central government, and if there is no constitutional rule, central governments can use their spending power to implement equalization. In general, multilevel negotiations prepare the legislative decisions, but representatives of governments, usually ministers of finance or senior civil servants in finance departments, negotiate in the shadow of hierarchy. The uncertain outcome of unilateral central decisions motivates regional and local executives to agree on a joint proposal even if it does not meet their expectations. They are more willing to agree if central funds turn the perceived redistributive policy into a positive sum game of equalization. Second, if a national community of citizens is represented by a democratically elected parliament, central legislation legitimizes redistribution between governments, although those regional and local communities which lose in the distribution of revenues may disagree. Central legislation also legitimizes the choice of a norm of distributive justice, which usually determines fiscal equalization over a longer period. Third, institutions of central governments establish procedures for negotiating fiscal equalization and legislative decisions. These institutions can provide for a formal representation of regional or local governments with the risk that they may use veto power in decisions. However, they allow governments ruling over poor territories to raise their voices. Besides, they ensure the continuity of multilevel negotiations and thus facilitate a regular evaluation of the effects of fiscal equalization and a revision of the rules. Intergovernmental commissions responsible for implementing fiscal equalization (like the "Governments Grants Commission" in Australia), conferences of ministers or administrative networks of responsible civil servants in the departments of finance ensure the stability of the policy arena. Finally, established procedures and norms of distributive justice generate continuity, as does the veto position of governments profiting from distribution. Fiscal equalization may be permanently disputed in intergovernmental politics or academic discourses, but its path-dependent evolution ensures its continuity.

In multilevel governance beyond the state, economic and fiscal disparities are more pronounced than within states. Yet none of the conditions exist here which facilitate fiscal equalization within a state. Macro-regional federations like the EU provide for institutional stability. Their legislative and executive institutions can use their budget power. With the structural funds, the EU has introduced a redistributive policy to support governments in economically underdeveloped regions and rural areas. Beyond that, the expenses of the EU have redistributive effects between member states, like revenues contributed by member states according to their economic capacity, which is measured in terms of the Gross National Income and revenues from value-added tax. The "NextGeneration" fund, which the EU established in 2021 to meet the economic crisis caused by the COVID-19 pandemic and the challenge of climate change, has increased these redistributive effects (Deutsche Bundesbank 2022). Funds are allocated, however, in task-related procedures and according to performance-related criteria, and the share of a member state mostly depends on conditions that the recipient government must fulfil. Likewise, international organizations rely on mandatory contributions of their member states, determined according to different criteria but mostly their fiscal capacity. To an increasing extent, they receive fees for specific services, contributions from trust funds or voluntary donations from governments or private actors (Goetz and Patz 2017; Graham 2017; Katz Cogan 2016). Many international organizations spend on aid for underdeveloped countries or people in need. In contrast to fiscal equalization, redistributive effects are not intended in the first place and programmes lack continuity because the available funds depend on the "resourcing strategies" of an organization's executive staff (Goetz and Patz 2017: 9).

Different reasons explain why fiscal equalization does not appear on the agenda of international politics: First, authorities, related tasks and conditions for fulfilling tasks differ significantly among states, with the consequence that measuring disparities as relations between fiscal capacities and fiscal need is next to impossible. Second, taxpaying citizens in democratic governments support foreign aid to countries in need. Yet this does not mean that they would support equalizing transfers to other states. Even for the EU, data indicate a certain willingness to support transfers to member states in need only among left-oriented and rich citizens (Kleider and Stoeckel 2019). Third, autocratic governments' willingness to pay for intergovernmental transfers is presumably limited. Likewise, citizens, parties and governments in democracies have reservations about subsidizing autocratic regimes which they perceive as corrupt and incapable of appropriately using fiscal grants. Finally, governments of great powers like China, Russia and the US compete with their engagement in countries of the Global South. While each of these governments claims to support economic and social development, it suspects that the other governments seek influence and domination over this part of the world. For these reasons, reducing social inequality through financial transfers from rich to poor governments meets many obstacles in international or global multilevel governance, and a system of fiscal equalization is unattainable.

Nevertheless, territorial disparities between national governments matter in international multilevel governance. Distributive justice between nations is a general topic of debate in global politics. It appears in various policies as an issue on the political agenda, for example in negotiations on measures to curb migration, to protect the natural environment and biodiversity or to mitigate climate change. In global climate policy, compensation payments for developing countries were discussed for three decades before the Climate Conference in Sharm El-Sheikh in November 2022 finally agreed on a "loss and damage fund". Even if such a decision benefits all participating governments and their citizens, demands for financial compensation accentuate the redistributive character of a policy. Given the complication of policymaking by such an issue linkage, international organizations and NGOs have gained importance as mediators shaping discourses and advocating norms of distributive justice. This has changed the character of multilevel governance in these policy fields. However, there is no guarantee that these actors can help to separate the substantial policy problem from distributive interests and conflicts.

CONCLUSION

Economic diversity is an objective reality characterizing levels of governance, whereas economic and fiscal disparities are based on the political assessment of this reality. The former is a necessary consequence of material conditions and technologies. They enable a division of labour between territories and induce the mobility of people, goods, firms and financial capital. Disparities result from an unregulated market, but also from the domination and exploitation of resources and people both inside and between jurisdictions, be it in production, trade or politics. Contemporary disparities can be traced back to a long history of domination and exploitation, which continue to a certain extent in contemporary societies and politics. The rise of financial capitalism and the divide of societies into those that profit from mobility and those who cannot escape their fate by leaving their location have aggravated the problem of social and territorial inequality. The divide between territories petrifies social disparity.

The widening gap between rich and poor people, countries and regions has been intensively studied and criticized in academic discourses and in politics. It is less the spatial diversity but disparity that matters for politics. Therefore, the horizontal dimension of multilevel governance deserves more attention in research. The definition of disparity instigates ideological conflicts. They affect debates about centralization or decentralization of authority and separating or sharing power. Fiscal disparities resonate in divergent interests of officeholders in institutional reforms. These discords complicate agreements on the redistribution of authority and especially weaken intergovernmental institutions that serve as safeguards against centralization. Inevitably, disparities turn into distributive conflicts in multilevel policy coordination and downgrade the effectiveness of negotiations in general and joint-decision systems in particular, but also complicate governance by standards, yardstick competition, experimental policy and policy diffusion in which governments participate under equal terms.

Centralization of authority is one option to avoid deadlocks or performance deficits in multilevel governance, which result from distributive conflicts. Yet it does not guarantee an appropriate allocation of resources, given the information asymmetries between upper- and lower-tier governments and the ideological orientations of a central government. A policy regime of fiscal equalization holds multilevel governance together and stabilizes decentralization, although the rules and effects of redistribution of funds are matters of permanent intergovernmental conflict. Yet without fiscal equalization, disparity surfaces on the agenda of multilevel politics in many policy fields to be coordinated. In national governments, but more so in macro-regional and international multilevel governance, economic disparities constitute enormous challenges and threaten the sustainability of governance systems. A political-economic approach to multilevel governance draws attention to these challenges and provides a framework for research on their causes, consequences and chances for managing the ensuing problems while preserving diversity.

NOTE

1. Frank Stilwell brilliantly illustrates income inequality on the global level by a virtual parade of the world's nearly 5 billion adults who walk past the attentive observer within an hour. If each person is, according to Stilwell's scenario, visualized in height in proportion to their annual income and if all are lined up in a row with the poorer people coming before the wealthier people, then the observer should see after half an hour people that measure 68 centimetres, those passing after 45 minutes are 1.6 metres tall. The "really rich people" measuring 4 metres arrive at the 55-minute mark. Finally, as Stilwell notes, "at the 59-minute mark, they are a towering 21.5 metres. With about 10 seconds to go, their height reaches 100 metres. Then, in the last two seconds of the grand parade, a truly amazing phenomenon occurs. The height of the giants rises from 250 metres to over 3,000 metres, about as tall as the highest mountain in the UK. ... Even the alert onlookers find it hard to vis-ualize just how tall they are because clouds shroud the tops of their bodies." (Stilwell 2019: 2). Updated data are published by the World Inequality Lab, a group of researchers initiated by Thomas Piketty (Chancel et al. 2022).

6. Identity politics and differentiated division of authority

One of the topics which Hooghe and Marks set on the agenda of research for multilevel governance concerns the identity of communities, as Kleider rightly pointed out (Kleider 2020: 793–4). The social logic of politics implies the mobilization of communities against the functional reasoning of policy specialists, and mobilization occurs when activists or political leaders appeal to the commonalities, shared values and coherence of the members of a community. As research on regional authority revealed, the mobilization of communities and their effects on multilevel governance vary significantly between regions (Hooghe and Marks 2016: 100–121). This finding corresponds to society-centred approaches to federalism, which consider the division of authority "as a device by which the federal quality of the society are articulated and protected" (Livingston 1952: 84) and federal institutions as reflecting societal diversities (ibid.: 87–8). As Hooghe and Marks point out, the observed differentiation of authority between jurisdictions contributes to the accommodation of diversity, but also causes continuous tensions and induces institutional changes in multilevel governance (Hooghe and Marks 2016: 110).

This theoretical reasoning and the findings apply to the regional structure of unitary states and federations alike. While it was for a long time considered an aberration from the standard model of state organization, scholars have discussed differentiated distribution of authority since the 1970s as asymmetric federalism (Agranoff 1999; Tarlton 1965; Watts 2005), constitutional asymmetry (Popelier and Sahadžić 2019b) and differentiated decentralization (Allain-Dupré, Chatry and Moisio 2020; Bird and Ebel 2007). Research on differentiated integration in the EU (Leuffen, Rittberger and Schimmelfennig 2013; Schimmelfennig and Winzen 2020) and regionalism in international relations of states (Börzel and Risse 2016) revealed similar structures of multilevel governance. Like findings on asymmetric federalism, studies on multilevel governance beyond the state refer to national or regional identity as one of the driving forces of differentiation (Katzenstein 2005: 76–103; Schimmelfennig and Winzen 2019).

This chapter suggests rethinking this strand of research and theorizing in three aspects: First, it reviews the concept of identity for analysing the political expression of socio-cultural diversities in multilevel polities. As identity describes the social construction of communities, this chapter suggests focusing on identity politics. Accordingly, societal diversity matters as identity claims of distinct *demoi* or other communities. These claims cause authority conflicts in the horizontal dimension of multilevel governance. Second, in multilevel political systems, identity politics appears not only at the regional level. We observe complementary and competing efforts to construct identities at least at the regional, national and macro-regional levels. Identity politics at different levels can generate an integrating idea of multilevel citizenship that legitimizes authority division in multilevel governance. However, it is also a source of contestation of authority and power. Third, differentiated integration or asymmetric distribution of authority have been discussed as procedures or institutional designs to attenuate conflicts between diverse communities. However, by institutionalizing divides, the risk of undermining multilevel governance increases. Institutional asymmetry implies not only difference but self-rule of constitutionally separated jurisdictions, all the more as identity politics is closely related to a populist understanding of people and democracy. Rethinking the political process of identity formation, the tendency to objectify communities and the inherent risks of differentiation and asymmetric division of authority sheds new light on these approaches to accommodating diversity in multilevel governance.

IDENTITY POLITICS: THE POLITICAL CONSTRUCTION OF COMMUNITIES AND *DEMOI*

Many scholars agree that the identity of communities (groups, societies, peoples) is relevant to explain collective action, political conflicts, the coherence of institutions and institutional change. What identity means has been a matter of controversial debate. As a social category affecting territorial politics and multilevel governance, collective identity comprises constitutive norms defining membership, social purposes of the community, comparisons with other communities and cognitive models of political or material conditions and interests (Abdelal et al. 2006: 696). Yet, as Kleider notes, "despite a rich literature on the implications of territorial identities, we still know relatively little about how identities are formed in the first place" (Kleider 2020: 794). What is more, we cannot even take for granted that empirically identified norms, purposes, distinctions and perceptions of a community matter in the behaviour of people and their choices or activities in politics. We know that identity is constructed, but how this occurs, whether in top-down processes of political leadership or bottom-up processes of deliberation, is still an open question (Checkel 2016).

Leaving aside the theoretical and methodological difficulties raised by the concept, this chapter posits that it is not identity, in the first place, that matters in multilevel governance, rather it is identity politics. Political leaders and parties define identity to justify their power and mobilize support for their policy. In multilevel politics, referring to the identities of a community or *demos* is a most relevant discursive strategy in the permanent contests for power. It presumes an internal coherence of the people, which elected officials claim to represent, and criteria by which the community of people differs from other people. Coherence and distinctness suggest that individuals belong to a community, that their collective action differences them from other communities, and that their particular public interests should be recognized in political institutions and procedures.

The term identity politics originated in the literature on social movements. Just as the concept of identity, scientists have used this term with various meanings (cf. Bernstein 2005; Fukuyama 2018; Heyes 2020; Tully 2003). In research on multilevel governance, it applies to regionalist or nationalist ideologies and campaigns against a concentration of power at the centre or the sharing of power in a multilevel polity. It also refers to the political mobilization of people who feel excluded or underrepresented in politics and demand recognition or rights to self-determination.

As a rule, the politicization of identity addresses communities which aim at becoming a *demos*. Like spatial economies, communities lack a clear and regular demarcation. Yet, just as spatial economies turn into territorial economies within the boundaries of jurisdictions, the territorial organization of governments turns a community into a *demos*. A *demos* exists as a political institution. Boundary rules define who is and who can become a citizen, and institutions enable legal and prevent illegal collective action. Apart from these rules, effective collective action requires and entails a sense of commonality, as well as mutual trust among citizens in others' willingness to seek the common good, to comply with basic norms and duties, and to respect individual freedom and human rights.

Considering the plurality of individual persons and the lack of obvious commonalities beyond their membership, a *demos* appears as an "imagined community" (Anderson 1998). Public communication shapes the imaginings of a *demos*, but cannot precisely determine an identity, not the least as the meaning of identity is usually more or less contested (Abdelal et al. 2006: 700). Therefore, it is primarily politics that shapes the "corporate identity" (Benhabib 1997: 37) of a *demos* and motivates citizens to identify with a *demos*. Adding to social ties in small and function-specific communities, identity politics and identification of private persons with a citizenry contribute to ensuring the coherence of a *demos* and for committing citizens to fulfil civic duties (ibid.: 45–8). Identities of *demoi*, more than those of other communities like tribes, religious communities or different kinds of associations, "are deployed strategically as a form of collective action to change institutions; to

transform mainstream culture, its categories, and values, and perhaps by extension its policies and structures; to transform participants; or simply to educate
legislators or the public" (Bernstein 2005: 62). Yet identity politics also
means "any kind of political intervention which intentionally targets a group
in which people share common essential attributes – like race, gender, sexual
orientation, religion or ethnicity – with the perceived aim of gaining sectional
advantage" (Younge 2019: 2). The first definition emphasizes internal, and the
second external, aims and potential effects.

Internally, identity politics constructs identity as an "attachment that people
feel" for their imagined community (Anderson 1998: 141) and fosters loyalty,
trust and solidarity among those who belong to it. A sense of belonging rests
on a common language and participation in political discourses. Against this
background, identity politics promotes ideas, values, norms and attitudes that
members of a community share. Therefore, it operates with symbols and narra-
tives on historical legacies, traditions, experiences, ways of living and beliefs.

Externally, identity politics determines how the community differs from
others, how it relates to others, and whether it is privileged or disadvantaged
compared to others. Marking distinctness from a comparative perspective
is more than a way to shape the perceptions of members. It serves to clarify
the political determination of a community in relation to other communities,
be it those at the same level or those at upper or lower tiers of a multilevel
political system. Externally oriented political strategies strive for substantial
advantages in competition or cooperation with other communities. These
advantages can refer to the recognition as a distinct community, the right to use
a native language in official communication or cultural practices, the authority
to autonomously decide on specific policies, representation in upper-tier institutions or the right to participate in political processes with or without a veto
right. Identity is also an argument of political leaders who claim independence
from a unitary or multilevel polity.

To understand the effects of identity politics in multilevel governance, two
aspects need to be highlighted: First, identity constructions are ideas, but they
reflect socio-economic conditions and cultural practices. Regardless of their
justification in politics, claims referring to identity often reflect economic
disparities. In the context of multilevel governance, the "sectional advantages"
mentioned in Younge's definition cited above point to political strategies of
mobilizing internal cooperation and exerting external pressure determined to
maintain beneficial conditions and resources or compensate for disadvantages.
Certainly, economic interests alone cannot explain the rise of identity politics.
For instance, independence movements often emerged in conquered territories
or after a change of state borders had divided existing communities. In consolidated states, however, economic interests and identity claims often overlap.

Second, politics which refers to the identity of a *demos* tends towards populism (Brubaker 2020). Both conceive the *demos* as a homogeneous political community, both indicate a strategy directed against the domination from above or by other communities, both appeal to the whole people to mobilize support for a political leader or a party, and both claim legitimacy by speaking for the people. If populism is a "thin-centred ideology" (Mudde 2004: 544), the ideology of identity is no less thin as it neglects distinct interests and conflicts and simply advocates an abstract common interest of a *demos* or community. At a glance, populism seems to speak for the people in general, whereas identity politics refers to a specific *demos*. In reality, however, this difference disappears since populists mostly characterize the people by distinct features. They often enrich their thin ideology with different concepts of identity. They advocate national identity against multilateral international politics or regional identity against intergovernmental politics.

COMPLEMENTARY AND COMPETING IDENTITY POLITICS IN MULTILEVEL GOVERNANCE

In the introduction to a book summarizing a decade of research on citizenship and national identity (Miller 2000), David Miller points out three tendencies which threaten the social foundation of democracy: first globalization, with the state losing its "capacity to determine the cultural make-up of its citizens"; second, sub-state nationalism in peaceful and violent forms, third, "new forms of identity politics" of communities who, beyond their citizenship, demand recognition of their distinct religion, ethnicity, gender etc. (ibid.: 1–2). In a critical reflection on these tendencies, Miller argues against advocates of a pluralist concept of identity, who take the diversification of identity for granted and make the case for multilevel citizenship (Maas 2017). This discussion on the concept of citizenship and identity reflects empirical observations which Miller put in a nutshell twenty years ago. Yet considering multilevel governance, his description of the fragmentation of identity misses important variations in the vertical and horizontal dimensions of multilevel governance; but so does the concept of multilevel citizenship.

First, if we take identity as a relevant argument in politics, it does not only matter in democracies but also in non-democratic governments or international organizations. In democracies, identity politics refers to values of equality, solidarity and pluralism (Miller 2000). In autocracies and illiberal or divided democracies, the new forms of identity politics mentioned by Miller often turn into radical nationalism. In many states around the world, parties in governments or heads of government imposed an "ethno-religious nationalism" as a reaction to postmodernity and globalization (Juergensmeyer 2019). In macro-regional and international organizations, identity politics promotes basic norms, values and political principles and thus constitutes the bond that stabilizes institutions and intergovernmental cooperation. However, ideological and value conflicts among national governments weaken this bond. In brief: Identity politics reflects the socio-cultural, political and institutional diversity of the constituent units forming a multilevel polity.

Second, like economic disparities, identity politics and divides between *demoi* materialize differently at the core levels of governance. The ties that associate citizens with communities vary with the density of communication and the diversity of individuals and social groups. Other things being equal, they tend to be stronger in smaller territories and at the local or regional level than in larger territories and upper tiers. Data available for federations show significant variations between countries (Kincaid and Jedwab 2019), but they support the plausibility of this hypothesis. Institutional conditions of a state and identity politics of the central government attenuate the effect of size. Given the fact that effective boundary rules and legal membership exist in a central state, but not at the regional and local level, national citizenship has a strong bearing on peoples' identity. Established measures to promote nationhood by central governments contribute to this. Cities and municipalities are most important for the social and cultural engagement of people and the provision of basic public services whereas the rise of regional governments reveals a policy change responding to the spatial diversity of economies and to regionalist movements requesting recognition of distinct communities and self-rule (Hooghe and Marks 2016). Therefore, identifications of citizens with local and regional communities add to nationality and amalgamate into multilevel identities.

Third, to explain the political dynamics in multilevel governance, it is less the fluctuating multilevel identities but the diversity of identity politics at different levels and territorial jurisdictions that matters. In the vertical dimension, between different levels, the substance and strategies of this politics vary, but in principle, they work well together. Therefore, emphasizing national identity as a prerequisite for democracy does not contradict the normative appeal of multilevel citizenship, which presumes loyalty, trust and solidarity in smaller and larger communities. In contrast, identity politics in the horizontal dimension applies to different communities and it constructs them as distinct. The claims made with identity politics differ, and they usually emerge on the agenda of specific communities, either those that present themselves as particularly important, attractive or successful or those that complain about discrimination, disadvantages and injustice. This unilateral identity politics can cause permanent tensions among governments and complicate multilevel governance due to conflicting claims. Moreover, it can instigate a self-reinforcing development of disintegration, if parties or a political elite in a jurisdiction demand recognition, participation rights, authority or autonomy and governments or parties in other jurisdictions follow suit with similar demands.

Such differing identity claims can be observed at the local level, where large cities request a special status as megapolis or smaller local municipalities fight against losing their autonomy in territorial consolidation. However, while empirical studies have revealed that the effects of local government reorganization rarely meet expectations, they found no indications that these disappointments have led to lasting mobilization against the reforms (Tavares 2018). From time to time, looming identity conflicts surface in local politics and policymaking, yet without significantly affecting multilevel governance. In contrast, the rise of regionalism and competitive nationalism has significantly changed territorial politics in states, macro-regions and international politics. A very rough sketch of these changes must suffice in this context.

Regionalism, the idea of "the persistence of subnational and transnational differences, identities and commitments" (Hueglin 1986: 439) appears as an ideology or political project of parties, governments or social movements. The term usually refers to "regions" of states and not to "macro-regions" of the world. It emphasizes the economic, social and political distinctness or discrimination of a region and the demands for more autonomy from the centre and the "majority society". As a new political movement in Europe and Northern America, it has gained momentum since at least the 1970s (Agnew 2013; Hueglin 1986, Keating 1998; Swenden 2006). Originating in specific regions, it rarely achieved political relevance in all territories throughout federal or unitary states. This movement initially started in peripheral regions. Later, it gained ground in politically and economically strong regions and set off a "dynamic of uneven development" (Spencer and Wollman 2002: 172). In economically flourishing regions, political leaders, business people and unions justify autonomy claims with the performance principle, presuming a right of regional governments and citizens to benefit from successful policies and from the efforts of working people and private companies in their region. They refer to the joint economic achievement of public and private actors to construct a "legitimizing identity" (Beyme 2007: 23; translated by author). Typical instances of this kind of identity politics of rich regions emerged in Alberta and Quebec in Canada, Bavaria in Germany, Basque Country and Catalonia in Spain, Flanders in Belgium, and Scotland in the UK. In economically disadvantaged regions, political leaders promote a "resistance identity of the underprivileged and excluded" (ibid.; translated by author), often in reaction to autonomy claims from rich regions. In both types of regions, identity politics serves to strengthen the regional level against the central state. The proposals for distributing authority, however, differ, as outlined in Chapter 5. Governments of disadvantaged regions call for financial assistance from the central government and cooperation in public services to compensate for their lack of sufficient fiscal capacities. Identity politics in rich regions aims at decentralization of authority or autonomy. This is especially the case in multinational societies; that is, in states with communities whose members share a sense of belonging to a distinct "nation" (Lecours 2021: 18) within a "majority nation". Regional nationalist movements or parties call for independence from an existing state. Secessionist politics in Quebec, Basque Country, Catalonia and Scotland are the most prominent examples. A similar kind of sub-state nationalism is likely to emerge after a change of state borders through occupation or the break-up of an existing state when minority communities feel dominated within the newly created state. The dissolution of the Soviet Union and the nation-building after the decolonization in Africa and the Arabic Peninsula exemplify these conflicts.

Sub-state regionalism seems to have contributed to the decline of nationalism, together with globalization and state failure in parts of the world. This was at least a hypothesis discussed in the literature on the transformation of the state towards multilevel governance (Sørensen 2004: 83–102; Loughlin 2000). However, the idea that a nation of citizens constitutes the societal condition of collective self-determination (Miller 1995: 11, 80–118) has never disappeared. After World War II, this idea arguably resurged in different types of plurinational multilevel political systems (Keating 2015). Sub-state regionalism challenging the homogeneity of nation-states was only one process contributing to this conversion, while the other was the formation of macro-regions based on transnational regionalism.

Macro-regionalism attracted the attention of scholars as a realist alternative to the "post-Westphalian" global governance approach. It originated in the optimistic intellectual climate of the 1990s (Télo 2014: 20). For a long time, research focused on European integration. Meanwhile, scholars applied a comparative approach to international relations. The label of regionalism in this context can mean a field of research, a process of forming regions or the construction of identities (Balogun 2021; Costa Buranelli and Tskhay 2019). Here, in line with Hueglin's definition mentioned above, it describes regional identity formation through the "emergence of shared feelings of loyalty, solidarity, and commonality among member states and their citizens therein" (Balogun, 2021: 5). In large territories, where not only spatial distance but also state borders or different languages constrain communication and interaction, institutions and elite discourses are more important for constructing identity than at the national or sub-national level. Identity politics translates specific cultures and norms prevailing in member states into an "institutional identity" which stabilizes corporate actorness even in weakly formalized patterns of cooperation (Acharya 1997; Oelsner 2013). Like regionalism in states, macro-regionalism complements state nationalism, all the more as it draws on norms and cultures which evolved in member states (Katzenstein 1996).

The EU has been considered the most advanced form of a macro-region with institutions forming a corporate identity of a transnational *demos* (Checkel 2016). The identification of citizens with Europe first appeared as a presumed "permissive consensus" of the people. Opinion polls confirmed a multilevel identity of European citizens, which is embedded in national identities. They also showed a significant minority of citizens who perceive themselves as exclusively national (Börzel and Risse 2020: 27). This ambivalence mirrors an incoherent political construction of a European identity. Looking at the identity politics that appeared in the debates in member states and the European Commission, Vivien Schmidt identified four visions of the EU: first, "the EU as a borderless problem-solving entity ensuring free markets and regional security", second, "the EU as a bordered values-based community", third, "the EU as a border-free, rights-based post-national union", and fourth, "the EU as global actor 'doing international relations differently' through multilateralism, humanitarian aid and peace-keeping" (Schmidt 2009: 24). There is no doubt that the development from the European Communities of six member states to the contemporary EU of 27 members created a unique polity in a macro-region that stands out as to both its institutional consolidation and its scope of authority. However, recent trends towards intergovernmentalism in European politics and divides among member state governments on salient policy issues reveal that macro-regional and national identities are less complementary than scholars had observed before the Euro crisis (Börzel and Risse 2020). Whether the external pressures of military threat or migration fosters the evolution of the EU towards a state is in doubt (Kelemen and McNamara 2022). While identity politics in member states varies, the different visions of Europe point towards differentiated integration (cf. next section).

Since about the turn of the century, identity politics in states has countervailed the evolution of multilevel identities of citizens. Yet even this revitalization of nationalism does not materialize in all parts of the world and varies significantly in those parts where it can be observed. In failed states, foreign governments, international organizations, private corporations and "warlords" compete for influence. In the best case, they provide basic governance functions of limited statehood (Börzel and Risse 2021); in the worst case, they fuel looming identity conflicts and violence. In emergent powers like Brazil, India, Iran, Turkey or South Africa, governments adhere to a populist version of nationalism claiming that the political leader represents a uniform nation. This identity politics comes with a policy aiming at strengthening the position of these countries in economic and political competition in the world. While cooperating in loose alliances, these governments abstain from macro-regional integration to maintain their national autonomy. Populist nationalism also emerged and has become increasingly influential in European countries (Bergmann 2020). Politics in the UK and the US reflect a neoliberal nationalism which rejects regulation of markets by international organizations and instead tries to regain control over economic policy (Harmes 2019: 87–119). A competitive version of nationalism emerged in the so-called great powers, China, Russia and the US, and likely determines the future of international and global governance. The US government and its allies in Europe, Canada and Australia present themselves as advocates of liberal values and human rights; China propagates a specific form of "democracy" where the will of the people is defined by a technocratic Communist Party; Russia has turned towards a cultural nationalism rooted on the history of the old Russian empire. Mainly driven by economic interests and therefore based on "rational calculations on how to further the national interest" (Hanrieder 1978: 1277), this competitive nationalism also reveals strategies of identity formation covered in fuzzy catchwords like values, competing political-economic systems or missions of a nation.

Whether this sketchy summary is empirically sound or not can be disputed. And yet, the following hypotheses are sufficiently plausible and give reasons for rethinking multilevel governance.

First, although it is uncertain whether and how identity politics influences people's sense of belonging to a community, it is the driving force of the "social logic" in multilevel governance (Hooghe and Marks 2016). Concerning the distribution of authority, it shapes the direction of change. If identity politics is strong at all levels, we can expect a permanent contestation of power. It may trigger a balancing process stabilizing multilevel governance based on multilevel citizenship, as can be observed in integrated federations. If identity is more strongly enunciated at the upper than at the lower tiers, or the other way around, it induces centripetal or centrifugal dynamics.

Second, states and national identity politics still prevail over sub-national or macro-level regionalism. Therefore, they constitute a constant condition in the evolution of multilevel governance. Neither identity politics at other levels nor multilevel identity has significantly weakened the impact of state nationalism. In the era of globalization, economic competition, the populist return to the nation-state and the contestation of Western domination have stimulated identity politics that frame nations as unique, based on specific values, histories, achievements and visions for the future (Bergmann 2020; Kaldor 2004). Furthermore, different versions of state nationalism rest on the history and the institutionalization of a *demos* in a state. Understood as a community of citizens with political rights, national identities are complementary. On this basis, international cooperation and macro-regional integration have "rescued" states against the globalization or de-nationalization of economies and societies. Yet the more identity politics defines a *demos* in terms of ethnonationalism, the more divides obstruct multilevel governance beyond the state level.

Third, whereas citizenship backs nationalism in a state, regionalism within states reflects the diversity of societies. Accordingly, it surfaces in specific regions and either provokes countervailing movements in other regions or diffuses to other regions (Hooghe and Marks 2016: 122). In any case, identity materializes differently in regions. The same applies to macro-regionalism, where the cultural and institutional diversity of states limits the consolidation of integration, and where these national features lead to multilevel governance with distinct identities.

The heterogeneity between nations and regions and unilateral or competing identity claims are a source of permanent power contestation in multilevel governance. Governmental actors representing distinct communities advocate not only policy-specific interests but also the right to self-determination for their *demos*. In practical multilevel politics, the social logic of governance becomes manifest in strategic interactions. Political executives prioritize preferences determined in domestic politics against coordinated action with other governments. They accentuate divergences rather than options for compromise, focus on distributive consequences of policies rather than joint benefits, and justify strategies of confrontation in intergovernmental relations with the presumed will of their people. Besides the effectiveness of multilevel governance, the stability of a division of authority is threatened through identity politics. As Hooghe and Marks put it:

> Normatively distinct communities produce ripples in the structure of governance because they attract rule. They produce local concentrations of authority that break the coherence of jurisdictional design across a country. The outcome then reflects not just heterogeneity of *policy* preferences, but something more fundamental and difficult to accommodate, heterogeneity of *polity* preferences. (Hooghe and Marks 2016: 17)

Considering that identity politics is likely to escalate conflicts and has ignited conflicts in many so-called multiethnic societies or multinational federations, scholars have made the case for differentiated multilevel governance as an approach to accommodate diversity and moderate conflicts (e.g., Kymlicka 2005). Whether and under which conditions this approach succeeds is still an open question.

FROM DIFFERENTIATED INTEGRATION TO ASYMMETRY OF AUTHORITY: ACCOMMODATING DIVERSITY OR DIVIDING GOVERNANCE

Differentiated multilevel governance can be explained as a compromise between the functional and social rationality of dividing authority. It is widely applied as an institutional design to reconcile the exigencies of complex tasks with the demands of identity politics. From a series of country studies on fiscal centralization and decentralization (Bird and Ebel 2007), Richard Bird and Robert Ebel conclude: "When examined closely, virtually every country, federal or unitary, large or small, appears to offer some evidence of asymmetry in practice – between rich and poor, urban and non-urban, capital cities and frontier territories, and territorial or non-territorial groupings based on race, religion or language" (Bird and Ebel 2006: 506). In a similar vein, Liesbet Hooghe and Gary Marks state: "The mobilization of territorial communities has created a patchwork of differentiated governance within the state that is the new normal" (Hooghe and Marks 2016: 18). In the literature on the EU, increasing differentiated integration has become a topic of research and controversial discussions (for a synopsis see Gänzle, Leruth and Trondal 2020a). Given the different research fields, it is not surprising that the terms applied in this context, like "asymmetric federalism", "asymmetric decentralization", "differentiated decentralization" or "differentiated integration" diverge. This conceptual confusion can be reduced by distinguishing integration, division of authority and policy coordination, as suggested in Chapter 3.

Integration means the coming together of governments to form a new level of governance. Accordingly, differentiated integration designates a specific process or political strategy which aims at forming and holding together a multilevel polity divided by identity conflicts. In the EU, it has been labelled as integration with "multiple speed", "variable geometry" and "sectoral differentiation". It developed in sequences of enlargement of the number of member states, the variation of membership in specific policies like the Schengen Agreement or the European Monetary Union, and the establishment of institutional pillars that differ according to the mode of decision-making between supranational and intergovernmental politics (Stubb 1996). Temporal, spatial and institutional differentiation characterizes the formation of macro-regions and global governance in general. Similar processes also characterize the history of federal systems. When the German federation was founded in 1871, a fusion of the federal government with the government of Prussia created significant institutional differentiation. In settler societies in the Americas and Australia, the integration of indigenous people occurred long after the state formation by the colonizers and in special institutional arrangements. Likewise, processes of disintegration start with identity politics and secessionist policies in one territory. They may end up in a withdrawal of a government from a multilevel system. Over time, other governments may follow suit and thus destabilize the architecture of multilevel governance.

As an institutional design of multilevel systems, the asymmetric division of authority aims at coping with societal diversity and solving identity conflicts. It should stabilize integration or prevent disintegration. In federations and regionalized states as well as in macro-regional and global multilevel governance, this design privileges a government or constrains the power of a government compared to others on the same level through a centralization or decentralization of authority that differs between territorial jurisdictions. Usually, a constitution, statutes or treaties enshrine such asymmetry. It can also be acknowledged as a "constitutional convention"; that is, a non-formalized rule derived from a widely accepted interpretation of constitutional law. To discern the asymmetric division of authority from the differentiated exercise of authority (Gamper 2021: 19; Popelier and Sahadžić 2019a: 6), there must be some kind of legal basis or acknowledgement. Moreover, institutional asymmetry encompasses "differences in status, distribution of competences and fiscal power" (Popelier and Sahadžić 2019a: 6). Status means the special position of a government in the multilevel polity including its right to co-decide in central institutions; competence designates the right to decide and act on specific policy issues; and fiscal power indicates the authority over revenues and expenditures (Sahadžić 2021: 42).

In international organizations, asymmetric authority often concerns the status of governments as permanent and non-permanent or full and associated members. Here and in national multilevel governance, population groups with a long history of ethnic or cultural distinctness are recognized as political communities to guarantee their existence. Recognition typically comes with special rights of members of the community, for instance, to form a corporation to exercise authority in a territorially or functionally defined jurisdiction. Within states, regions enjoy a privileged status if the constitution grants them full governmental autonomy in spelled-out matters including legislation, whereas other regions serve as administrative sub-units of the central government. Some regions may also be over-represented in institutions or procedures at the upper tier and/or profit from specific veto rights.

Status differentiation of constituent units of a multilevel polity can but does not necessarily entail a differentiation of competences in policymaking. In this respect, asymmetry refers to a standard set of decentralized policies. Privileged governments hold special competences and decide over additional policies, whereas restricted governments decide over fewer policies than all other governments. Accordingly, the central government holds either more or less authority in the territorial jurisdictions concerned. An asymmetric distribution of authority of the first kind regularly refers to policies that relate to the distinctness of communities such as language, education and culture. Beyond that, a widely used procedure to flexibly differentiate authority is the right of lower-tier governments to opt out from general legislation or intergovernmental agreements. Mostly a choice open to all governments, it entails asymmetric authority if it privileges certain governments ruling over distinct communities. In another way, a government can gain privileged authority by being exempt from specified constitutional rules or laws. Restricting asymmetry reduces the scope of authority of selected governments, for instance, if a central authority fulfils a normally decentralized policy in certain jurisdictions. It can also subject a government to specific legal or executive provisions, to central supervision or to direct rule either in general or under specified conditions. Autocratic governments use such restrictions to control dissenting people and undermine their ambitions for autonomy. A case in point is China's establishment of Ethnic Minority Autonomous Regions where local legislation must be submitted for approval by a standing committee of the National People's Congress (Buhi 2019: 120). Democratic governments restrict autonomy to prevent violent conflicts in divided communities or if the formation of an effective government fails. This occurred in the UK when the government in London introduced direct rule over Northern Ireland from 1972 to 1998 and again from 2002 to 2007. Central rule or supervision makes lower-tier governments dependent on the will of a central authority. Within states, the number of dependent regions has significantly declined since the 1950s (Hooghe and Marks 2016: 116–8). In contrast, the privileging asymmetric distribution of competences has been more and more used to empower distinct communities.

An asymmetric distribution of authority over revenues and expenditures has significant consequences for the balance of power in a multilevel polity. Concerning revenues, the authority to determine and collect taxes differs, for example in Spain, where the Basque Country and Navarre are privileged, and in Canada, where Territories largely depend on federal grants, whereas provinces decide on and collect a significant share of taxes. In general, legislative acts or statutes of central governments or the conditionality of funding by international organizations like the IMF or the EU can constrain expenditure autonomy and limit the spending power of a government, but such restrictions depend on specific circumstances and apply for a limited period. Irrespective of whether fiscal authority is symmetric or asymmetric, the effective fiscal capacities and hence the power of governments differ according to economic disparities. Fiscal equalization redistributes revenues to the benefit of specific regions or states to compensate for these disparities (cf. Chapter 5), whereas grants allocated by a central government can de facto restrict the autonomy of governments and invigorate identity politics in multilevel fiscal policy.

Table 6.1 summarizes different manifestations of differentiated authority. During the last decades, comparative research has shed light on these institutional asymmetries in multilevel governance, inquired into the causes and tried to evaluate the effects. Unfortunately, the different conceptualizations of asymmetry have inhibited an accumulation of evidence. Based on the available literature, we can mark some important trends.

First, literature on the EU (Gänzle, Leruth and Trondal 2020b; Schimmelfennig and Winzen 2020) and international authority (Hooghe, Lenz and Marks 2019; Zürn, Tokhi and Binder 2021) indicates multiple

Table 6.1   *Asymmetric distribution of authority*

	Privileging	Constraining
Status	– full, permanent membership of constituent government – recognition – autonomy (right to legislate) – overrepresentation, veto power	– associated, non-permanent membership – dependence – conditional autonomy – underrepresentation
Competences in policymaking	– broader set of policies – legislative competences – special right to opt out; exemption from central rules	– narrower set of policies – special legal provisions – central supervision or direct rule
Fiscal authority	– extended authority to collect taxes for selected governments	– dependence on central grants (spending power of the central government)

asymmetries in the division of authority, which have also been observed at the regional and local level in unitary and federal states (e.g., Agranoff 1999; Allain-Dupré, Chatry and Moisio 2020; Beyme 2005; Burgess 2006: 209–225; Keating 1999; Popelier and Sahadžić 2019b; Watts 2005). Hooghe and Marks found a rising number of "autonomous regions" with a specific status. According to the authors, the constitutionalization of this status institutes an effective safeguard of autonomy (Hooghe and Marks 2016: 109–10). Their data also show a remarkable institutional dynamic. Priviledged regions, for which a central government granted specific authority or rights, often turn into standard regions, while standard regions often turn into regions privileged by asymmetry. Apparently, this demonstrates the volatile nature of a distribution of authority in multilevel governance as outlined in Chapter 3.

Second, identity politics drives the asymmetric division of authority. Where politics claims to represent a distinct community, it demands autonomy. In matters concerning their distinctness, regional governments with special status exercise self-rule instead of shared rule. In consequence, institutional asymmetries "segment political institutions along territorial lines, insulating local elites and raising the salience of differences between the region and the center" (ibid.: 109). In other words: While societal distinctness and territorial segmentation refer to the horizontal dimension of a multilevel system in the first place, that is the relations of constituent units like states, regions or local governments, they regularly affect the vertical dimension. Charles Tarleton, who was among the first to draw attention to asymmetry in federations, made a similar argument. He defined symmetry as "the level of conformity and commonality in the relations of each separate political unit of the system to both the system as a whole and to the other component units" (Tarlton 1965: 868). Accordingly, asymmetry in the form of a special status of autonomy for selected constituent governments divides multilevel governance through the separation of authority between jurisdictions and levels. It seems incompatible with power sharing and establishes high hurdles for multilevel policymaking.

Third, the endurance of asymmetric division of authority cannot be taken for granted. If entrenched in constitutional law, veto rights in amendment procedures or constitutional courts might serve as safeguards against change. Nonetheless, if communities or their governments hold specific powers, they face contestation by other governments. Therefore, asymmetric decentralization is difficult to stabilize. If a central government grants special powers to a government or organized community which claims to represent marginalized minorities, it tries to accommodate diversity by restoring justice. This arrangement appears as a self-enforcing institution because both governments benefit compared to alternative outcomes or conflict escalation. However, in the horizontal dimension of multilevel governance, asymmetry initiates a distributive conflict with other governments holding fewer competences. These governments often aim to catch up with privileged governments and demand equal decentralization of authority or try to block increasing asymmetry by further decentralization (Hombrado 2011). The central government is thus confronted by opposing institutional interests of bargaining coalitions, which as Christina Zuber pointed out, "are more stable than the issue-based ad hoc coalitions between equal units in a more symmetrical system" (Zuber 2011: 554). The idea that an asymmetric design of a multilevel polity can accommodate diversity contrasts with the probability of power conflicts between differentiated constituent units (ibid.: 565). This explains the ambivalent assessment in comparative research. Scholars found cases where asymmetry helped to integrate distinct communities and cases where it led to an escalation of conflict and disintegration (Watts 2005: 6).

As this literature confirms, societal diversity is a reality in multilevel governance and identity politics is the primary cause of a differentiated distribution of power. Autonomy for distinct communities or nations is still conceived as an institutional design to cope with identity conflicts in multinational societies (Watts 2005). There is, however, empirical evidence that this strategy of constitutional politics entails two problematic effects. On the one hand, there is no guarantee that a special status and autonomy meet the demands of distinct communities. As Lecours has demonstrated by comparative case studies, it is not the status of autonomy or the extent of authority that matters. Identity conflicts can only be managed by a regular renewal of recognition and the adjustment of a differentiated distribution of authority to the changing ways in which distinct communities perceive and articulate their identity and express their claims. Lecours concludes: "Autonomy that is subject to ongoing discussions, negotiations, and adjustments is a better nationalist management strategy than autonomy presented as a definitive and ultimate settlement" (Lecours 2021:

196). However, the regular adjustment of authority provokes expectations and claims in non-privileged communities. In negotiations, actors representing these communities argue for symmetric institutions in multilevel governance and thus legitimize their demands for extended authority. For both reasons, the asymmetry of power in the horizontal dimension of multilevel governance is an unstable constellation (Basta 2017; Zuber 2011). This instability must be managed in institutional policy which needs to include all governments in multilateral negotiations.

Like fiscal equalization, constitutional amendments and institutional change concerning the division of authority are responsibilities of a central government. In practical politics, the substance of legislation in these matters is regularly negotiated among actors representing all affected governments. The corresponding policy in the EU and international organizations requires decisions with unanimity on treaties determining the delegation or pooling of authority. In contrast to constitutional amendments in states, the EU or international organizations cannot create a shadow of hierarchy motivating negotiating actors to find an agreement. Instead, member state governments face the shadow of ratification of agreements by their parliaments.

In line with Fritz W. Scharpf's theory of the "Joint Decision Trap" (Scharpf 1988), empirical research on constitutional change in multilevel governments (Benz 2016) and treaty amendment in the EU (Christiansen and Reh 2009) proved that intergovernmental negotiations usually end with compromises on marginal changes of the division of power. Over time incremental change accumulates, but a sequential process can also "advance backwards" (Benz and Sonnicksen 2018) when later agreements revise previous achievements. This development, first and foremost, must be expected in constitutional disputes on an asymmetric division of authority. The more identity politics and enduring claims for autonomy impede a compromise on an acceptable division of authority, the more responses from parties or people in less-empowered governments may express rising resentment and lead to an escalation of conflicts (Basta 2017). Under these conditions, negotiating intergovernmental agreements are likely to end in stalemate due to a "spiral of competitive claims" (Hooghe and Marks 2016: 147). Notwithstanding this risk of failure, "dynamic autonomy" as suggested by Lecours (2021: 9–15, 194–208) seems a viable option for coping with societal diversity, even if autonomy institutionally divides governments. The need to permanently negotiate and adjust the division of authority can stabilize relations between policymakers of different jurisdictions (Breda 2023); all the more, if a government or international organization orchestrates constitutional negotiations.

Multilevel policymaking matters to accommodate diversity for another reason as well. Comparative research on conflict resolution in divided societies suggests combining decentralization with power sharing, which scholars have recommended as a basic strategy for accommodation (O'Leary 2013: 19–30). Literature on post-conflict countries also emphasizes the relevance of shared rule (Keil 2019: 152). These propositions stand in contrast to the predominance of self-rule in regions with a specific status. Given the instability of this kind of asymmetric decentralization in multinational societies, scholars have proposed consociational arrangements which divide authority between levels and jurisdictions but provide for proportional representation of communities in central institutions, establish governance by negotiated intergovernmental agreements, and allow governments to veto intrusion of other governments into their jurisdiction and to ward off negative externalities (Lijphart 1977: 25–52). In contrast to joint-decision systems in constitutional policy, consociational arrangements create cross-cutting cleavages by including representatives of different societal sectors. However, as long as politics focuses on the identity of people, it is not a given that confrontation can be avoided.

CONCLUSION

Like economic disparities, diverse identities of communities or *demoi* are a reality. However, in politics, they appear as constructed reality. Therefore, not identities per se but identity politics matters in multilevel governance. Identity claims are voiced in ethnic communities and territorially organized *demoi*. In multilevel governance, they cause conflicts and divides in the horizontal dimension which affects the relations between governments at upper- and lower tiers. Identity politics gives voice to marginalized minorities, but it divides regions and nations, despite efforts to promote multilevel citizenships in macro-regions like the EU. Strategies of differentiated integration seem to show a middle way to foster complementary identities at different levels, whereas asymmetric division of authority seems to cope with diversity within levels.

However, a realist analysis unveils a general problem of multilevel governance. The rise of identity politics and the underlying populist concept of *demos*, which implies a substantial corporate identity of a *demos*, are conducive to decentralization, self-rule, differentiated integration and asymmetric distribution of power. This trend toward differentiated multilevel governance complicates the management of complexity per se, but even more under the condition of economic disparities. In consequence, the social logic of multilevel governance becomes manifest in diverging rational calculations of political actors in wealthy and poor states or regions. The former profit from decentralization, autonomy and asymmetry because this allows them to prevail in economic competition, develop the advantages of their spatial economy and profit from increasing revenues. Governments of poor states or regions also prefer decentralization and autonomy in general, but their interests in promoting development and providing a standard of living for their citizens on an equal basis with other territories speak for sharing legislative, executive and fiscal power with a central government (for EU member states see Schimmelfennig and Winzen 2020: 26–42; for sub-national regions, Beyme 2007: 23). It is this divergence of policy interests which promotes differentiated structures of multilevel governance. Yet asymmetry of authority inhibits policy coordination concerning institutional change or fiscal equalization and complicates dealing with external effects of private production or consumption. For these reasons, the reality of differentiated multilevel governance and the normative assessment of this reality should be reconsidered.

Regarding the trend towards differentiation and asymmetries, a critical analysis of the policies that drive this process can shed light on the underlying strategies of responsible actors. In general, identity politics claims to increase loyalty and solidarity among citizens, to protect values, to assert the rights of minorities and to restore justice to a *demos*. However, we should not ignore that these arguments regularly conceal specific interests. A populist version of identity politics claims to be following the will of a *demos* but in fact seeks to increase citizens' loyalty to their government by raising demands against other communities or governments. Political leaders also blur fiscal or institutional interests with identity claims, as do regionalist or nationalist parties. By disguising their interests as values or rights of a community and by constructing a corporate identity of people that obscures the plurality of individuals, they turn intergovernmental conflicts into divides. At the same time, they mobilize the people of a territory against centralized authority or coordinated policy-making in multilevel governance.

Politics of integration at upper tiers can curb an escalation of divides in the horizontal dimension. An asymmetric division of authority can moderate identity conflicts. However, the success of these strategies is uncertain. Therefore, as Hooghe and Marks suggest, we should conceive multilevel governance as a dynamic process of integration and disintegration. Yet, it is not only the interplay of the integrating functional logic and the disintegrating, bottom-up social logic that drive this dynamic development but also political leaders' or parties' competing or mutually outbidding claims for power. Multilevel governance therefore requires a constant balancing of power.

7. Policy coordination and power

The previous chapters draw attention to three characteristic features of multi-level governance that suggest rethinking the concept and theory. First, Chapter 4 discusses the interplay of politics and policymaking within and across jurisdictions including the specific problems resulting from institutional varieties of governments. Chapter 5 explains why multilevel governance typically reveals economic diversity and causes distributive conflicts due to disparities between spatial economies and fiscal imbalances between governments. Chapter 6 addresses societal diversity, focusing on the political construction of distinct communities through identity politics and the asymmetric division of authority as a typical way to mitigate societal divides. Taken together, these varieties and imbalances combine into complicated conflicts. They raise the question of whether and how responsible actors can settle these conflicts when they coordinate policies across levels or can revise the division of authority in cases where they are confronted with new challenges.

Answering this question requires reflecting on power in multilevel governance. Theories of policymaking emphasize different social mechanisms and conditions to explain "who gets what, when and how", as Harold Lasswell expresses the basic research question of political science. While Lasswell studied how the "influential" and "powerful" actors achieve their preferences (Lasswell 1936: 3–18), recent theorizing applies more differentiated analytical frameworks. They consider policy arenas that vary with the type of policy, actors and their preferences, the institutional context, patterns of interactions or sequences and feedback in the policy process (e.g., Cairney 2019; Weible 2023). Studies on the coordination of policies across multiple levels of governance profit from these concepts. What is more important, however, is rethinking the concept of power.

The power to make binding decisions and implement decisions on specific matters results from the division of authority. Effective power to shape policy outcomes materializes in strategic actions and interactions within institutions. In multilevel policy coordination, it is mainly institutions and politics inside governments that limit actors' options for strategic action, whereas the division of authority between levels provides opportunities to accomplish policies by the coordinated use of power. Yet, mutually interfering power complicates governance. The complexity of multilevel governance modifies the character of power and suggests rethinking this concept. Based on the analytical framework outlined in Chapters 2, 3 and 4, the following section highlights distinct features of multilevel policymaking. The second section identifies types of power that appear particularly relevant in coping with the complex patterns of conflicts. The third section discusses the need for permanent restructuring of power to make multilevel governance work.

ARENAS, ACTORS AND INSTITUTIONAL CONTEXT OF MULTILEVEL POLICYMAKING

Addressing the complexity of governance, theories of multilevel policymaking focus on actors and their interactions, presuming that they follow their preferences under constraining and enabling institutional conditions or power structures (e.g., Falkner 2011; Holzinger 2008; Putnam 1988; Scharpf 1997). There is no need to review these theories and the related research in greater detail. Instead, some distinct features of policymaking in multilevel governance should be highlighted to explicate the focus on power and dynamics of structures in the following sections. The character of policy arenas in multilevel governance, the diversity of actors with variable preferences and the different manifestations of institutions in the dimensions of multilevel governance are particularly relevant.

As pointed out in Chapter 2, multilevel policy coordination usually focuses on two levels. The first, lower-tier level encompasses the jurisdictions in which private activities or public policies cause external effects or disparities that are addressed in multilevel governance. An upper-tier government or political authority and its jurisdiction constitutes the second level, where responsible governmental actors take the lead in coordinating policies through guidance or incentives, setting standards and monitoring their effects, and organizing experimental governance, yardstick competition, policy transfers or horizontal cooperation. Interactions of governmental actors from these levels constitute a specific policy arena.

Policy shapes politics in this arena, though it does not determine politics (Lowi 1972: 299). In multilevel governance, no less than in governance at one level, constitutional, regulative, distributive and redistributive policy agendas mobilize different actors and generate different power relations among these actors. The policy arena created through coordination between two levels and the specific patterns of interaction and power are embedded in the wider context of politics, markets and societal interactions across all or most scales of multilevel governance. Private actors or actors from additional levels participate, although without having political authority or adopting responsibility for decisions. Embeddedness particularly influences policy agendas – that is, the framing of the complex problems and options for solving them – while functional and territorial boundaries demarcate responsibility and power for policymaking.

In these arenas, actors seek to realize policies that conform to their preferences. The post-functional approach to multilevel governance (Hooghe and Marks 2009, 2016), similar to the actor-centred institutionalism that addresses policymaking in complex configurations (Scharpf 1997), suggests deriving policy preferences from rational and social orientations of the responsible actors. Generally speaking, governmental actors must rationally assess the pros and cons of a specific division of authority and policy coordination to manage interdependence, but they must also consider the concerns of the people that they represent. Likewise, the preferences of non-governmental actors reflect their interest in solving specific problems, but also the expectations addressed to them by members of the association or community for which they stand.

How actors frame their policy preferences depends on the role they play in multilevel governance. The preferences of executives directly involved in multilevel policymaking overlap but are not identical with the preferences of domestic institutional actors, such as cabinets, parliaments or parliamentary assemblies and majority parties. Specialized in a multilevel policy, they are motivated to cope with external effects and distributive conflicts. Inside governments, party ideologies, coalition agreements among governing parties, consociational arrangements with interest associations or an elite consensus determine the policy choices of governmental actors. Concerning the distribution of authority, domestic actors who are not directly involved in multilevel governance prefer autonomy, in contrast to executives who benefit from a shift of power towards multilevel governance (Fossum and Laycock 2021; Wolf 1999). Private actors and independent experts provide information or services in multilevel governance (Mende 2021: 177–81). Their preferences often neither relate to a *demos* nor to the authority or power of governments. Hence conflicts emerging with the participation of these actors tend to cut across the conflicts among the governmental actors. While increasing the complexity, cross-cutting cleavages open chances for all actors to review their preferences in the light of potential policy outcomes and adapt their preferences in order to settle conflicts in the processes of policymaking.

This diversity and flexibility of preferences during the process of policymaking allows political leaders, in their role as "chief negotiators" (Putnam 1988: 435) in a "double-edged process" (Evans 1993: 397), to seek a policy that is acceptable to their counterparts in policy coordination and their domestic constituents. They can achieve this aim by various strategies in processes of bargaining and deliberation, but also in efforts to restructure interactions to circumvent intractable conflicts (ibid. 400–23). Yet institutions can limit this flexibility. In multilevel governance, the degree of institutionalization varies between the different dimensions. It is strongest within governments, where accountability relations can rigidify preferences. In the vertical dimension of multilevel governance, joint-decision systems significantly constrain the choice of governmental actors in policymaking, while other governance modes operate with incentives or persuasion and provide room to manoeuvre. In the horizontal dimensions, intergovernmental councils or regional associations of governments promote cooperation, while agreements on a joint position in multilevel negotiations tie the hands of governmental actors. Private actors participate in multilevel governance mostly ad-hoc and informally in hearings, policy networks or committees of experts. In general, the institutional rigidity of domestic politics contrasts with the elasticity of inter-level, intergovernmental or public-private relations. Yet even institutions of a government adapt when arenas of multilevel policymaking consolidate. Research on the "Europeanization" of national governments, parliaments or administration has drawn attention to these institutional adjustments within governments to the evolution of multilevel governance.

In consequence, actors directly or indirectly involved in multilevel policymaking face complex, overlapping and variable conflicts over authority and policies. Such patterns of conflicts open chances for pragmatic coordination. However, competitive party politics or adamant autocratic rulers, territorial disparities and identity politics can instigate confrontation. Multilevel policymaking is therefore threatened with traps of coordinated action. In such a situation, actors face problems that require them to coordinate their policies, but they fail to find an effective solution and therefore perpetuate an insufficient outcome. Research on multilevel governance has so far focused on the "Joint-Decision Trap" (Scharpf 1988), a theoretical model that reflected the problems of German federal democracy, namely the incompatibility of party confrontation in parliamentary governments and the need to find intergovernmental agreements in cases of power-sharing. Research on comparative federalism and the EU has discovered how actors can avoid these traps (Falkner 2011; Héritier 1999; Painter 1991). The rise of alternative modes of multilevel governance (cf. Chapter 3) seems to have reduced the risk of gridlock or responded to policy failure. However, none of these modes are immune to coordination traps either. Institutional constraints and domestic politics can block the participation of governments in voluntary cooperation, experimental governance and governance by standards. They can prevent addressed actors in lower-tier governments, such as parliaments, cabinets or administrative agencies, from taking monitoring and best practices into consideration. Governance also fails if distributive or identity conflicts among governments cannot be settled in negotiations and if these conflicts obstruct governance by standards, yardstick competition, policy transfer or horizontal cooperation.

Under these conditions, power relations determine whether governance ends in stalemate leaving mutual adjustment as the only option, or whether policies can be coordinated. In multilevel governance, the dispersion of authority across levels and jurisdictions suggests a limited impact of power compared to the concentration of authority in a central government. Nonetheless, countervailing powers never cancel each other out. Policy outcomes largely depend on how authorized actors in multilevel coordination balance their power. In addition, different types of "transboundary" power materialize in multilevel governance. Structuring these power relations can help to evade coordination traps.

TRANSBOUNDARY POWER IN MULTILEVEL GOVERNANCE

The dispersion of power in multilevel governance results from the division of authority in the first place. Authority signifies the power to rule. It is legitimized by institutions or constitutions, assigned to levels of governments or international organizations, confined by jurisdictions, and in the hands of actors holding offices in governments or governmental organizations. Besides the power derived from authority within a jurisdiction, multilevel governance generates power that reaches beyond jurisdictions and across the boundaries of levels. This kind of transboundary power to shape coordinated policies is essential in multilevel policymaking. It is the topic of this section.

In social science, power is an ambiguous concept that is used with different meanings (Dowding 2021). A special issue of the "Journal of Political Power" provides an instructive summary of "the changing faces of power" (Gallarotti 2021). An appropriate analytical lens that emerged in these discussions distinguishes "power-to" and "power-over" (Pansardi and Bindi 2021; Haugaard 2022). "Power-over" describes the capacity of an actor to dominate, to make others act or behave in a certain way or to abstain from certain actions against their own will. It characterizes the relationship between a superior authority and subordinated individuals or corporate actors. In contrast, "power-to" enables actors to achieve their preferred options despite resistance or inhibiting conditions, which they accomplish often by coordinated action.

In their seminal book on multilevel governance in the European Union, Liesbet Hooghe and Gary Marks introduce power along the lines of this distinction, as follows:

> On the one hand, power or political control may be conceptualized as control over persons. *A* has power over *B* to the extent that she can get *B* to do something he would not otherwise do. ... By contrast, power conceived as the ability to achieve desired outcomes entails power over nature in the broadest sense. According to this conception, I have power to the extent that I can do what I wish to do. ... We argue ... that one reason why government leaders shift authority away from the central

state is precisely because this may enable them to achieve substantive policy goals. (Hooghe and Marks 2001: 5; cf. also Hooghe and Marks 2016: 16–17)

The authors emphasize power-to as a means to achieve goals through multilevel governance. In contrast to authority limited to and concentrated in jurisdictions, the dispersal of authority and policy coordination allows governmental actors to extend their power to solve problems or achieve policy goals beyond their jurisdiction. This transboundary power prevents domination, though it certainly does not rule out predominance in case power is not balanced. The unilateral power to decide or enforce a policy is acceptable to prevent deadlock under specified conditions. In general, however, dividing authority to self-rule or establishing shared rule in multilevel governance requires all responsible actors to coordinate their power to achieve common goals, although each of them seeks to realize a preferred outcome. In this process of interaction, three basic types of power appear relevant. The first materializes in strategic interactions between executives, the second emerges in communicative interaction, and the third is executed as a last resort.

Bargaining Power

To implement their preferences through strategic interaction in politics, individual actors apply bargaining power. This kind of reciprocal power changes the incentive structure of others by credible offers, threats or both (Dowding 2019: 67–77). In multilevel policymaking, it is based on the resources actors can offer in a trade-off, on veto rights or rights to opt out of a policy. The bargaining power of actors increases the more they can offer, the less they suffer from coordination failure compared to others, and the more they profit from autonomy. These sources of bargaining power shape the "connected games" of multilevel and domestic politics.

First, actors preferring a change of a policy through coordinated decisions and action can propose a deal by announcing concessions or compensations and reciprocate in sequential moves quid pro quo. Concessions lead to package deals and usually require linking different policy issues, whereas financial compensations provide unspecific benefits (Scharpf 1997: 125–30). Actors achieve a deal if their preferences do not exclude any agreement; that is, if the aggregated costs and benefits amount to a positive win-set for all of them (ibid.: 119–21). Otherwise, bargaining power does not suffice to change the status quo or an existing policy. In international, European and national migration policy, governments typically seek to settle distributive conflicts by compensations or package deals. However, these deals often fail because they do not meet the expectations of negotiating governments, all the more so, as migration is difficult to control and the burdens for affected governments are uncertain.

Multilevel governance of migration policy indicates another problem limiting the power to make deals. Intergovernmental agreements regularly fail because they cannot overcome the resistance of parties or people of the involved governments. Even when executives are authorized by their government to offer package deals or compensation payments, the commitments they make in bargaining processes must be credible, and their fulfilment must be feasible. Heads of a government may enjoy wider room for manoeuvre than policy specialists because they are able to link issues in different policy fields. They can increase their zone of agreement by claiming leadership and authority within their government, a strategy which allows them to strengthen their constructive bargaining power in multilevel policymaking (Putnam 1988: 451). Yet, in democracies, their hands are tied by mandates of parliaments or expectations of parties in parliament, and in autocracies, political leaders must satisfy elites and pacify potential opponents. Given these complications, executives often turn from a strategy of making offers for a bargain towards binding themselves to an explicit or pretended will of their government or their people to back up their bargaining position (Schelling 1960: 22). Precommitments enable them to obtain higher concessions from other negotiating parties in bargaining, provided that they can afford to threaten with a veto. It increases individual bargaining power, but with the risk that the win-set shrinks or disappears.

A second source of bargaining power derives from the right to veto a coordinated policy. Inspired by the veto player theory elaborated by George Tsebelis (2002), many scholars have derived the chances for policy change from veto rights (for a good overview: König, Tsebelis and Debus 2010). Veto players are capable of preventing a decision on a proposed policy. Therefore, they compare the potential consequences of a proposal not only with their preferred policy but also with the status quo. The term status quo needs to be qualified. The "default conditions" in case of failure of policy coordination can deviate from the existing state of affairs, as Elinor Ostrom emphasized (Ostrom 2005: 211). Over time, a non-decision can deteriorate a problem and increase the pressure on governments to cope with the foreseeable consequences. The status quo also prevails only if coordination requires joint decisions. Under different institutional conditions, failure to coordinate policies due to vetoes may allow an authorized government to decide unilaterally. To advance policy change in multilevel governance, this government then can make a first move in policymaking that induces other governments to respond. The "cooperative game" of negotiations thus turns into a "non-cooperative game" of governments which mutually adjust their policies in an uncoordinated way. Still, coordination can be achieved via policy emulation. Governance by standards, monitoring or yardstick competition can induce this constructive response. However, a non-cooperative game often progresses through "thrust and riposte" (Painter 1991: 275) or an escalation of mutual sanctions, and the achieved changes in the status quo can turn out as harmful or remain disputed.

The complexity of multilevel governance affects veto power no less than the power to make deals. Veto players represent corporate or collective actors. Focusing on collective veto players that decide with a simple or qualified majority, Tsebelis discussed their coherence (Tsebelis 2002: 38 –63). To analyse this problem in governments interacting in multilevel governance, we should distinguish two types of veto players. On the one hand, executives directly participate in negotiations on agreements, the selection of standards and yardsticks or the search for best practices, and they can issue their veto in these venues. On the other hand, domestic actors not directly involved in multilevel policymaking scrutinize how these processes develop and evaluate the outcome from the outside. Some of these actors, like parliaments or courts, have the power to overrule the outcome of multilevel policy coordination by their veto against ratification or implementation. They decide as "external" veto players (Benz 2004: 880) on the fate of agreements negotiated by executives. As mentioned above, the preferences of negotiating executives and "external" actors differ. Besides, external actors like parties in parliaments differ in their perception of multilevel policies from the directly involved executives. Internal veto players compare the achieved outcome with the default conditions. External players focus on the expected outcome. This especially applies to majority parties in parliament who face critical opposition parties, but also to political elites in autocracies who must demonstrate success to consolidate their power. Therefore, it is not unlikely that external actors veto the bargaining outcome achieved by executives even though it would improve the status quo, and thus cause "involuntary defection" (Putnam 1988: 438). Such an outcome can also result from negotiating actors' bargaining strategy to threaten with a veto. Intended to induce other actors to make concessions, they can run into the trap of either self-committing themselves to veto a decision or provoking external veto players to do so. Endorsing veto threats by appeals to the people, a strategy that is especially used by populist governments or parties, bears a particularly high risk of provoking governance failure.

Finally, individual governments can threaten with exit, either to opt out from policy coordination or, as a last resort, to withdraw from a system of multilevel governance (polity exit; Jachtenfuchs and Kasack 2017: 603–37). By tabling the exit option, a government indicates its preference for autonomy. This constitutes bargaining power, if political leaders credibly threaten to execute this option. In contrast to exit from a multilevel polity that changes the structure of multilevel governance, opting out from coordinated policy prevents an individual government from being committed to implementing a policy or complying with decisions or standards. If institutional rules or agreements allow governments to opt out from a joint policy, such a "policy exit" reduces the scope of coordination to those jurisdictions whose governments agree, while the government using this option faces a new situation as others change their policy in a coordinated way. In contrast to polity exit, opting out can attenuate conflicts. In Canada, the federal government accepts a provincial government's decision to opt out of intergovernmental agreements to reduce the veto power of individual provinces, provided that opting out does not obstruct the aims of a coordinated policy and that those provincial governments using this option adapt their policy accordingly (McRoberts 2023). In the EU, opting out is also widely accepted and practiced in contested policies to circumvent vetoes of national governments (Duttle et al. 2017). The corresponding mode of enhanced cooperation aims at advancing integration. It enables non-participating member states to opt in later on.

Executives engaging in multilevel policymaking, especially policy specialists, tend to prefer coordinated policy to institutional or policy-specific autonomy. Pressure for polity exit usually arises in domestic politics. Executives can translate this pressure into bargaining power and may achieve significant policy change. In 1933, for example, the government of Western Australia negotiated an agreement with the Australian federal government which included permanent support of the state through fiscal equalization, after a majority of voters of the state had endorsed an initiative for secession (Lecours and Béland 2019). In the UK, the pressure for secession in Scotland prompted the British government to concede significant legislative authority to the Scottish government. In Canada, the provincial government of Quebec used the same strategy to achieve a distinct status, although the intergovernmental agreements preparing formal amendments to the constitution failed in ratification (Benz 2016: 180–185). The secession of the UK from the European Union demonstrated the high risk of this strategy. Calls for autonomy raise identity claims and provoke a climate of confrontation inside and between governments. Under these conditions, negotiators have a hard time finding a compromise or package deals or getting an agreement ratified. Therefore, opting out from a coordinated policy is preferable in multilevel bargaining.

Multilevel governance of climate policy illustrates how the different types of bargaining power interact in the arenas of multilevel policy coordination. In the global negotiations on commitments to reduce greenhouse gas emissions, the need to reach a consensus allows every national delegation to veto a decision, even though decision rules have remained a matter of dispute (Kemp 2016). In consequence, global climate policy, like international environmental coordination in general (Beaudoin 2023), progressed incrementally and went through crises and deadlocks before the Paris Agreement finally committed

UN member states to reduce global warming to maximally plus 2°C and pos-
sibly 1.5°C compared to the preindustrial level.

The Kyoto Protocol, which delegates of governments adopted in December
1997 and entered into force in February 2005 after a complicated ratification
process, had already committed governments of industrialized states to reduce
greenhouse gas emissions according to individual targets. This governance
approach by a negotiated treaty proved successful, in so far as most governments met their reduction targets. Yet, by introducing international emission
trade and a "Clean Development Mechanism" that allowed governments to
fulfil their commitments by emission-reducing projects in developing countries, economically rich countries profited from their financial capacities to
make deals. Moreover, the Kyoto Agreement lost its effectiveness when two
large states, which have historically been responsible for a significant share of
emissions, decided to opt out: the US did not ratify the treaty and the Canadian
government decided to revoke its approval in 2011 after the Conservative
Party gained a majority in parliament.

Faced with accelerating climate change, negotiations turned to a different
governance mode, following a proposal by President Obama at the 2009
conference in Copenhagen. Intended to avoid a veto by the US Senate, this
"radical departure from the previous model of environmental governance"
(Milkoreit 2019: 1027) introduced a "pledge-and-review system". Instead
of joint decisions on binding agreements, global climate policy now aims
at voluntary commitments of member states combined with monitoring and
benchmarking of national implementation. While this policy turn failed in
Copenhagen, the US executive gained the support of the Chinese government.
With the Paris Agreement, governments adopted the new governance mode. It
changed the linkage of international and national politics and thus reduced the
risk of involuntary defection due to external vetoes. At the 2022 Conference of
the Parties (COP 27) in Sharm El-Sheik, less-developed countries succeeded
in revising the deal settled at Kyoto. The compensations for countries suffering
from global warming indicated their increased bargaining power as a coalition
of governments.

Similar stories of bargaining over the transformation of fossil-based society
and successes and failures to meet the goals of climate policy could be told
about national climate mitigation and adaptation. Multilevel governance in
states varies significantly according to the territorial organisation of a government, the type of government, the legal order, the structure and development
of the economy, the organization of society etc. Irrespective of these distinct
features, bargaining power in national multilevel governance differs from what
we observe in international governance in two significant respects.

First, party politics shapes bargaining among governments. In unitary states
with majority democracies or presidential governments, the governing party

has the power to decide, although it cannot ignore competition with opposition parties or the demands of political elites. In federal and regional states, inter-governmental relations often include governments formed by different and competing parties or party coalitions. In consequence, the zone of agreement (or "win-set") in policy coordination shrinks. Independent of the state organ-ization, party polarization affects the bargaining power of many countries. It has particularly encumbered climate policy in the US (Selin and VanDeveer 2020). Antagonist positions on the appropriate policy approach, whether global warming should be mitigated by advanced technologies or changes in consumption, whether governments should provide incentives to reduce emis-sions or raise emission costs and to what extent they should protect industries or vulnerable people from higher costs, has politicized climate change more than other policy issues (Marquardt and Lederer 2022). These conflicts make compromises or package deals difficult and increase the impact of veto power.

Second, the transformation of industry revises old and generates new eco-nomic disparities between regions and local jurisdictions. The transition from non-renewable to renewable energy sources has significant territorial effects, like policies to reduce the emission of greenhouse gases, whether by regulation or carbon tax. These variations in costs and benefits for industries and energy consumers influence the preferences of regional and local governments in climate politics. Their bargaining power is closely connected to exit threats of industry while the transformation to meet the climate policy targets is hardly possible without the cooperation of governments and private corporations. Under these conditions, regional governments tend to veto intergovernmental coordination or opt out of agreements or implementation. Therefore, coordi-nated energy policy has reached its limits even in countries where it has a long tradition, like in Germany (Benz and Broschek 2020).

Veto and exit threats appear as a unilateral use of power by an individual government. Nevertheless, as long as a government remains in a multilevel political system, it lacks unrestricted autonomy and its power materializes in bargaining processes. Accordingly, no government and no actor involved in policymaking can dominate others. Certainly, bargaining power is not equally distributed and power structures are characterized by imbalances. In the vertical dimension, national governments profit from their fiscal resources, veto power and exit options in global and macro-regional forms of multilevel governance. Within states, central governments are in a stronger position to bargain with regional and local governments, all the more so when the latter fail to find a common position against the central government. In the horizontal dimension of multilevel governance, economic and societal diversity causes imbalances in regional or local governments' bargaining power. Bargaining power is also not balanced between executives and domestic institutional actors like parliaments. It is a truism in the literature on federal systems and the EU that executives, in their role as gatekeepers between domestic and multilevel politics, profit from information asymmetries, their options to strategically use institutions and their ability to shape ideas in the "two-level game" (Moravcik 1993). Nonetheless, complaints about the domination of central governments, governments in rich countries or regions or executives are often exaggerated. They neglect the reciprocity of bargaining power and the countervailing powers preventing domination in multilevel governance. In this context, epistemic power, in particular, can compensate for imbalances of bargaining power.

Epistemic Power

External effects or disparities caused by public policies or private activities are often not immediately evident, their causes complex, and their conse-quences difficult to forecast. Therefore, reasoning and expertise are essential in multilevel governance. These are sources of epistemic power, the power "to influence what people think, believe, and know, and ... to enable and disable others from exerting epistemic influence" (Archer et al. 2020: 29). This type of power has been defined in the philosophy of science to identify injustice in the development of knowledge. If we consider knowledge as a crucial condition for legitimate governance (Goodin and Spiekermann 2018) and knowledge creation as a social process, it makes sense to understand the ability to shape shared knowledge as a kind of political power. In politics, evidence-based reasons, knowledge gained by scientific methods, experience of special groups and rational arguing add up to this power to persuade others. Actors profit from their knowledge to define problems, frame policy issues, provide information and evaluate the effects of alternative solutions. All these components of policymaking are matters of dispute, as is knowledge as such. Epistemic power emerges from these disputes and increases to the extent that actors recognize a specific knowledge as valid, based on reliable experience and sound reasons and supported by the scientific community. In this way, knowledge turns into collective power. Actors sharing this power are part of an "epistemic community" (Haas 1992), which usually consists of independent experts or specialists in public administration but can also include laypersons with particular experience.

In multilevel governance, it seems appropriate to distinguish two types of epistemic power. The first draws on analytical and empirical knowledge of problems and ways to solve them. Usually, it applies to processes of agenda setting and influences the framing of issues and conflicts. The second type of epistemic power refers to the assessment of governance outcomes and is held by actors who participate in performance evaluation. Analytical epistemic power requires scientific expertise, but civil society organizations or representatives of communities with specific experiences can also contribute empirical knowledge. In governance by standards, yardstick competition and experimental governance, experts from public administration or private consultants hold the power to evaluate. Their ex-post assessment changes power relations among officeholders who have to anticipate the potential effects of an evaluation on bargaining processes and on the implementation of policies. Likewise, courts and lawyers apply epistemic power in matters of law and civil rights. While they cannot enforce the law, their binding judgement significantly affects the distribution of authority and the bargaining power of political and private actors in multilevel policymaking.

Not by coincidence, the concept of epistemic communities emerged in studies on international politics. It is also no coincidence that research on global governance discovered expertise as a source of "epistemic authority" (Liese et al. 2021; Zürn 2018: 52–3). International organisations lack the legal authority to compel member state governments or private actors in the transnational arena to comply with decisions. Therefore, they rely on persuasion by information and arguing. Epistemic power is also relevant in international multilevel governance which often leads actors into uncharted waters, confronts them with fluctuating constellations of actors and conflicts and lacks guidance from rules or routines established in institutions.

Research on international administration has emphasized the power of expertise and, in consequence, scholars have argued against a "realist" approach to politics. Certainly, the staff of international organisations seek to extend their power, yet they mostly rely on "expert authority" (Busch and Liese 2017; Sendling 2017) or "moral authority" (Barnett and Finnemore 2004: 25–7). Thomas Risse described "arguing" as a mode of policymaking in international relations that changes power structures (Risse 2000), presumably due to the position and reputation of experts in international administration and the juridification of international politics. These studies confirm the relevance of epistemic power. It obviously prevails in international organizations because their administrative staff lacks legal authority and bargaining power to challenge national governments or private companies (Littoz-Monnet 2017). In the EU, executive agencies have stabilized networks between officials of the European Commission and civil servants delegated by responsible departments of national governments. While a bargaining style of interactions emerges when chief negotiators negotiate on binding regulations, specialists in administration in general coordinate their policies through exchanging information and knowledge (Benz 2023). In a similar vein, international, European and national courts constitute an arena of communication concerning the definition of jurisdictions, authority, rights and the rule of law (Sandholtz 2021; Vosskuhle 2010). The epistemic power of administrative communities and court judges substantially impacts the bargaining power of governmental and non-governmental actors in multilevel governance.

The evolution of new modes of multilevel governance has increased the relevance of expertise. Coordination by experimental governance, standards and monitoring, yardstick competition and policy transfer essentially operate with epistemic power. It also shapes traditional intergovernmental negotiations in states, in which authorized executives to a considerable extent rely on the work of specialists in public administration who regularly prepare formal decisions or agreements, often with the help of scientists or consultants. In a case study on multilevel policymaking in Switzerland, Céline Mavrot and Fritz Sager convincingly demonstrated the empowering effect of vertical epistemic communities, which include non-governmental actors and policy specialists (Mavrot and Sager 2018). The political culture of Swiss consensus democracy facilitates this practice, but it can also be observed in other democratic federations (Poirier and Saunders 2015: 487).

In the international and national contexts of multilevel governance, climate policy is a case in point demonstrating how epistemic power counterbalances bargaining power. Climate policy gained significant momentum after the United Nations established the UN climate regime with the "United Nations Framework Convention on Climate Change (UNFCCC)" in 1992. Part of this regime is the "Intergovernmental Panel on Climate Change" (IPCC), an advisory body of experts. Set up in 1988, the Panel initially was to elaborate a comprehensive review of the state of knowledge on climate change. It now exists as a permanent institution and regularly reports on the rise of global warming, assesses the consequences, and indicates trajectories to mitigate climate change without recommending specific policies (Fischlin 2017: 8). The panel developed into a special kind of international organisation with a secretariat, an executive committee, working groups and a plenary where all member states of the UN are represented. This organization orchestrates the work of hundreds of experts, including officials from national governments, scientists from universities or research institutes and delegates from "Observer Organizations". A Task Force selects experts to draft and revise the reports of the IPPC. Since its foundation, the epistemic power of the Panel has increased along with its reputation and the public awareness raised by the reports, as the Nobel Peace Prize awarded to the Panel in 2007 for its work on climate change proved.

The IPCC is unique as it engages in analysing the causes and consequences of global warming and evaluates the achievements of national climate policy. In addition, it combines two sources of epistemic power which often are separated in other cases of multilevel governance. The Panel is well known for its network of scientists, but it also established a multilevel administration to draw on expertise from officials of international organizations and national ministries. Within states, administrations of central and regional governments have established their own epistemic communities in a more or less permanent form. City networks constitute additional epistemic communities in climate policy. They connect local civil servants from different countries (Kern 2019; Kern and Bulkeley 2009).

Given these multiple layers of epistemic communities, the epistemic power of the IPCC does not dominate multilevel climate governance. In fact, knowledge generation is divided among different expert bodies, networks or venues of deliberation, not least when it comes to deciding on national, regional or local measures to reduce greenhouse gas emissions or to adapt society to global warming. Within states, expertise tends to be fragmented between policy fields like economy, energy, transportation and environment. In many governments, technological and market-based approaches compete with social science approaches. The former have been advanced by advisory bodies in the EU and global climate politics (Anfinson 2023; Meckling and Allan 2020), while the latter seem to have gained more attention at the regional and local levels. Besides the fragmentation of epistemic power, the choice for specific policy approaches indicates that bargaining power frequently trumps the power of knowledge and reasoning in multilevel governance.

Nonetheless, actors short of bargaining power can compensate for this disadvantage by epistemic power. In global climate policy, the least developed countries increasingly gained influence by applying a style of deliberation in debates that aims at persuasion. Instead of forming coalitions as a bargaining strategy, they operate as epistemic communities to issue policy proposals designed to cope with climate change (Gray and Cointet 2023). The voice of representatives speaking for these countries can no longer be ignored by the most powerful players like China, the EU and the US. In the negotiations of the Paris Agreement, they successfully argued for fixing the 1.5°C target, and in later Conferences of the Parties, they advanced negotiations on compensation for damages.

Power of the Last Resort

Multilevel governance is not compatible with domination. A central government in a unitary state holds superior authority. However, if it coordinates policies with regional agencies or local governments, it avoids ruling from the top, either because it must consider the competences of lower-tier governments or cope with information asymmetry. In federations, federal law takes precedence over the law of regional or member state governments. Yet, in contrast to domination through unilateral action, precedence implies a ranking of divided powers and calls for balancing authority. The hierarchical structure of a political order in governments or international politics divides authority to fulfil different functions, and multilevel governance integrates these functions in coordinated policymaking. Hierarchy allows for reducing complexity by assigning "nearly decomposable" functions (Simon 1962: 474) according to different degrees of abstraction to institutional levels, whereas subordination in a political order ignores complexity (Simon 1962: 468). Such functions are interdependent. Precedence serves as a principle to solve conflicts between more abstract and more specific decisions or actions. It does not rule out the need for coordination of policies across the different levels.

Although not implying domination and subordination in political systems, the hierarchy of authority relations constitutes a specific source of power in multilevel governance, a power that normally remains in the shadow and is only used as a last resort. It allows an authorized agency to intervene in case participating actors in multilevel governance cannot solve their conflicts and uncoordinated unilateral policymaking causes significant harm, injustice or instability. This authority to decide or act unilaterally can derive from the constitutional rules of a multilevel polity, but actors involved in a multilevel policy process can also implicitly acknowledge or explicitly delegate this power. The scope of authority and the effects of power vary accordingly.

A far-reaching, but disputable power of the last resort typically arises in a state of emergency. The pressure on governments or agencies to respond immediately and with effective measures calls for a concentration of power in the centre and in the executive. Responsible executives may use their emergency power to mobilize resources of public and private actors. Yet, to cope with problems as fast and effectively as possible, they either avoid the complicated bargaining processes in the connected venues of multilevel governance or strongly pressure for an agreement. The singularity of a crisis situation and the need to resort to exceptional action justify this proceeding and motivate compliance among all actors involved in multilevel governance. In general, emergency power should only apply in a unique situation that requires urgent action. However, as can be observed in the EU, the various coordination problems that arise in weakly institutionalized multilevel governance can lead to a recurrent shift of power to executives and the mobilization of exceptional funding for specific policies. As Jonathan White observed for the EU: "When circumstances are cast as unique, it is difficult to keep them in proportion, for who can say what the proper proportions of a unique challenge are? Political discourse becomes consumed with one issue, leaving the scrutiny of others to suffer" (White 2019: 197).

In multilevel constitutions, subsidiary competences are another source of power of the last resort. Usually, the principle of subsidiarity is meant to safeguard decentralization and self-rule. However, it can also allow a central government to legislate if coordination problems of decentralization cannot be solved by modes of multilevel governance. The Federal Constitution of

Switzerland, for example, obliges the cantonal governments to harmonize certain rules for education and presumes that they are able and willing to do so. Nonetheless, Article 62 Section 4 of the Constitution states that the federal government can pass the necessary regulation when the cantons fail to coordinate their legislation in relevant matters. In the shadow of this power of the last resort, in 2007 the Swiss Conference of Cantonal Ministers of Education drafted an agreement which 15 cantonal governments adopted outright during the following three years, while in the other 11 cantons, voters declined ratification in a referendum but governments amended their law in line with the concordat (Schnabel 2020: 203–18). Other federal constitutions assign supplementary or ancillary legislative authority to the central government provided that central legislation is necessary and proper to fulfil essential public tasks.

If the power of the last resort is based on legislative authority, it seems to presume statehood. In general, central governments of states hold this power, and they can use it also in international multilevel governance, for example by withdrawing from agreements, revoking their commitments to treaties or suspending their membership in international organisations. Yet not only states profit from the power of the last resort. National governments can delegate emergency power to an international organization to avoid unintended outcomes of bargaining. For example, according to the "International Health Regulations", the World Health Organization can define an outbreak of an infectious disease as a "public health emergency of international concern". It can oblige member state governments to take measures to prevent the spread of the disease across borders. If conflicts escalate and the risk of a military confrontation rises, the UN Security Council, with the consent of the affected government or conflict parties, can send military forces to maintain peace. This power delegation works as a strategy of precommitment and "abdication of power" that protects actors against the dilemmas of collective action and coordination traps (Elster 1979: 37–47, 88–103).

The third and most limited power of the last resort is held by courts. In multilevel governance, they are called to settle authority conflicts or disputes over commitments inherent in authority. In this way, they can significantly modify the constitution of a multilevel polity, as has been observed in federations and in the EU (Aroney and Kincaid 2017; Schmidt 2018). International courts or arbitration panels finally decide on the implementation of treaties regulating civil rights or international trade. The power of courts is limited to arbitration in disputes. The direct effects of judgements depend on whether the parties in a legal conflict accept the authority of the court and whether executives of a state or an association of states enforce the implementation of a court decision. Courts nonetheless indirectly influence bargaining over authority among governments or over the substance of law among governmental and non-governmental actors. With the growing juridification of multilevel governance inside and beyond states, the power of the last resort executed by courts has become stronger.

The power of the last resort usually remains in the shadow, only to be mobilized when multilevel policymaking via different modes of coordination is in danger of failing or has failed. Private interest groups or civil society organizations may call for the intervention of an authorized central agency that settles conflicts through final decisions or actions. Executives negotiating on policy coordination in multilevel governance tend to avoid such a transferal of their power. As a rule, power of the last resort mainly entails indirect effects and influences the behaviour of actors in multilevel governance. Anticipating the uncertain consequences of an intervention from central authorities or a judgement of courts, participants in multilevel governance seek to find compromises in bargaining. They prefer to cooperate, to fulfil standards or to participate in yardstick competition. Therefore, "the problem-solving capacity of hierarchical authority structures reaches beyond the narrow limits of hierarchical coordination" (Scharpf 1997: 205).

RESTRUCTURING POWER RELATIONS

In the complicated policymaking across borders of jurisdictions, strategic bargaining among executives is crucial for the success and the outcome of coordination. While engaging in bargaining in pursuance of their preferences, responsible executives must accommodate conflicting interests of governmental and non-governmental actors in a policy field as well as meet expectations of communities of citizens, parliaments or majority parties of the government which they represent. Bargaining power is dispersed among the involved executives and limited due to their accountability. Therefore, unintended coordination failure is likely. This is the reason why epistemic power is important in multilevel governance, especially in agenda setting, the search for policy options or the evaluation of these options or outcomes. It can influence the preferences of actors, mediate between multilevel bargaining and politics within governments, and focus strategic bargaining on solving problems instead of playing out power games to maximize distributive benefits or autonomy. To prevent bargaining from running into a dead end, the shadow of the power of the last resort motivates actors to find compromises or fair deals in bargaining. Hence, bargaining power, which actors apply in pursuance of their preferences, does not determine whether multilevel governance succeeds or fails in managing interdependence and in coping with distributive or identity conflicts. Instead, the combination of different types of power matters, all aiming at shaping coordinated policies rather than dominating multilevel governance. In addition, the dynamics of power structures make multilevel governance work.

The inherent dynamics of multilevel governance allow actors to modify the power structures. Given the institutional diversity, the conflicting rule systems and the heterogeneity of actors, the chief negotiator's main task in multilevel governance is "structuring or creating order and direction out of complexity" (Zartman 2002: 84), in policy coordination across levels of government no less than in international multilevel governance. Usually, selected actors or agencies manage processes of governance. In bargaining processes, they structure the agenda, organize negotiations and combine bilateral deal-making with a multilateral search for compromises. They can also shift the balance between bargaining and epistemic power or mobilize the power of the last resort. Informal adjustments of governance processes to favourable or unfavourable circumstances advance policymaking. Over time, structuring power relations may entail institutional reforms that redistribute authority between levels or amend formal rules of policymaking (Héritier 2007: 46–8). In multilevel policymaking, shifting policy processes between levels or venues, reorganizing actor constellations or changing the mode of governance are the most important ways to circumvent obstacles.

"Venue shopping" is a widely used strategy in multilevel governance. In federations and regionalized states, constitutional rules on the distribution of competences are more or less detailed but never cover all aspects of a policy. Within the framework of constitutional law, policymaking can be centralized or decentralized by reframing a policy problem (Painter 1991: 278) or interpreting competence categories (Cairney 2006). Moving the responsibility for a policy to another level changes power structures in multilevel coordination and opens ways for achieving policy change. Renate Mayntz explained amendments in financial market regulation as a result of "uploading" policymaking from states and the EU to international politics (Mayntz 2015). These venue shifts modify the prevailing conflicts. What is more, they change the bargaining power of the actors involved. A government which has legislative power at the national level and may have veto power in the EU is in a weaker position when negotiating with the US government in international relations. In the polycentric and loosely coupled "regime complex" (Abbott 2012) of global climate policy, alternating meetings in the Conferences of the Parties of the UN Climate Change Regime, the G7 and G20 summits have maintained the continuity of communication and negotiation and together constitute a "successful UN climate summitry" (Kirton, Kokotsis and Warren 2022: 209). The veto power of individual governments loses its impact because strategies to prevent agreements in one venue do not necessarily impact policymaking in others.

A variation of venues of multilevel policymaking changes actor constellation. The interplay of administrative committees, meetings of ministers, hearings of experts or civil society, and parliamentary bodies increases the chances of amending the division of authority in multilevel governments (Benz 2016). In global climate policy, the continuous exchange of experiences in dialogues, the establishment of distinct negotiation tracks, and the preparation of the agenda in working groups appear no less relevant for coming to agreements than the organization of the global conferences into different groups of state representatives, the inclusion of experts and non-governmental stakeholders, and, last but not least, the informal meetings of executives to make deals or find compromises (Bulmer, Doelle and Klein 2017). The sequence of processes in different venues and their linkage significantly influences policy outcomes. In the German federal system, the *Länder* governments typically seek an agreement before they negotiate with the federal government. To coordinate their positions, they use committees of specialists and generalists in administration and meetings of ministers or heads of government. This way, they reduce conflicts but also the win-set in ensuing negotiations with the federal government The effect of this sequence on policy outcomes is most obvious in policies changing fiscal equalization. As a rule, ministers of finance elaborate a proposal which rules out losses compared to the status quo for any single *Land*. The formal federal-*Länder* negotiations then turn into bilateral distributive bargaining on the share of the federal government. In general, only marginal changes in fiscal equalisation are feasible in such a process. In other federations, fiscal equalization reforms are prepared by a panel of experts who define norms of distributive justice. The federal government thus can shape the agenda of ensuing negotiations with regional governments and achieve substantial policy changes (Benz 2021: 122–43).

Actor constellations particularly vary with a shift from generalists to specialists or from political actors to experts with the consequence that epistemic power is strengthened against bargaining power. Research on multilevel administrative governance has recently emphasized this particular power dynamic (Bach and Ruffing 2018). Besides, structuring power relations can also increase or decrease the number of participating actors by organizing committees or sub-committees in negotiations or by forming coalitions of governments. In federations, regional governments often coordinate to pursue specific interests in multilevel governance or to defend their authority against the intrusion of the central government. These coalitions may connect governments led by the same parties or party coalitions, whereas others include governments with similar interests in policy fields. In the international context, the "climate club" of states, founded in 2022 at a G7 summit following a proposal by William Nordhaus, reduces the number of governments to solve the free-riding behaviour of states in climate policy (Nordhaus 2015) but aims at an incremental widening of the number of actors who are willing to cooperate. Clubs and coalitions significantly change bargaining power, either by facilitating agreements among a limited group of governments or by increasing the credibility of coordinated veto threats.

In contrast to shifting policies between levels or venues and shaping actor constellations, changing modes of governance either requires a central authority or an agreement of lower-tier governments. In international and national politics, new modes of multilevel governance based on experimental policies, standards, benchmarking and monitoring have been introduced or at least supported by international organizations (like the IMF and the OECD), the European Commission (Schäfer 2006) or ministries of central governments. To avoid the hurdles of changing institutionalized joint decision-making, new modes of governance are often attached to existing ones. Like the creation of new levels of governance, change of governance modes mostly occurs through "layering" (Mahoney and Thelen 2010: 16), rather than, for instance, a displacement or conversion. The variability of patterns of coordination increases the chance for policy change.

In multilevel governance, chief executives of governments and/or international organizations structure and restructure interactions to avoid deadlocks or ineffective policies caused by bargaining power and to advance policies supported by epistemic communities. As a rule, domestic actors or institutional rules hardly constrain the room for manoeuvre to shape processes, actor constellations and modes of multilevel governance. Thus, executives gain leadership over "meta-governance" (Jessop 2015). However, they also face a dilemma, as Jacob Torfing rightly pointed out:

> Metagovernors who tend to be metagoverning too much and too tightly risk strait-jacketing the participants in interactive governance arenas and thus undermining their willingness to participate and invest in joint problem-solving. By contrast, if metagovernors do too little and are too weak and vague, it might give rise to underperformance, stalemate and disintegration and thus lead to governance failure. (Torfing 2022: 576)

Finding the middle way in structuring power is anything but easy.

CONCLUSION

The "governance-turn" in political science has indicated that the state no longer concentrates supreme power to govern societies – if it ever did so. Instead, power spreads among different institutions and levels of government and among governmental and non-governmental actors. Governing appears as a process of coordination and requires continuous adjustment of policymaking to changes in societies and in the international context (Pierre 2000a). The rise of multilevel governance accordingly changes political power, and theories of power have reflected this change. The division of authority across levels has entailed transboundary power relations. This chapter highlighted bargaining power, epistemic power and power of the last resort. These types of power characterize the relations of actors involved in multilevel policymaking. To explain policymaking and policy outcomes, bargaining power is particularly relevant, all the more as it reflects institutional conditions and the resources of actors. In addition, however, we need to consider how it is influenced by epistemic power and power of the last resort.

In the literature on global governance, scholars have outlined similar concepts, some of them putting more emphasis on the reciprocity of power in policy coordination and others on the domination of actors over others. The focus on enabling power does not ignore the second aspect. Yet the division of power in multilevel governance impedes domination. In multilevel governance, actors use power to cope with interdependence reaching beyond their jurisdiction and at the same time meeting the expectations and preferences of the people and peoples' representatives in jurisdictions. This power is not distributed equally among all actors. Power structures are imbalanced. Yet instead of leading to domination, imbalances provoke contestation of power. Policymaking in multilevel governance thus appears as a process that simultaneously aims at solving conflicts between actors with different preferences and at balancing power. In this process, bargaining power, epistemic power and power of the last resort have complementary effects and drive the dynamics of power structures. This does not mean that governance ends in a balance. Rather, an imbalance is likely to persist. In practice, it causes contestation and gives rise to safeguarding strategies and balancing mechanisms. For analysing multilevel governance, it raises the question of how power can be legitimized.

8. Legitimizing power in multilevel governance

The legitimacy of multilevel governance has been a matter of continuous discussion in political science. Given the many new ideas that have emerged during this discussion, it seems superfluous to propose rethinking this concept, its theoretical implications, the critical evaluations of legitimacy deficits or suggestions for preventing them. Analyses and proposals reveal different concepts of legitimacy and accordingly highlight different challenges (DeBardeleben and Hurrelmann 2007; Kohler-Koch and Rittberger 2007; Peters and Pierre 2004). Accountability of executives and experts in multilevel governance has been a central topic in discussions which have focused on the scrutiny of power by parliaments and citizens (Benz, Harlow and Papadopoulos 2007; Keohane 2004; Papadopoulos 2010). From other theoretical perspectives, scholars have made the case for the participation of citizens or NGOs in multilevel policymaking (Archibugi and Cellini 2017; Grote and Gbikpi 2002) or deliberative democracy (Bohman 2007).

In analyses of the legitimacy of multilevel governance, the distinction between input and output legitimacy suggests a differentiated perspective. Introduced to categorize theories of democracy and to formulate a "complex theory of democracy" in an early publication (Scharpf 1970: 21–8), Scharpf applied this analytical framework in his studies on European politics. He argued that deficits in the transmission of the peoples' authentic will into political processes can be compensated if multilevel governance ensures effective and acceptable outcomes (Scharpf 1999). While Scharpf clarified the conditions for effectiveness in terms of policies and decision procedures, others identified output legitimacy with governing based on "expert knowledge and moral integrity" (Zürn 2018: 52). Vivien Schmidt emphasized throughput legitimacy resulting from feedback between input-processes and output generation via transparency and accountability (Schmidt 2020: 39–54), an idea which conforms to Scharpf's model of a complex democracy. Based on this theoretical framework, scholars have discussed various democratic dilemmas of multilevel governance (Hurrelmann and DeBardeleben 2009).

This chapter draws on this literature, yet with a different perspective. The concept of transboundary power outlined in Chapter 7 suggests considering different types of power. Without claiming to cover all aspects of the academic discussion on this subject, the following sections seek to answer the question of how the specific manifestations of power and the emerging power structures characterizing multilevel governments can be legitimized.

It needs to be noted that legitimacy, meaning the acceptability of power and political decisions, can be justified by different reasons, like values, religious beliefs, scientific knowledge or law. In line with many contributions to the academic discussion, this chapter takes democratic legitimacy as an essential normative standard, supposing that in modern societies, political power must serve the general will of the people. The implications of this definition are not self-evident. Disputes concern the meaning of "people", the concept of general will, the ways people can express their policy preferences, and the organization of a polity that makes democracy work according to normative standards. Therefore, this chapter starts with clarifying the concept of democratic legitimacy. It explains why democracy can only work in a territorial jurisdiction; that is, a state and its regional and local governments. Yet, if complex problems transgress the boundaries of jurisdictions, ignorance of these effects makes democratic decisions undemocratic, as long as governments do not adopt responsibility in multilevel governance. The ensuing sections address the question of how power and the execution of power can be legitimized in politics transgressing territorial jurisdictions of governments, although conditions for democratic legitimacy do not apply in the arenas constituted in the vertical and horizontal dimensions of multilevel governance. The third section suggests a pragmatic solution to the democracy dilemma. It explains how democracy-compatible modes of legitimizing multilevel politics and policymaking can complement democratic legitimacy generated within governments.

LEGITIMACY AS DEMOCRATIC LEGITIMACY

The definition of legitimacy as democratic legitimacy is a normative statement. It connotes that political decisions to solve social conflicts or provide essential public goods should be acceptable for all whom they affect. In addition, it entails that only those who are affected can determine what is acceptable, provided that they take into account the interests of others concerned. Clarifying the consequences of this normative statement for practical politics helps to identify the basic legitimacy problems of multilevel governance.

First, identifying those affected by political power is essential but difficult. It seems to be feasible for a specific policy. Yet even cost-benefit analyses for clearly defined projects like road construction can hardly demarcate who benefits and who bears the costs defined according to acknowledged criteria. It is even more difficult to define who is affected by political power in general. In practice, the territorial organization of political power in a state has pragmatically solved this problem. It presumes a congruence of the scope of power, which the jurisdiction of the state delineates, and the people (*demos*) consisting of citizens who are subject to power and decide on its acceptability. The congruence principle, requiring a similarity of authority patterns of those who govern and those who are governed, rather than geometrical isomorphy (Eckstein 1969: 291), therefore constitutes a fundamental condition of democracy. The people include those who are members of a polity ruled by a government, and this membership defines citizenship.

Second, political power is acceptable if it serves the common welfare of citizens. In principle, citizens should determine in deliberation that is guided by the "unforced force of the better argument" (Habermas 1981: 52–3, translated by the author), what the common welfare implies and whether the use of political power conforms to this idea. Yet this procedural rule is also a normative idea. In practice, political parties formulate alternative proposals for policies claiming that they serve the welfare of the people. These proposals are discussed in various public forums. The parties in power and holders of executive offices decide on and implement a policy proposal under the scrutiny of a critical opposition in parliament, the media and the electorate. The commitment to justify their policies, the supervision by the parliamentary opposition or media and the risk of losing their power motivate elected officeholders to govern according to the common welfare. The "general will" of the people constitutes an abstract idea. Its substance in terms of the common welfare or public good and the specific policies it requires are matters of permanent discussion and contestation in politics and in the public.

Third, democracy entitles citizens to participate in public deliberation, parties, interest organizations and elections on an equal basis. They can express their opinion in different ways. In debates on specific issues and policymaking, they are represented by authorized actors who speak for them in the processes of governing. Having neither sufficient expertise nor time to control the execution of power, citizens elect members of parliaments and/or the executive whom they trust and hold accountable in retrospect. The parliament delegates power to execute to the cabinet and administration, defines the mandates of the cabinets by party programmes, legislation or resolutions and controls the executive accordingly (Caramani 2017: 55–7). In brief, democratic legitimacy requires that representatives are not only authorized but also accountable.

Fourth, a government must be empowered to work towards the welfare of the people. At the same time, its power must be limited so that opinions expressed in public or organized interests can influence politics and policymaking. Constitutional law guaranteeing citizen rights, division of power between the executive, the legislative and the judiciary, as well as checks and balances between governments at different levels evolved in the history of governments as institutional provisions to limit power. Majority rule, a strong executive and a professional administration are critical conditions for effective governing. The principle of democratic legitimacy requires limited and effective government. How the organization of a polity balances institutions that enable and those that limit power determines the quality of democracy.

This summary of the basic conditions for democratic legitimacy points out a fundamental dilemma: On the one hand, the increasing complexity of problems facing governments requires that they take responsibility for the external effects of their policies. They must consider the will of people outside their jurisdiction and should give those affected a voice in policymaking. This is the purpose of multilevel governance. By including representatives of people affected by complex problems, although in different ways depending on the level where people are politically organized, it contributes to governing according to principles of democracy. On the other hand, democratizing multilevel governance seems to be impossible, if we apply the standard of representative democracy outlined above. Political scientists have searched for ways to align these contradictory requirements by discussing the following questions: Can we presume a "multilevel" *demos* (either a transborder *demos* or multiple *demoi*) or is democratic legitimacy realizable if the *demos* is substituted by functional equivalents like stakeholders or associations? How are citizens represented and how can they hold their representatives accountable? Which conditions and which modes of governance promise effective policies that are acceptable for the people concerned? Can the power dynamics be controlled to avoid an increasing or persisting imbalance? Considering these questions, the following sections review the legitimacy of the three types of power that shape multilevel politics and policymaking. Evidently, this rough sketch of reasoning can only indicate an analytical perspective. It should demonstrate how the differentiated conceptualization of power can contribute to rethinking the democratic legitimacy of multilevel governance.

LEGITIMIZING TRANSBOUNDARY POWER IN MULTILEVEL GOVERNANCE

If we understand multilevel governance as the dispersal of authority and coordinated governing under the condition of divided authority, legitimacy concerns both aspects of politics. Whenever actors at different levels claim authority, they must justify their claim with appropriate and acceptable reasons. However, the crucial question concerning legitimacy is how authorized officeholders use their power in interactions with other governmental and non-governmental actors.

Entrenched in constitutional law, international treaties or statutes, the consensus achieved in the negotiations and ratification of these basic documents seems to legitimize rules establishing the division of authority. As a matter of fact, constitutions, treaties and statutes are "incomplete contracts" which reflect that "actors are only bounded rational and cannot anticipate all possible contingencies" (Aghion and Holden 2011: 182). Therefore, the division of authority is a matter of permanent interpretation and renegotiation in processes of multilevel policymaking. Irrespective of the different procedures of making or amending constitutions, treaties or statutes on the one hand and governing according to the established rules on the other hand, both types of politics include actors representing governments or organizations from different levels and jurisdictions. In multilevel governance and meta-governance, outcomes result from the reciprocal use of bargaining power and epistemic power, if not the power of the last resort and the adjustment of power structures to specific conditions and situations. Therefore, this section focuses on legitimizing these types of power and highlights accountability, deliberation and power balancing as essential legitimization mechanisms.

Accountability

Bargaining power prevails in multilevel governance and essentially shapes policy coordination as well as the negotiation of constitutions, treaties or statutes determining the division of authority. Given the primary responsibility of governments to make binding decisions, members of cabinets or senior public officials first and foremost apply this power in policymaking. These political executives represent citizens in central and lower-tier jurisdictions. Therefore, the democratic legitimacy of bargaining power results from processes in domestic politics where multiple *demoi* express their views of the public welfare. For federal, regionalized and unitary governments, the precedence of central law seems to speak for a hierarchical order of democracy giving prevalence to the will of the *demos* over the will of *demoi*. However, a hierarchical legal order may cast a shadow of hierarchy over multilevel governance but cannot render policy preferences of lower-tier governments irrelevant. Beyond the state, no *demos* exists to express the global public interest. In the EU, even the establishment of European citizenship and the directly elected European Parliament have not ended debates about the no-*demos* thesis. Overall, bargaining power is legitimized by democracy organized in territorial jurisdictions at different levels.

Scholars have discussed whether direct or participatory democracy can integrate multiple *demoi* into a community of citizens who feel concerned by specific policies. Heidrun Abromeit argued for referenda in functional governance arrangements cutting across boundaries of territorial jurisdictions, assuming citizens declare their membership in these jurisdictions according to how much a policy affects them (Abromeit 1998: 95–136). Philippe Schmitter (2006) suggested that the participation of selected "stakeholders" representing affected groups in policy-specific governance arrangements can generate legitimacy. However, the selection of those who "have some legitimate claim to participate" (Schmitter 2006: 168), like the self-declaration of voters as members of a policy-specific governance arrangement, can hardly avoid arbitrary results. Participation of civil society and interest groups can improve the quality of multilevel policymaking, but it cannot replace the legitimation of bargaining power of authorized officeholders in procedures of representative democracy.

For practical reasons, executives who act for a government or international organization are the responsible agents in multilevel policy coordination and negotiate essential agreements on rules, conditions for grants, standards, procedures of monitoring or yardstick competition, etc. Democratic legitimacy of their bargaining power derives from the executives' accountability to parliaments or assemblies of citizens representing local, regional or national or, if they can be presumed to exist, transnational *demoi*. Institutions of representation and accountability procedures are organized within territorial jurisdictions on the basic levels of multilevel governance. Paradoxically, the democratic processes and the scrutiny and control by parliaments or parliamentary assemblies tend to inhibit effective policy coordination. This dilemma has been discussed at length in the literature on global governance (e.g., Dahl 1994), governing the EU (e.g., Scharpf 1999) and democracy in federal systems (e.g., Benz and Sonnicksen 2017). It particularly arises in joint-decision systems because the accountability of executives in domestic politics reduces their flexibility to adjust preferences, to settle package deals or to find compromises in negotiations. Yet it also can impair other modes of governance, if, for example, parliaments reject policies that comply with standards, refuse to participate in experimental policies or yardstick competition or disregard the outcome of monitoring.

Deficits in effectiveness rarely result from a deadlock of policymaking. Under the pressure to cope with complex problems, actors in multilevel governance agree on deals or compromises and majority parties in parliaments normally endorse the achievements of the cabinet they have elected. Outcomes may be sub-optimal but incrementally change the status quo. Vetoes can be avoided if an opposing government explicitly or implicitly opts out of an agreement, provided that this does not offend the interests of people in other governments or undermine policy coordination. In case of governance failure, interest organizations may increase the pressure to resume intergovernmental negotiations. In general, regulative policies can be more effectively coordinated in multilevel governance than policies with redistributive effects. Nonetheless, as bargaining power delegated to executives aims at satisfying the preferences of different *demoi* and as these preferences are defined in domestic politics, multilevel policymaking is affected by veto- and exit threats that limit the range of feasible alternatives.

In principle, there are two options to solve this dilemma: The first loosens the constraints resulting from the accountability of executives in domestic politics without causing executive domination. The second establishes forums of transborder deliberation among actors not directly involved in policy coordination, particularly among external veto players, to facilitate the adjustment of policy preferences.

The first option takes advantage of institutional complexity. To make complex systems effective and adaptive, system theory argues for loose coupling of sub-systems (Orton and Weick 1990: 204). Theories of federalism have adopted this idea (Landau 1969,1973), and comparative research on federal democracies has confirmed the advantages of loose instead of tight linkages between intergovernmental relations and democratic processes in governments (Benz and Sonnicksen 2021). Instead of executives negotiating with their hands tied by instructions and subject to strict controls of their strategies and behaviour, loosely coupled multilevel and domestic policymaking evolve in sequences of mutual adjustment. Executives allow parliaments or their committees to monitor multilevel policymaking, report on intermediary results or critical conflicts and finally justify their decisions and the outcome. Policy coordination in the multilevel arena switches between confidential and public negotiations and develops in different venues and actor constellations. International climate policy proceeds exactly according to such a loosely coupled design, as outlined in Chapter 7. Politics in the Swiss federal system also provides examples of flexible linkages of distinct policy arenas like intergovernmental negotiations in the executive, consultation with civil society, debates and majority decisions in parliaments, and, in the last resort, a referendum (Armingeon 2000). In the EU and federations, opting out has evolved as a strategy to loosely couple multilevel politics and democracy (Scharpf 2017: 331–2). Many more exemplary cases could be added.

The second option complements the first one by implementing elements of deliberative democracy. In general, democracies require citizens' engagement in public deliberation. This process is essential to form an opinion about the public interest by taking into consideration the opinions and concerns of other citizens. Likewise, transborder deliberation among citizens, interest organizations and responsible office-holders can contribute to developing their mutual understanding of the joint problems requiring multilevel policy coordination and options of coordinated action (Scharpf 2000: 118–20). Such processes can be organized through the participation of selected groups of citizens, as experiments to include civil society in EU governance demonstrate (Kohler-Koch and Quittkat 2013). More important and effective, however, are forums of deliberation among members of parliaments who scrutinize multilevel policies, civil servants who prepare these policies, and party representatives and members of nongovernmental organizations who serve as intermediaries between politics and citizens. Therefore, interparliamentary relations, administrative networks, and communicative processes in integrated multilevel parties, private interest organizations or civil society organizations provide venues for transborder deliberation. The organization of these patterns of deliberation raises many practical problems that call for further research. Furthermore, the internet and social media have changed the quality of deliberation, with consequences that cannot be neglected. Empirical research does not allow for general conclusions, but studies on digital communication among diplomats and civil servants have indicated new divides between member states in the EU and between urban and rural municipalities (Bicchi and Lovato 2023: 213; Roy 2021: 99–102). Nonetheless, communication across levels among actors who monitor multilevel policymaking and hold executives to account are promising strategies to improve effectiveness and democratic legitimacy.

Accountability relations link executive governance in multilevel systems to intra-governmental democratic processes. This is an essential condition for legitimizing bargaining power, although it does not suffice to democratize multilevel governance. Reciprocal bargaining power in multilevel governance is rarely balanced. Regardless of institutional rules providing for fair procedures, equal voting rights and veto rights, or exit options to protect essential concerns of minorities, actors in multilevel governance use bargaining power in search of advantages for their government or organization. Unilateral domination can be prevented by the aforementioned rules, and the chance to contest arbitrary or unauthorized power initiates balancing mechanisms. Still, an inherent tendency towards power imbalance remains. This dilemma of persisting imbalance is typical for systems of checks and balances, but it exceedingly appears in multilevel governance, where power asymmetry reflects economic disparities, societal diversity and different governance capacities. In consequence, democratizing bargaining power cannot guarantee the equality of citizens in different jurisdictions, if it is not complemented by the capacity to restructure and balance power (cf. Chapter 7).

Another problem of legitimacy in multilevel governance should not be ignored. The conditions legitimizing bargaining power apply to representatives of democratic governments. However, as mentioned in Chapter 4, executives who are not democratically legitimized regularly participate in global or macro-regional governance as well as in unconsolidated democratic federations. Likewise, private actors, whose claims to represent societal interests are doubtful, regularly influence policy coordination across jurisdictions. Yet most private actors participate with limited bargaining power in multilevel governance. More powerful are holders of private capital who can threaten to exit from local, regional or national jurisdictions, if governments do not coordinate market regulation in response to transborder mobility. In contrast, representatives speaking for autocratic governments can have significant bargaining power in multilevel governance. Excluding these governments from policy coordination is not a viable option in the face of multiple interdependence between governments and societies. Yet their participation is also no reason to deny the democratic legitimacy of multilevel governance in total. If a policy is accepted by citizens who can hold executives accountable in democratic governments, their approval can be taken as an indication that it may also be acceptable for citizens in non-democratic governments. This assumption holds if policies conform to general principles like distributive justice and recognition of people's diversity. Furthermore, if people cannot voice their grievances, independent experts from international or non-governmental organizations can uncover and communicate their concerns. Thus epistemic power can contribute to bringing justice to citizens who are subject to autocratic rule. However, this kind of power is not legitimate per se. It needs to be compatible with democratic legitimacy.

Deliberation

The power of experts has been a matter of controversial debate in political science and the public. On the one hand, terms like "expertocracy" or "technocracy" indicate negative or at least ambivalent connotations, whereas terms like "expert authority" or "evidence-based" governance present their function in a favourable light. The first terms usually address the power of specialists in public administration, whereas the second refer to professional advisors or scientists. In multilevel governance, both types of experts participate and both have significant impact due to their special experience and knowledge. However, even if knowledge is essential for good governing, as such it does not legitimize epistemic power.

The concept of "epistemic authority" (Zürn 2018: 45–61), which emerged in the literature on international politics and global governance, implies legitimacy. Michael Zürn explicates that epistemic power can turn into authority if it results from a process of "enduring reflection about the worthiness of the authority" by those who are subject to it. Despite their limited rationality and capacities to scrutinize specific decisions, subordinates can engage in a "permanent monitoring and consideration of the standards that make an authority appealing and trustworthy" (ibid.: 46). In the international realm, Zürn identifies reflexivity as "epistemic foundation" of both the political authority to make binding decisions and the epistemic authority to provide interpretations of the reality that confront politics and to elaborate policy options. This foundation of authority essentially characterizes "the relationship between international organisations and states" (ibid.: 53), but reflexivity also emerges from relations between different authorities, political as well as epistemic, that cooperate to coordinate policies and mutually limit their separate powers.

It can be disputed that "an epistemic foundation" is sufficient to legitimize the authority to make binding decisions. However, the notion of reflexivity points in an appropriate direction to determine the legitimacy of epistemic power. Zürn rightly emphasizes that legitimacy in this context does not mean democratic legitimacy (ibid.: 69). Independent experts and specialists in administration are not accountable to parliaments or citizens. Their authority derives from a scientific or professional rationality of their interpretations and policy proposals. Both rationalities refer to processes of knowledge generation and denote rules to be followed in these processes. The epistemic power of experts is not recognized because they have knowledge or enjoy reputation as experts, but because their knowledge conforms to scientific standards. It must be gained according to appropriate methods, and the accessibility of data and methods must enable other experts in the field to review their findings. Hence, the process of knowledge generation requires reflexivity in the sense of verifiability, revisability and consideration of standards of good scientific practice. Experts, regardless of whether they work in academia, public administration or jurisprudence, can claim epistemic authority only if they accept a critical evaluation of their knowledge and never claim it to be indisputably true.

For this reason, epistemic power cannot be legitimized through democracy. Yet, the legitimization of this power derives from processes that in crucial respects resemble democratic processes, and in other respects match with multilevel governance. Scientists are not accountable to the people, but responsible to the scientific community. They do not pursue specific purposes like public welfare; instead, they contribute to solving problems of mankind or particular groups of people. Ideally, scientific evidence is proved in open deliberation. Inquiries and expertise are published and discussed in public, in the scientific community in the first place but also in politics, business, media and the general public. In this process, knowledge is tested and contested in an exchange of theoretical or empirical reasons. Finally, the better reasons decide which knowledge is recognized and accepted as long as it is not contested and revised. Legitimacy of epistemic power (or epistemic authority) thus results from processes that correspond to a cosmopolitan deliberative democracy, a democracy that, lacking a real *demos*, complies with the idea of a *demos* by including a plurality of "political and social agents" in inclusive processes of arguing and struggles to make political power accountable (Archibugi and Held 2011: 448–55). Yet, knowledge must also be applied to specific contexts. If policymakers take the evaluations and recommendations resulting from evidence-based benchmarking and monitoring as law-like instructions in multilevel governance without checking their applicability in different jurisdictions, epistemic power turns into technocratic rule. As Pierre Salmon has emphasized for yardstick competition, the essential function of these modes of governance is to reduce information asymmetries between executives and citizens and to "rescue accountability" (Salmon 2019: 60–70), provided that comparative evaluation stimulates public discussion.

In contrast to democratic legitimacy that results from clearly defined and institutionalized procedures, epistemic power is legitimized in informal processes and according to standards defined in science. Therefore, legitimacy deficits are difficult to discover and more difficult to sanction. Typical problems concern the selection of experts, the ambivalent role of specialists in public administration who prepare or implement political decisions, or the neglect of deviating opinions or experiences of minorities like indigenous people. Moreover, experts who consult on politics are also influenced by politics and are rarely fully unbiased. Yet, like an imbalance of bargaining power, deviations from normative principles of epistemic authority can be and are regularly contested. The division of authority in multilevel governance favours the exchange of arguments, which is essential for both creating and legitimizing epistemic power.

Arguing instead of bargaining does not render epistemic power democratic, but its legitimacy draws on the idea of deliberative democracy. While representative forms of democracy motivate actors in power to pursue the public interest, deliberation can determine what the public interest means in specific policies. In theory, it calls for arguing among rational actors and the inclusion of all affected people on an equal basis. Participants should seek common knowledge to understand reality, to find the acceptable norms for evaluating reality and to solve joint problems. In practical politics, deliberation occurs in different, but connected, "epistemic communities" that not only include scientists or experts from administration but also emerge in non-governmental organizations, media and citizen participation (Lafont 2020). Deliberation does not end in a binding decision by authorized and accountable officeholders. Rather, it generates epistemic power. This power is legitimized as knowledge, evidence-based opinion or relevant experience, and it has an impact on policymaking through the persuasiveness of reason. Therefore, epistemic power legitimized in deliberation complements representative democracy in general. In multilevel governance, it is essential because deliberative processes are not bound to jurisdictions of governments. Deliberation justifies policies by arguing and critically reviewing policy outcomes, whereas representative democracy transfers policy proposals that, based on the outcome of deliberation, appear acceptable into binding decisions and actions.

Balancing Power

As outlined in Chapter 7, bargaining among representatives of governments or other governmental or non-governmental organizations and deliberation in epistemic communities often evolves in the shadow of the unilateral power of the last resort. The authority of legislatures, political leaders or courts to decide unilaterally is legitimized and limited by constitutions or treaties. However, the actual use of this power shortcuts processes of bargaining and deliberation. What is more, it can induce a permanent concentration of power and weaken the limiting effects of a division of authority. In a crisis of multilevel governance, the emergency power of central governments suspends the bargaining power of regional or local governments and public-private partnerships or renationalizes policymaking in international governance. Given the external effects and interdependence of economies, societies and public policies across jurisdictions, subsidiary competences provide gateways to centralization rather than protect decentralized power. Court authority is limited to arbitration and jurisprudence, but they more and more decide on "mega-political" issues; that is, matters of outright and utmost political significance that often define and divide whole polities. (Hirschl 2008: 94). Though authorized and required to prevent governance failure or solve conflicts, the power of the last resort can undermine the legitimacy of multilevel governance through accountability of representatives and deliberation.

The same applies to the power that allows actors to restructure venues or patterns of interaction and to vary modes of coordination. In general, a chief negotiator takes the lead in a critical situation, but to manage bargaining processes, he or she must cooperate with others. As William Zartman pointed out for international conflict resolution, "all the hands that can be brought to the task can help. The only requirement is that all efforts be well coordinated ..." (Zartman 2007: 16). Like the continuous adaptation of institutions to everchanging challenges and conditions, shifting processes between levels or arenas, variation of actor constellations or altering modes of coordination in multilevel governance are negotiated with a "wide range of policy actors" in a "coordinative discourse" (Schmidt 2010: 3), mostly in confidential exploratory talks and private negotiations. These discourses and the resulting changes emerge during the process of policymaking without being planned ex-ante. They reveal the institutional elasticity of multilevel governance, however, they are difficult to scrutinize or control ex-post in accountability processes.

In terms of legitimacy, the shadow of power of the last resort and the elasticity of multilevel governance are ambivalent. On the one hand, both increase the chance of successful policy coordination in multilevel governance, even if distributive or identity conflicts have to be solved. Therefore, both contribute to output legitimacy. On the other hand, process management can make policy processes opaque and impede democratic accountability and democracy-conforming deliberation. In addition, the power of the last resort increases the risk of "authority migration", irrespective of whether it remains in the shadow or is used in a specific policy process. Given the incompleteness of formal rules, political actors may exploit institutional flexibility by "deliberately and strategically seeking to shift authority as a political strategy" (Gerber and Kollman 2004: 397). Authority migration may result from an upward or downward movement of power in the vertical dimension (ibid.: 397) but can also bear upon power structures in the horizontal dimension of multilevel governance. Within states, authority migration tends to strengthen central governments in relation to regional or local governments. In macro-regional or global governance, it leads to decentralization and re-nationalization of politics, when governments in large states with supreme economic or military capacities presume leadership. For this reason, studies on multilevel governance should not neglect arbitrary domination or consider it irrelevant, neither within nor beyond the state (Barnett and Duval 2005: 10–23). Even if the enabling dimension of power ("power-to") rather than the constraining dimension ("power-over" or "domination") is essential in multilevel governance, researchers and actors in practice should consider "the duality of power, which entails constant awareness of the potentially dominating aspects, while seeking out the empowering sides of power" (Haugaard 2022: 194).

As long as multilevel governance remains in place, authority migration and the concentration of power meet resistance. The division of authority presumes a balance of power. Hence, whenever actors feel disadvantaged by an imbalance of power, they can initiate processes to restore the balance. Theoretically speaking, power structures are balanced if the power of an actor is not contested by any other actors concerned, provided that contestation is not prohibited. While authority is legitimized by constitutions or agreements, effective power can only be legitimized if all involved and affected actors can challenge its conformity with constitutional norms or agreements. In addition, power can be considered balanced if actors can effectively react to the power applied against them with corresponding countervailing power. This definition of balance is assumed in realist approaches to international theory as a power balance among states. In game-theoretical models, it appears as an equilibrium. However, such a constellation rarely exists in practical politics. Instead, multilevel politics evolves as a process in which actors permanently contest imbalances and mobilize counteracting power. What game theory defines as equilibrium appears as never-ending balancing in real politics. And instead of a balance among states, suggested in international relations theories, the challenge is to balance the power of institutional actors in the different dimensions of multilevel governance. It is not a balance, but the permanent process of balancing which constitutes legitimacy. Therefore, we need to determine what guarantees the permanence of balancing and what qualifies this process.

In research on federal systems, scholars have not only discovered imbalance as a characteristic feature of multilevel polities but also identified "political safeguards" as mechanisms inducing processes of balancing (Wechsler 1954; Kramer 2000). They have emphasized the stabilizing effect of an integrated party system, assuming that members of parliaments and holders of executive offices lose their interest in expanding power through authority migration if they are affiliated or accountable to multilevel parties (Riker 1964: 129–36; Filippov, Ordeshook and Svetsova 2004). Others have drawn attention to "institutional safeguards" (Thorlakson 2006). Jenna Bednar convincingly argues that no single political (party system) or institutional safeguard (division of power, representation of lower-tier governments in central institutions; referenda, constitutional courts) alone is sufficient, whereas a system of complementary safeguards can prevent power imbalance (Bednar 2009). In multilevel governance, it is the combination of division of authority and modes of coordination in a particular – national or international – institutional context that determines the system of safeguards. In general, the dispersal of authority, the interdependence of problems or policies in territorial jurisdictions and the interactions of actors as such reveal imbalances and motivate actors to contest power and initiate processes of balancing. From the perspective of the initiating actor, efforts to revise power relations can succeed or fail. Counterreactions from actors profiting from the power imbalance being addressed can inhibit changes. However, they cannot prevent the dynamics of safeguard processes and the continuity of power balancing.

Safeguard strategies and the ensuing mechanisms of adjusting power prevent a self-enforcing imbalance in multilevel governance. The common term "checks and balances" qualifies the normative implications of a division of authority and presumes an end of balancing. However, if a balance is defined as a constellation of power that is not contested by any of the concerned actors, the process of balancing matters as an end in itself. It serves to prevent an imbalance of power and thus legitimizes power negatively through the opportunity of contestation and the availability of institutional and political safeguards that set in motion the process of balancing. The following propositions clarify what preventing imbalance means and indicate under which conditions a process initiated by safeguards qualifies as balancing.

– First of all, contestation of power imbalances and safeguards against authority migration should inhibit a concentration of power and the risk of domination. This does not suggest that power should be restricted through a strict separation of authority. Multilevel governance aims at overcoming the limits of power that result from the demarcation of jurisdictions.

Therefore, balancing should avoid both the concentration and fragmentation of power. Instead, it maintains institutional differentiation and integration in line with economic and social diversity and the challenges of complexity.

- Second, balancing aims neither at centralization nor decentralization. Instead, "noncentralization" should be the normative guideline. Daniel Elazar introduced this concept to characterize federal democracy as "the structured dispersion of powers among many centres whose legitimate authority is constitutionally guaranteed" (Elazar 1987: 34). He described noncentralization "as a matrix of governments, with power so distributed that the rank order of the several governments is not fixed" (ibid.: 36). Balancing then aims at determining the rank of actors representing governments and other actors involved in multilevel governance for specific policies and conditions to which a policy applies. At the same time, it preserves the elasticity of the order regarding levels, jurisdictions and the relation of multilevel and domestic politics.

- Third, balancing should avoid rigid power structures. Constitutional law or treaty rules and courts interpreting the substance of these rules serve as safeguards to prevent imbalance. However, overregulation of the division of power by constitutions or treaties or juridification through court judgments contradicts the idea of balancing (Benz 2016: 191–7). Authority is legitimized by constitutional rules, but these rules cannot guarantee a balance of power. While protecting the division of authority against actors' attempts to expand their power, these rules must also enable them to adapt multilevel governance to changing tasks (Bednar 2009: 52–6). Rigid rules constrain policymaking, whereas adjusting a constitutional design serves to achieve specific policy goals. Therefore, balancing power is a matter of politics in the first place. In multilevel systems, legal proceedings serve to arbitrate conflicts on authority, but courts should avoid decisions that constitutionalize policy conflicts. They should rather "rely on a combination of constitutional ambiguity with specific forms of elite behaviour, …, which serve to keep disagreements over constitutional matters from openly unfolding in society" (Hurrelmann 2023: 243). Leaving constitutional disputes in abeyance maintains the process of balancing power.

- Fourth, balancing requires considering the different sources and faces of power. Focusing on authority conflicts while neglecting imbalances in bargaining power or epistemic power foregoes an important potential of balancing. Strengthening the bargaining power of lower-tier actors, for example, by pooling resources or coordinating the use of veto power, can counterbalance the centralization of authority. Epistemic power of independent committees of experts can offset the bargaining power of executives or external veto players as well as the authority of governmental actors to decide in the last resort. Like executives, experts should be called to account in public forums like parliaments, parties or public discourses.

- Fifth, balancing power should prevent polarization in multilevel governance. Polarization obstructs balancing processes because it turns interaction and bargaining among actors into a confrontation of opposing groups or alliances and their leaders. Apart from the probability of deadlocks or an escalation of conflicts, it advances a concentration of power within two camps and hence contradicts the first criteria of balancing. In principle, the division of power in multilevel governance, the coordination of policies across borders of jurisdiction, the interplay of bargaining among executives representing governments and the deliberation of civil servants or other experts in epistemic communities protect governance against polarization. Nonetheless, antagonistic politics in states and international politics threaten balancing multilevel governance, irrespective of which kinds of safeguards are in operation. In party politics and international relations, polarization is difficult to attenuate. A pragmatic policy of détente seems to revise a self-enforcing confrontation, a policy that avoids polarizing rhetoric, focuses on interests and the potential of compromises instead of emphasizing values, and relies on communication through different, official and informal channels to prevent misperceptions and to explore options for coordinated action.
- Sixth, imbalances of power often reflect economic disparities and discrimination against communities. Therefore, claims for justice and mutual recognition characterize a process of balancing that can lead to attenuating conflicts. In many cases, coalitions of political leaders or executives representing economically disadvantaged countries, protests organized by civil society organizations or campaigns of discriminated communities contest an imbalanced power structure by stimulating public discourses and mobilizing opposition (Steffek 2023: 11–13). By drawing attention to basic standards of governance, they compel representatives of governments or international organizations to respond to the claims raised.

Certainly, power imbalance persists, all the more under the condition of economic disparities and asymmetric distribution of authority. However, as long as multilevel governance empowers and enables actors to effectively contest power, we can assume that power of the last resort in multilevel governance is legitimized. Power contestation and processes of balancing power maintain the institutional checks and the plurality of actors and venues of policymaking which constitute essential prerequisites of democracy. If power balancing ends in structural gridlocks or escalating conflicts, it indicates legitimacy deficits.

DEMOCRACY ACROSS BORDERS

The previous sections outlined how the different types of power in multilevel governance can be legitimized and whether they conform to standards of democracy. Taken together, the democratic legitimacy of power in multilevel governance seems to be based on shaky ground. Bargaining power can be legitimized in democratic processes, but the incongruence of policy coordination between levels and jurisdictions on the one hand and accountability and public deliberation within governments on the other hand is a source of tension between effectiveness and democratic legitimacy. Likewise, the legitimacy of epistemic power through arguing conforms to the idea of deliberative democracy, but there is no guarantee that the participation of experts and processes of consultation and knowledge transfer conform to this idea. As to the power of the last resort, output legitimacy can be taken as a normative benchmark, but affected actors may disagree on the need for unilateral decisions and the assessment of the output. Moreover, opportunities to use the unilateral power of the last resort can entail a concentration of power or institutional conflicts.

Given their different normative foundation, the three types of power can cause legitimacy conflicts, such as those that have built up in the EU during recent decades, as observed by Vivien Schmidt. She described the incongruence of multilevel governance and democracy as "split-level legitimacy" (Schmidt 2020: 57). At the European level, experts of the Commission elaborated proposals for the harmonization of regulation in the Common Market, which executives in the Council turned into binding decisions. Despite the expanding power of co-decision of the European Parliament, input legitimacy resulted from the approval of market integration and European policies by a majority of citizens in national democracies. After the turn of the century, the enlargement of the Union and the Euro crisis exposed the distributive effects of EU policies. This led to a politicization of European governance in member states, where parties opposing European integration emerged and attracted voters. The contestation of global governance signified similar tensions when divides between national governments undermined the epistemic authority of international organizations and when the approval for global governance in national democracies waned (Zürn 2018). In multilevel governance inside states, the enduring debates about the weakness of regional parliaments compared to the bargaining power of executives (Kropp 2015) or the epistemic power of "technocrats" in multilevel administration (Beer 1978) indicate comparable tensions between modes of legitimacy. In federations, where democracy is established at all levels, frictions between arenas of policy coordination and accountability relations reveal tensions between methods of legitimization (Benz and Sonnicksen 2017).

In politics, these tensions provide reasons for contesting power imbalances. As mentioned in the previous section, a balance of power is difficult to stabilize in multilevel governance. Nonetheless, it constitutes an idea guiding multilevel politics. Balance refers to power relations between upper- and lower-tier governments, executives and parliaments, political representatives and civil servants or governmental and non-governmental actors. Yet it also implies that the three modes of legitimacy concerning bargaining power (democratic legitimacy resulting from accountability and public deliberation in governments), epistemic power (legitimacy through arguing in deliberation) and unilateral power of the last resort or power to manage processes (output legitimacy) indicate complementary sources to justify power. Therefore, instead of discussing alternative types of democracy (like participative democracy, direct democracy, deliberative democracy, associative democracy, etc.) or legitimacy (input versus output), it seems more promising to think about combining different ways of legitimizing power.

From a normative point of view, democratic legitimacy must be taken as the primary mode. In multilevel governance, the concept of democratic legitimacy is realized in a representative government according to the principles defined above. The tensions between democracy and multilevel governance do not speak against the applicability of this concept. Yet they call for complementing representative democracy and accountability inside governments with multilevel deliberation (Scharpf 2000: 118–20). Participation of citizens or civil society organizations, or innovative forms of democracy like mini-publics, cannot replace representative democracy. Like discourses among experts, they can, however, constitute additional venues for legitimizing epistemic power. Unilateral power of the last resort is necessary to make complex governance work, as is the continuous restructuring of patterns of interaction in multiple venues. Both can complement democratic legitimacy and deliberative legitimacy, as long as unilateral power remains in the shadow and restructuring does not aim at migrating power or authority by stealth. Structuring venues and processes must prevent the "reasoning" of experts from dominating democratic politics or party politics from neglecting expertise presuming that they fulfil the "will" of the people (Caramani 2017).

The normative complementarity of the three types of power contributes to the balancing process. Epistemic power often contrasts with bargaining power, and the "shadow power" of the last resort can shift the balance in favour of knowledge-based politics if a central authority follows proposals from experts and, in consequence, increases pressure on negotiating actors or finishes bargaining by a final decision. Such a balancing can result from and may be intended by a change of modes of governance. Without going into details, it is obvious that the different modes reveal a trend towards a specific type of power. Joint decisions, the implementation of central guidelines or grant programmes, and cooperative policies are negotiated among executives. In these negotiations, participants face the dilemma of managing complex tasks while taking into account domestic actors' preferences for policy outcomes and autonomy. Bargaining power is part of the strategies of executives to cope with this challenge, but the power of the last resort is no less relevant given the risk of gridlocks. Expertise is often used as a strategic tool to counter bargaining power in joint policymaking. In experimental governance, governance by standards, yardstick competition or policy transfers, epistemic power shapes a policy, whereas authorized actors organize these processes and design standards, targets or benchmarks. In these processes, experts play a significant role and shift negotiations towards arguing instead of bargaining. The trend towards mixed modes of governance in policy fields (e.g., Tömmel and Verdun 2009) or differentiation of structures that lay the ground for a variety of modes of governance (e.g. Falkner 2011; Jordan et al. 2018: 97–228; Scharpf 2001, 2006) can be interpreted as ways to balance power. In any case, they reflect the dynamics of politics in multilevel governance.

No mode of legitimization works in reality as presumed in theory, not only in multilevel governance but in political systems in general. Even well-established democracies are all but perfect. This is the reason why they need to be embedded in social structures of civil society and international regimes, in addition to institutions guaranteeing the rule of law and welfare regimes (Merkel 2004). Likewise, democracy in governments is embedded in multilevel governance, which should motivate citizens and their representatives to assume responsibility for the external effects of their decisions and actions and to support executives in the efforts to coordinate policies across borders. In turn, multilevel governance is embedded in politics at the different levels and gains legitimacy from democracy in governments. As long as power created by multilevel governance is compatible with democracy and as long as power structures in multilevel and democratic politics are continuously balanced, we can consider multilevel governance as legitimized in a democracy-conforming way.

CONCLUSION

As democracy requires a congruence of a *demos* and the jurisdiction of a government, power executed in multilevel governance cannot be democratic. This is one of the conclusions that follows from the reasoning outlined in this chapter. However, this argument does not entail that multilevel governance is undemocratic. The second conclusion is that multilevel governance can be legitimized in line with the normative principles of democracy. The different types of power emerging in multilevel governance are either linked to democratic processes organized in governments or they complement these processes in a way conforming to the principle of democratic legitimacy. Executives applying bargaining power of multilevel governance must give an account of their negotiation behaviour and the outcomes of policy coordination to parliaments and citizens. Epistemic power and the shadow of power of the last resort can counterbalance the constraining effects of intragovernmental accountability. The *demos*-constraining effect of multilevel governance can be compensated by democracy-conforming deliberation in cross-border communities of actors who provide different kinds of expertise. In addition, power structures inside and between jurisdictions can be balanced if they are contested and revised through safeguard mechanisms. The division of power in multilevel governance and the different modes of governance constitute conditions and provide procedures for safeguarding power against imbalances and establishing a permanent balancing of power.

These modes of legitimizing multilevel governance cannot guarantee stability. On the contrary, balancing indicates that an enduring balance of power is never achievable. This way, multilevel governance remains elastic and adaptable to cope with the ever-changing challenges of complex tasks that call for coordination across levels. Elasticity, however, implies a permanent trend towards imbalance. If balancing processes fail, an imbalance of power can escalate conflicts, polarization and confrontation. In the last consequence, multilevel governance might be dissolved, when national governments presume sovereign power and turn to an antagonist strategy of foreign policy that implies threatening, if not applying military power. Calls for democratic accountability and deliberation across boundaries of jurisdictions cannot prevent this vicious cycle of confrontation. Presumably, the only chance to stop such a development is to engage in balancing processes according to the normative principles outlined above, which is anything but easy in practice, but worth the effort.

9. Conclusion: multilevel governance in times of political polarization

Until recently, scholars assumed a continuous trend towards multilevel governance. Research on intergovernmental relations and policymaking in federations or regionalized governments endorsed this perception, which concepts like polycentric or interactive governance reflect. Michael Zürn described global governance as multilevel governance, also characterizing it as "*conditio politica* of the twenty-first century" (Zürn 2010: 82).

Only a few years after publishing this statement, Zürn observed an increasing contestation of the global order (Zürn 2018). Since 2022 at the latest, contestation has turned into confrontation among the great powers China, Russia, the US and the EU. In the shadow of this development, conflicts intensified in many parts of the world. In the EU, Brexit and divides among member states over the rule of law, migration, climate policy and fiscal policy appear as "multiple, interconnected but quite different crises", which "shake the very foundations of the European project" (Cotta and Isernia 2021: 3). Within states, distributive and value conflicts obstruct policy coordination, while the centralization of regulation and redistributive policies and decentralization of public services divide authority for interdependent functions and increase the need for multilevel governance. The polarization in party politics deepens divides between governments or communities of different jurisdictions. The confrontation between actors who are responsible for coordinating policies across borders reflects polarized debates about multilevel policies in governments and societies (McCoy, Rahman and Somer 2018). Economic competition causing disparities and the rise of a new nationalism or regionalism driven by identity politics at different levels of government are the main causes of this development.

Does this mean that research on multilevel governance is outdated and that we should address the new reality of politics after the failure or decline of multilevel governance? This book suggests a different conclusion. It argues for rethinking multilevel governance considering the changing reality. It makes the case for maintaining and advancing the division of authority across levels and searching for appropriate coordination to cope with interdependence. Even if divides and confrontation obstruct coordinated efforts to manage complex problems in many policy fields and even if central governments in states try to concentrate power and seek autonomy in international relations, multilevel governance remains a relevant concept to understand the evolution of politics. It covers different aspects of politics and policy, structures and processes, institutional rigidity and power dynamics, varieties of institutional and societal conditions, and legitimacy, effectiveness and adaptability. The first section of this chapter summarizes the theoretical perspectives related to these aspects. Considering the recent changes in politics and societies, it focuses on how multilevel governance influences political polarization and how it works under this condition. The second section outlines avenues for further research and practical implications of the concept of multilevel governance.

MULTILEVEL GOVERNANCE AND POLITICAL POLARIZATION

In a political system dividing authority, polarization between parties, interest organizations, communities of citizens or officeholders in different institutions threatens the performance of governance. In multilevel systems, political polarization no less complicates governance, irrespective of the specific institutional design or division of authority and the modes of coordination to deal with the incongruence of jurisdictions and policy issues. However, multilevel governance can also reinforce polarization. The different approaches to multilevel governance indicate potential causes which may take effect under specific conditions.

Multilevel Governance as a Source of Polarization

With their actor-centred approach that significantly advanced research, Hooghe and Marks (2016) shed light on the vicious cycle of dispersal of authority across levels and escalating conflicts between levels and jurisdictions. They emphasize the conflict between functionalist reasons for dividing or sharing authority and the interest of communities to preserve their right to self-rule. Research on party politics demonstrates that this conflict has become a main source of confrontation in politics and policymaking. It divides parties advocating open borders for people, goods, capital or services and nationalist or regionalist parties. The former argue for harmonizing regulation in multilevel governance, the latter defend state-centred or decentralized authority to regulate societies and provide public goods and services (Kriesi et al. 2006). The divide in party politics appears in electoral campaigns and debates in national or regional parliaments. In this way it translates into polarization in the horizontal dimension of multilevel systems and, in consequence, instigates a politicization of the division of authority and policy coordination between levels.

This trend reflects the dualism of politics in multilevel governance (see Chapter 3). Here, conflicts on policies often immediately turn into more fundamental disputes on the distribution of authority – and the other way around. This intersection bears a high risk of conflict escalation among governments and increases the salience of issues in elections. It explains why party politics stirs up confrontation among actors responsible for coordinating policies in multilevel settings.

An institutionalist perspective on multilevel governance draws attention to two characteristic features of institutional diversity. First, institutions of governments or international organizations solidified during their path-dependent evolution. Their continuity contrasts with the flexibility of rules or informality in multilevel governance. The rigidity of institutions or routines at the different levels can entrench political divides, if executives try to coordinate policies across levels under rules that strictly tie their hands. Different policy regimes of governments constitute high hurdles for coordinating policies and a redistribution of authority. The impact of welfare regimes on EU social policy and of economic policy regimes on the international management of financial crises or the implementation of regional development programmes are cases in point. The other feature of institutional diversity concerns the types of government, especially the difference between democracy and autocracy. In relations between democratic and autocratic governments, value conflicts often complicate the regulation of interest conflicts. Representatives of democratic governments blame autocratic governments for violating human rights, and representatives of autocratic governments respond by claiming their autonomy and rejecting interference in their domestic affairs. The more disputes address such fundamental values, the more politics becomes polarized. This kind of inter-state polarization mainly occurs between national governments, fuels nationalism and hardens the political divides and institutional diversity between democracies and autocracies.

The society-centred perspective outlined in Chapters 5 and 6 explains polarization as a consequence of economic disparities and identity politics. Research focusing on Western democracies has revealed two cleavages in contemporary societies. One concerns the dispute between liberals and social democrats on the framing of the spatial economy as either diversity that stimulates productive trade or as disparity and social injustice. In multilevel governance, liberals advocate open borders and harmonized regulation, whereas social democrats address disparities and call for redistributive policies (Harmes 2019). If disputes aim at a shared understanding of distributive justice as a principle guiding policies, multilevel governance can foster a convergence of preferences. However, the conflict on economic diversity often overlaps with a second cleavage concerning identity politics (Hooghe and Marks 2012: 842–4). On the one side, Green-Alternative-Libertarians stand up for human rights and recognize the diversity of individuals and their cultures. They call for global justice and the preservation of natural and social living conditions in all parts of the world. On the other side, Conservative-Nationalists (or proponents of "traditionalism/authority/nationalism", ibid. 843) defend the economic interests and identity of a nation against global competition, immigration and intrusion of external authorities into domestic politics. Polarized disputes concern values, rights, rule of law and democracy. The protection of human rights, recognition of diversity, restitution of injustice and climate policy require coordinated policymaking in multilevel governance. In contrast, conservative identity policy aims at autonomy and self-rule of nation-states or regions within states and intensifies the antagonism between competing autonomy claims.

Polarization complicates the coordination of policies across levels for different reasons. Confrontation in bargaining processes reduces the influence of epistemic communities. Threatening deadlock situations provoke intervention and unilateral decisions by agencies holding power of the last resort. A change of venues, actor constellations or modes of governance is difficult in polarized politics. Actors tend to pursue their selfish interests in bargaining processes, all the more if they are committed to parties, organized interests or powerful elites. Depending on the specific circumstances, the dynamics of multilevel governance either lead to a disintegration or a concentration of power in the hands of central authorities and executives.

Sustainability of multilevel governance

Taken together, the different theoretical approaches outlined in the previous chapters reveal why multilevel governance can invigorate political polarization. Party politics manifesting societal cleavages in democracies, conflicts between democratic and autocratic governments, distributive and identity conflicts in the horizontal dimension of multilevel governance, and authority contestation between upper and lower-tier governments are the main indications of polarization. However, the different perspectives on multilevel governance also explain why a division of authority nonetheless still extends from the local to the global level of governance, why multilevel governance can continue in spite of polarization, and why it, against all odds, works to cope with complicated societal problems transgressing borders of jurisdiction.

Actor-centred approaches assume a differentiated concept of preferences of political actors and a mixed-motive character of interactions. They point out that multilevel governance opens ways to avoid coordination traps. Research on international politics following Robert Putnam's 1988 article (e.g., Evans, Jacobson and Putnam 1993; cf. for a summary da Conceição-Heldt and Mello 2017) and studies on joint policymaking in federations following

Fritz W. Scharpf's theory of policymaking (e.g., Benz, Detemple and Heinz 2016; Falkner 2011) revealed how actors use the connected processes in multilevel and domestic politics for their strategic management of conflicts. Executives and policymakers in public administration can take advantage of their boundary-spanning role to explore the preferences of their governments, parties in parliaments or private interest organizations. They seek to identify a win-set but also use their bargaining power and strategies to attain their preferred policies in multilevel coordination. Furthermore, actors can profit from the dual character of multilevel politics. By shifting authority upwards or downwards on the "ladder of scale" (Hooghe and Marks 2016: 12–15), they can dissolve gridlocks in policy coordination or change a policy in the preferred direction. They often modify modes of coordination, for instance when they turn to governance by standards, yardstick competition or experimental policymaking to avoid multiple veto points in joint-decision systems. Such adjustments of authority and governance modes can succeed without changing the institutions, as long as no authorized actor perceives and contests an imbalance of power.

Studies on parliaments, parties and interest organizations have uncovered another strategic response of actors to the challenges of multilevel governance. They describe the rise of multilevel relations between members of regional, national and European parliaments, the interactions of party officials in multilevel party organizations, and interest intermediation of private actors and civil society representatives who address different levels of government and international organizations. These mainly communicative relations reduce information asymmetries which regularly obstruct accountability of political executives in matters of multilevel governance. They also help to avoid decision traps and involuntary defection caused by external veto players, for instance, if a parliament opposes the ratification of a treaty or constitutional amendment after executives have negotiated an acceptable agreement on a draft.

An institutionalist perspective emphasizes the constraining effects of institutions and rule systems of governments and international organizations on policy coordination, but also the institutional flexibility of multilevel governance. This flexibility varies depending on the modes of governance. Central regulation and joint-decision systems establish rather rigid rules of policymaking. They can cause institutional tensions or frictions that entail either ineffective policy coordination or deficits in democratic legitimacy (Benz and Sonnicksen 2017: 14–16). Multilevel cooperation allows opting out and waivers enabling experimental policies of individual governments. It also supports governance by standards or yardsticks and voluntary horizontal partnership of states, regions or local governments. These modes significantly increase institutional flexibility, improve the conditions for managing tensions between multilevel and domestic politics, and mitigate political polarization.

Considering institutions not only as rule systems but also as results of a division of authority and power according to functions and territories, an institutionalist approach also draws attention to the multiple arenas linking multilevel and domestic politics. Executive multilevel governance includes negotiations between political leaders and their staff but also brings together specialists in public administration. Multilevel cooperation between ministers and senior civil servants occurs in policy-specific networks, but also in intergovernmental councils or executive agencies. Multilevel parliamentarism in the EU and international organizations has led to certain institutionalizations of assemblies or regular meetings of committees. In federations, party meetings and multilevel party organizations stabilize the informal communication of members of parliaments across levels (Thorlakson 2020: 70–101). The hierarchical organization of court systems guarantees a consistent jurisdiction, whereas EU and international courts communicate in informal dialogues in order to do justice to the plurality of the law in transnational multilevel governance. Likewise, NGOs and private interest organizations constitute policy-specific multilevel arenas. The interplay of these different arenas drives the dynamics of politics and policymaking in multilevel governance. Based on the ambiguity of institutions, it facilitates the harmonization of creative interactions in specific venues with the rule-oriented behaviour of officeholders in other venues.

Society-centred approaches explain polarization in the first place. However, they also inspire research on ways to de-escalate conflicts and to dissolve divides. As mentioned in Chapter 5, the framing of economic diversity as disparities calls for redistributive policies to mitigate injustice and social problems. As a response to identity conflicts, scholars discuss the differentiated distribution of authority or constitutional asymmetries which they observe in many federations including the EU. More often than not, governments in economically prosperous regions profit from autonomy, in contrast to economically disadvantaged regions where governments depend on the central government's fiscal assistance. Multilevel governance thus constitutes favourable conditions to accommodate the diversity of societies, provided that policies are coordinated between levels.

These economic disparities and the asymmetric distribution of power and finances bear upon bargaining power. In democratic governments, executives accountable to parliaments and citizens within their jurisdiction must justify the outcome of distributive policies. Discourses on fiscal equalization reveal contests between liberal parties preferring solutions by market mechanisms and social-democratic parties preferring solutions by politics. Likewise, Conservative-Nationalists oppose the demands for recognition of and distributive justice for disadvantaged communities recommended by

Green-Alternative-Libertarians. If multilevel policies end with agreements on fiscal equalizations and recognition of distinct communities, this is in most cases due to the strong epistemic power of experts and the de-politicization of conflicts between parties and governments.

AMBIVALENCE OF MULTILEVEL GOVERNANCE

From a normative perspective, multilevel governance appears as ambivalent. On the one hand, differentiation of political authority and coordination across levels is necessary for enabling politics to cope with the complicated problems of societies and public policies. On the other hand, the dispersal of power across levels inside and beyond states comes with several challenges. Multilevel governance does not cause polarization, but in times of increasing polarization in national and international politics, it can run into three kinds of traps:

First, efforts to coordinate policies can fail and prevent rather than enable the solution of problems or conflicts. The "Joint-Decision Trap" (Scharpf 1988) is the most obvious constellation. It compels actors to conclude agreements under institutional incentives that induce selfish behaviour and motivate actors to use veto power. Polarization reinforces selfishness and confrontation in bargaining. Other modes of coordination reduce the risk of non-decisions or ineffective policy coordination. However, they cannot compel public or private organizations to participate in multilevel policy, implement agreements, comply with standards or yardsticks or adopt best practices or experimental policies. The willingness of responsible governmental or non-governmental actors to engage in multilevel governance cannot be taken for granted in times of polarized politics.

Second, effective policy coordination can cause deficits in democracy. With the rise of populist parties in the course of increasing polarization, opposition against a perceived technocratic character of multilevel governance has become a problem for democracy on its own. Populists disapprove of representative democracy and thus principally question the institutional conditions for effective accountability of executives. Claiming to defend the interest of a *demos* against the intrusion of external governments or international authorities, they argue for autonomy and against multilevel governance.

Third, distributive conflicts, identity conflicts or continuing negative externalities can escalate political polarization if disputes on these issues turn into a contestation of perceived power imbalances. If worse comes to worst, this process leads to the secession of governments or the dissolution of multilevel governance. In contrast to deficits in effectiveness or democratic legitimacy, the collapse of an established structure of multilevel governance is an extreme case of failure with far-reaching consequences. Policy and legitimacy deficits can be remedied by adapted modes of governance and appropriate linkages of multilevel policymaking and politics in governments, whereas the dissolution of multilevel governance significantly deteriorates the conditions for coping with fundamental problems like climate change, social justice, migration or economic stability. Likewise, a centralization of power in the state impairs differentiated governance conforming to the diversity of economy and society. In general, the inertia of established institutions and the power of actors interested in maintaining them protect structures against dissolution. However, polarized politics can cause a stalemate in policymaking and hollow out multilevel governance.

For these reasons, multilevel governance can fail, and polarization bears the risk that deficits in effectiveness and democratic legitimacy turn into a self-reinforcing process of confrontation and disintegration. Instead of reducing deficits in governance and legitimacy by restoring the autonomy of central states, such a development worsens both problems. A concentration of political power limits capacities to manage complexity and increases the threat of democratic backsliding. Separation of power by secession or dissolution of a multilevel polity may increase the autonomy of democratic governments, but the challenge of coping with interdependence remains and therefore also the need to coordinate policies. In cases of identity conflicts, the secession or partition of a state often comes with an outburst of violence (Sambanis 2000: 446–59) and provokes a military intervention of external governments.

The conclusion to be drawn from this reasoning sounds paradoxical: On the one hand, increasing political polarization makes multilevel governance prone to ineffective policies and democratic deficits, if not to stalemate and disintegration. In addition, multilevel governance can exacerbate polarization due unresolved conflicts, veto power and contestation of authority. On the other hand, complex problems of societies cannot be solved or mitigated without multilevel governance. Even if a democratically legitimated world government would exist, such a government would have to interact with governments of macro-regions and states. And the more power is decentralized to nations, regions or local governments, the more interdependence must be coped with in coordinated policymaking. If autonomous governments neglect external effects caused within their jurisdiction and refuse to engage in multilevel governance, they would not only ignite conflicts, but also infringe the principle of democratic legitimacy that those who are affected by power must have a voice, either directly in accountability relations of a representative democracy or indirectly by their government in multilevel governance.

Therefore, against all odds of deficits, and contrary to calls for autonomy of nations or regions and the contestation of global governance, there are good reasons to make the case for multilevel governance. However, the dilemma outlined in this section must be addressed in research and dealt with in political practice.

CONCLUSIONS FOR RESEARCH AND PRACTICE

To better understand the evolution of multilevel governance, Liesbet Hooghe and Gary Marks implemented an outstanding research programme. Continuing and extending empirical studies along the lines of this programme has proven valuable in the past. Future work can enhance our knowledge of how the dramatic changes during the last few years have affected the dispersal of authority and can inspire the advancement of theory explaining these changes.

Considering the impact of polarization on multilevel governance, there is an urgent need for comparative research on the varieties of multilevel governance. Fritz W. Scharpf suggested more than twenty years ago to focus research on different modes of governance, which evolved in national governments, macro-regional unions of states and in international governance (Scharpf 2001: 4–5). With his research on the EU, Scharpf demonstrated the fruitfulness of such an approach to explain Europeanization or the effectiveness and legitimacy of governing Europe. From a comparative perspective, different institutions of governments involved in multilevel governance, economic disparities and identity politics must be considered as conditions that affect the operation of modes of governance.

Meanwhile, the attention of researchers has shifted from integration and the unravelling of centralized states towards the disintegration of multilevel governance beyond the state and the limited or declining influence of regional and local authorities. However, the concepts of integration and disintegration or centralization and decentralization can mislead the analysis of the observed developments. In established systems of multilevel governance, changes in both directions concur. They often reveal the adaptation of patterns of authority to changing tasks or conditions for fulfilling tasks. Still, we cannot neglect the possibility that multilevel governance can run into stalemate and unilateral politics replace coordinated action, even though the division of authority remains in place. Therefore, research on the adaptability and resilience of multilevel governance can advance our understanding of how complex governance arrangements operate and survive serious crises (VanNijnhatten 2021).

Comparative studies guided by a policy science perspective inquire into the effectiveness and legitimacy of multilevel governance. Both normative concepts overlap if we bear in mind that a policy is effective if it conforms to the expectations of people and that informed people would not accept and legitimize an ineffective policy. Hence democratic legitimacy appears as the essential normative standard to evaluate multilevel governance. However, if we apply the standard of representative democracy, policies resulting from multilevel coordination can only gain legitimacy through the approval of parliaments representing citizens in democratic governments; whereas the participation of stakeholders or civil society organizations does not suffice to "democratize" multilevel politics. In international governance, the inclusion of autocratic governments or defective democracies excludes affected people from deliberating on and effectively scrutinizing multilevel policies. Therefore, the essential question is not whether multilevel governance is democratic or not. Rather scholars should ask two sets of questions: (1) Is multilevel politics compatible with principles of democratic legitimacy? Does it allow fair deliberation on complex policies in structures that prevent an escalation of power imbalances? (2) How is multilevel politics linked to processes within governments or international organizations? Do these linkages enable parliaments or assemblies of member states and citizens to hold executives, who are responsible for coordinating policies, to account?

In addition to data collection and quantitative analyses, future research should engage in comparative case studies on instances of multilevel governance in different policy fields. Such studies can uncover the dynamics of authority patterns across levels, they can substantiate assumptions about the effectiveness and legitimacy of different modes of multilevel policy coordination, and they can help to understand the adaptability and resilience of multilevel governance. Combining different analytical perspectives, theoretical approaches and methods can contribute to advancing this research. In the first place, however, comparative research requires a precise concept of multilevel governance that serves to appropriately focus the analysis and apply it to different instances.

The outcomes of such research have significant practical relevance. Institutions like the European Commission, the European Parliament, the Committee of the Regions and various international organizations have adopted the term multilevel governance to characterize principles guiding the design of institutions and policies. In the OECD, an expert group works on topics related to multilevel governance in regional and fiscal policies, collects data on decentralization and recommends adaptive and innovative designs of better coordination across levels. In federations and regionalized states, governments search for appropriate modes of coordination of central and decentralized policies. Given the growing tensions in systems of multilevel governance, scientific research should put more emphasis on practical issues, for instance by comparing varieties of governance, by describing, explaining or evaluating them under different conditions, by comparing the impact of different institutions of governments or different actor constellations in multilevel politics, by searching for promising ways to cope with distributive conflicts and identity conflicts, and by identifying procedures for balancing power. So far, research has revealed problems and deficits of multilevel governance but also provided good arguments for distributing authority between levels and against a concentration of power in states. Given the current disruption of international relations and tendencies towards nationalization of politics, scholars have reasons to advocate for multilevel governance as a necessary condition to manage crises and turbulence. However, they must argue from a pragmatic point of view considering the complexity of the tasks at hand, the challenges of coordinated governance and the need to permanently balance power. Based on the conclusions drawn in the previous chapters, a pragmatic approach includes the following aspects:

The concept of multilevel governance draws attention to the complexity of policies made at different levels, the dynamics of power relations in multilevel politics and the need for balancing power. Thus, it does not assume a separation of power which, as a normative principle, predominates constitutional debates about centralization and decentralization. In a multilevel system, authority implies responsibility and therefore requires a clear demarcation. However, in designing multilevel governance, politics must distinguish between the separation of authority and the coordinated use of authority. Complexity calls for balancing differentiation and integration, and the necessary division of authority must be complemented by appropriate patterns of coordination across levels.

Considering the need to manage complexity resulting from economic and social diversity in local, regional, national and international contexts and the uncertainty of developments, theoretical considerations and empirical evidence speak for a "requisite variety" of structures (Ashby 1956: 202–13). Yet in contrast to system theory, the concept of multilevel governance emphasizes the need to establish appropriate linkages between parts of a system; that is, between levels and between multilevel politics and politics inside governments or governmental organizations. Empirical research on institutional evolution and actors' adaptation to the rise of multilevel governance has uncovered cross-level communication among members of parliaments, parties and civil society organizations as well as between civil servants in administration and judges of courts, especially in the EU and international governance. The effects of these informal discourses are uncertain, but scholars should not underestimate their potential. They can induce the participating actors to reconsider and change their preferences, diminish information asymmetries in accountability processes and reduce the risk of deadlock due to misperceptions, polarization and conflict escalation.

Research on policymaking in multilevel governance has discovered various modes of governance and analysed their advantages and disadvantages under different conditions. Actors holding the power to shape multilevel governance can profit from a menu of modes and adapt governance to changing conditions. This is an essential strategy to coordinate policies in multilevel politics, apart from alternating between venues and changing actor constellations in policymaking. Therefore, scholars should not regard multilevel governance as a given condition of politics. In line with theories of polycentric governance (Ostrom 2010), they should consider it as a continuous experiment that requires permanent learning and the recurring adaptation of policy preferences, interactions and effective power structures.

Multilevel governance requires rethinking legitimacy by pragmatically reconsidering power and democracy. By holding responsible actors to account, parliaments and citizens must legitimize how executives use their bargaining power and governments their unilateral power of the last resort. Epistemic power of specialists in administration, experts or non-governmental actors can be legitimized through deliberation, which means a procedure of knowledge generation, not a mode of democracy. To deal with global problems, multilevel governance cannot exclude actors from autocratic governments simply because they are not democratically legitimized. Yet, if multilevel policies conform to principles of justice and are supported by deliberating epistemic communities, we have reasons for assuming that they are acceptable even for citizens living under autocratic rule, although we never can take this for granted. Legitimacy also requires that power is balanced. Given the tendency for imbalances in multilevel systems, governance arrangements must provide for processes allowing contestation and the permanent balancing of power. If these basic prerequisites for legitimizing multilevel politics apply, nothing prohibits searching and applying additional and innovative forms of democracy, although they cannot replace patterns of representative democracy.

A final practical issue arises when multilevel governance fails, established modes of coordination dissolve in a process of disintegration or governments escalate confrontation through mutual unilateral actions. In these periods of backsliding into nationalism, separatism and hostile relations, populists call for strong leadership. Intendedly or unintendedly, they pave the way for authoritarian rule and ignite conflicts. To stop the dynamics of confrontation, multilevel governance needs to be restored. Yet restoring multilevel governance – or maintaining modes of coordination in a peaceful disintegration or secession – requires coordinated policies. To put it in another way: The inherent risk of failure and decline raises the question of the resilience of multilevel governance: How can structures and processes adapt to new critical challenges or self-reinforcing imbalances caused by turbulent changes in economy, society, environment and politics (Chandler 2014: 7–9)? Political leadership and centralized power of the last resort may be appropriate in a crisis. However enduring adaptability requires interactions among different kinds of actors, governmental as well as non-governmental, who cooperate in different patterns of interaction and venues. Adaptable and resilient structures of multilevel governance provide redundant links between levels which can be mobilized to mitigate conflicts and confrontation. When official negotiations between political leaders and intergovernmental cooperation have run into a dead end, informal communication of diplomats, civil servants and private actors can explore ways to come to an agreement or at least alleviate tensions. Multiple transborder relations among political executives, specialists, members of parliaments or parties and civil society organizations can improve the conditions for a policy of détente. Such a policy promises to break the vicious cycle of polarization and confrontation, if the different actors coordinate their courses of action.

Multilevel governance emerged in response to the increasing complexity of societal problems and public policies. In many states, it is confronted with the rise of nationalist populism, an ideology that neglects this complexity and causes increasing tensions and confrontation between governments. How multilevel governance can be maintained or restored under the condition of political polarization is a difficult problem for politics and an important topic for research. How it can be made effective and legitimized according to the standards of democracy remains a fundamental issue. These challenges call for rethinking the concept of multilevel governance, as well as related analytical approaches, theories and the results of empirical research.

References

Abbott, E. A. ([1884] 2006), *Flatland: A Romance of Many Dimensions*, R. Jann (ed). Oxford: Oxford University Press.

Abbott, K. W. (2012), 'The Transnational Regime Complex for Climate Change', *Environment and Planning C: Government and Policy* 30 (4), 571–90.

Abbott, K. W. et al. (2015), 'Orchestration: Global Governance through Intermediaries', in K. Abbott et al. (eds) *International Organizations as Orchestrators*. Cambridge UK: Cambridge University Press, pp. 3–36.

Abdelal, R. et al. (2006), 'Identity as a Variable', *Perspectives on Politics* 4 (4), 695–711.

Abels, G. and Battke, J. (2019), 'Regional Governance in the EU or: What Happened to the "Europe of the Regions"?', in G. Abels and J. Battke (eds) *Regional Governance in the EU*. Cheltenham UK, Northampton MA: Edward Elgar Publishing, pp. 1–14.

Abromeit, H. (1998), *Democracy in Europe: Legitimising Politics in a Non-State Polity*. New York: Berghahn Books.

Acemoglu, D. and Robinson, J. A. (2012), *Why Nations Fail. The Origins of Power, Prosperity, and Poverty*. London: Profile Books.

Acharya, A. (1997), 'Ideas, Identity, and Institution-building: From the "ASEAN Way" to the "Asia-Pacific Way"?', *The Pacific Review* 10 (3), 319–46.

Ackerman, B. (1991), *We the People. Foundations*. Cambridge MA, London: The Belknap Press of Harvard University Press.

Acuto, M. and Rayner, S. (2016), 'City Networks: Breaking Gridlocks or Forging (New) Lock-ins?', *International Affairs* 92 (5), 1147–66.

Adam, M.-A., Bergeron, J. and Bonnard, M. (2015), 'Intergovernmental Relations in Canada: Competing Visions and Diverse Dynamics', in J. Poirier, C. Saunders and J. Kincaid (eds) *Intergovernmental Relations in Federal Systems*. Oxford: Oxford University Press, pp. 135–73.

Aghion, P. and Holden, R. (2011), 'Incomplete Contracts and the Theory of the Firm: What Have We Learned over the Past 25 Years?', *Journal of Economic Perspectives* 25 (2), 181–97.

Agnew, J. (2013), 'The "New Regionalism" and the Politics of the Regional Question', in J. Kincaid, J. Loughlin and W. Swenden (eds) *Routledge Handbook on Regionalism and Federalism*. London, New York: Routledge, pp. 130–9.

Agranoff, R. (ed) (1999), *Accommodating Diversity: Asymmetry in Federal States*. Baden-Baden: Nomos.

Alcantara, C., Broschek, J. and Nelles, J. (2016), 'Rethinking Multilevel Governance as an Instance of Multilevel Politics. A Conceptual Strategy', *Territory, Politics, Governance* 4 (1), 33–51.

Aldecoa, F. and Keating, M. (1999), *Paradiplomacy in Action*. London, Portland OR: Frank Cass.

Allain-Dupré, D. (2020), 'The Multi-level Governance Imperative', *The British Journal of Politics and International Relations* 22 (4), 800–808.

Allain-Dupré, D., Chatry, I. and Moisio, A. (2020), 'Asymmetric Decentralisation: Trends, Challenges and Policy Implications', *OECD Regional Development Papers*, No. 10. Paris: OECD Publishing. doi: https://doi.org/10.1787/0898887a-en.

Allain-Dupré, D. et al. (2021), *The Territorial Impact of COVID-19: Managing the Crisis and Recovery Across Levels of Government (OECD Policy Responses to Coronavirus [COVID-19])*, 10 May. Paris: OECD Publishing. Available at: https://www.oecd.org/coronavirus/policy-responses/the-territorial-impact-of-covid -19 -managing -the -crisis -and -recovery -across -levels -of -government -a2c6abaf/ (Accessed: 1 May 2024).

Amin, A. (1999), 'An Institutionalist Perspective on Regional Economic Development', *International Journal of Urban and Regional Research* 23 (2), 365–78.

Anderson, B. (1998), *Imagined Communities: Reflections on the Origin and Spread of Nationalism*. Verso: London, New York.

Anderson, G. (2008), 'The Council of Australian Governments. A New Institution of Governance for Australia's Conditional Federalism', *University of New South Wales Law Journal* 31 (2), 493–508.

Andonova, L. B., Betsill, M. M. and Bulkeley, H. (2009), 'Transnational Climate Governance', *Global Environmental Politics* 9 (2), 52–73.

Anfinson, K. (2023), 'Capture or Empowerment: Governing Citizens and the Environment in the European Renewable Energy Transition', *American Political Science Review* 117 (3), 927–39.

Ansell, C. K. (2023), *Rethinking Theories of Governance*. Cheltenham UK, Northampton MA: Edward Elgar Publishing.

Ansell, C. K. and Torfing, J. (2022), 'Introduction to the Handbook on Theories of Governance', in C. K. Ansell and J. Torfing (eds) *Handbook on Theories of Governance*. Cheltenham UK, Northampton MA: Edward Elgar Publishing, pp. 1–16.

Ansell, C. K., Trondal, J. and Øgård, M. (eds) (2017), *Governance in Turbulent Times.* Oxford: Oxford University Press.

Archer, A. et al. (2020), 'Celebrity, Democracy, and Epistemic Power', *Perspectives on Politics* 18 (1), 27–42.

Archibugi, D. and Cellini, M. (2017), 'The Internal and External Levers to Achieve Global Democracy', *Global Policy* 8 (S 6), 65–77.

Archibugi, D. and Held, D. (2011), 'Cosmopolitan Democracy: Paths and Agents', *Ethics & International Affairs* 25 (4), 433–61.

Armingeon, K. (2000), 'Swiss Federalism in Comparative Perspective', in U. Wachendorfer-Schmidt (ed) *Federalism and Political Performance*. London: Routledge, pp. 112–29.

Aroney, N. and Kincaid, J. (eds) (2017), *Courts in Federal Countries. Federalists or Unitarists?* Toronto: University of Toronto Press.

Ashby, W. R. (1956), *An Introduction to Cybernetics*. London: Chapman & Hall.

Bach, T. and Ruffing, E. (2018), 'The Transformative Effects of Transnational Administrative Coordination in the European Multi-level System', in E. Ongaro and S. van Thiel (eds) *The Palgrave Handbook of Public Administration and Management in Europe*. London: Palgrave Macmillan, pp. 747–63.

Bache, I. and Flinders, M. (2004a), 'Themes and Issues in Multi-level Governance', in I. Bache and M. Flinders (eds) *Multi-level Governance*. Oxford: Oxford University Press, pp. 1–11.

Bache, I. and Flinders, M. (2004b), 'Conclusions and Implications', in I. Bache and M. Flinders (eds) *Multi-level Governance*. Oxford: Oxford University Press, pp. 195–206.

Bache, I. and Flinders, M. (eds) (2015), *Multi-level Governance. Essential Readings* (2 volumes). Cheltenham UK, Northampton MA: Edward Elgar Publishing.

Bakvis, H. (2013), '"In the Shadow of Hierarchy". Intergovernmental Governance in Canada and the European Union', *Canadian Public Administration* 56 (2), 203–18.

Balogun, E. (2021), 'Comparative Regionalism', in *Oxford Research Encyclopedia of International Studies*. Oxford: Oxford University Press. doi: https://doi.org/10.1093/acrefore/9780190846626.013.554.

Balthasar, A., Schreurs, M. and Varone, F. (2020), 'Energy Transition in Europe and the United States. Policy Entrepreneurs and Veto Players in Federalist Systems', *Journal of Environment and Development* 29 (1), 3–25.

Barcevi, E., Weishaupt, T. and Zeitlin J. (eds) (2014), *Assessing the Open Method of Coordination: Institutional Design and National Influence of EU Social Policy Coordination*. Basingstoke: Palgrave Macmillan.

Barnett, M. N. and Duval, R. (2005), 'Power in Global Governance', in M. N. Barnett and R. Duvall (eds) *Power in Global Governance*. Cambridge UK: Cambridge University Press, pp. 1–32.

Barnett, M. N. and Finnemore, M. (2004), *Rules for the World. International Organizations in Global Politics*. Ithaca NY: Cornell University Press.

Bartolini, S. (2011), 'New Modes of European Governance: An Introduction', in A. Héritier and M. Rhodes (eds) *New Modes of Governance in Europe. Governing in the Shadow of Hierarchy*. Houndsmills, Basingstoke: Palgrave Macmillan, pp. 1–18.

Basta, C. (2017), 'The State between Minority and Majority Nationalism: Decentralization, Symbolic Recognition, and Secessionist Crises in Spain and Canada', *Publius: The Journal of Federalism* 48 (1), 51–75.

Becattini, Giacomo (2004), *Industrial Districts*. Cheltenham UK, Northampton MA: Edward Elgar Publishing.

Bednar, J. (2009), *The Robust Federation*. New York: Cambridge University Press.

Bednar, J. and Page, S. E. (2016), 'Complex Adaptive Systems and Comparative Politics. Modelling the Interaction between Institutions and Culture', *Chinese Political Science Review* 1 (3), 448–71.

Beaudoin S. (2023), 'Revue Historique de la Gouvernance Mondiale de l'Environnement (1945–2022)', *Canadian Journal of Political Science* 56 (4), 790–810.

Beer, S. H. (1978), 'Federalism, Nationalism, and Democracy in America', *American Political Science Review* 72 (1), 9–21.

Behnke, N. and Benz, A. (2020), 'Federalism and Constitutional Change', in X. Contiades and A. Fotiadou (eds), *Routledge Handbook of Comparative Constitutional Change*. London: Routledge, pp. 167–81.

Behnke, N. and Mueller, S. (eds) (2017), *Better Together? The Purpose of Intergovernmental Councils in Federal States*. Abingdon: Routledge.

Behrend, J. and Whitehead, L. (eds) (2016), *Illiberal Practices: Territorial Variance within Large Federal Democracies*. Baltimore: J. S. Hopkins University Press.

Béland, D. and Lecours, A. (2007), 'Federalism, Nationalism and Social Policy Decentralization in Canada and Belgium', *Regional & Federal Studies* 17 (4), 405–19.

Bell, S. and Hindmoore, A. (2009), *Rethinking Governance. The Centrality of the State in Modern Society*. Cambridge UK: Cambridge University Press.

Benhabib, S. (1997), 'Strange Multiplicities: The Politics of Identity and Difference in a Global Context', *Macalester International* 4 (Article 8), 27–56. Available at: https://digitalcommons.macalester.edu/macintl/vol4/iss1/8 (Accessed 1 May 2024).

Benz, A. (2004), 'Path-Dependent Institutions and Strategic Veto Players – National Parliaments in the European Union', *West European Politics* 29 (5), 875–900.

Benz, A. (2007), 'Accountable Multilevel Governance by the Open Method of Coordination?', *European Law Journal* 13 (4), 505–22.

Benz, A. (2016), *Constitutional Change in Multilevel Government: The Art of Keeping the Balance*. Oxford: Oxford University Press.

Benz, A. (2017), 'Patterns of Multilevel Parliamentary Relations. Varieties and Dynamics in the EU and other Federations', *Journal of European Public Policy* 24 (4), 499–519.

Benz, A. (2021), *Policy Change and Innovation in Multilevel Governance*. Cheltenham UK, Northampton MA: Edward Elgar Publishing.

Benz, A. (2023), 'Only Words? Coordination and Power in Multilevel Administration beyond the State', in C. Knill and Y. Steinebach (eds) *International Public Administrations in Global Public Policy: Sources and Effects of Bureaucratic Influence*. London: Routledge, pp. 220–39.

Benz, A. and Broschek, J. (2020), 'Transformative Energy Policy in Federal Systems. Canada and Germany Compared', *Canadian Journal of European and Russian Studies* 14 (2), 56–78.

Benz, A., Broschek, J. and Lederer, M. (eds) (2021), *A Research Agenda for Multilevel Governance*. Cheltenham UK, Northampton MA: Edward Elgar Publishing.

Benz, A., Detemple, J. and Heinz, D. (2016), *Varianten und Dynamiken der Politikverflechtung*. Baden-Baden: Nomos.

Benz, A., Harlow, C. and Papadopoulos, Y. (eds) (2007), *Accountability in EU Multilevel Governance* (Special Issue of *European Law Journal* 13/4). Oxford: Blackwell.

Benz, A. and Sonnicksen, J. (2017), 'Patterns of Federal Democracy. Tensions, Friction, or Balance between Two Government Dimensions', *European Political Science Review* 9 (1), 3–25.

Benz, A. and Sonnicksen, J. (2018), 'Advancing Backwards: Why Institutional Reform of German Federalism Reinforced Joint Decision-Making', *Publius: The Journal of Federalism* 48 (1), 134–59.

Benz, A. and Sonnicksen, J. (eds) (2021), *Federal Democracies at Work. Varieties of Complex Government*. Toronto: University of Toronto Press.

Beramendi, P. (2012), *The Political Geography of Inequality*. Cambridge UK: Cambridge University Press.

Bergmann, E. (2020), *Neo-Nationalism. The Rise of Nativist Populism*. Cham, CH: Palgrave Macmillan.

Bernstein, M. (2005), 'Identity Politics', *Annual Review of Sociology* 31 (1), 47–74.

Beyme, K. von (2005), 'Asymmetric Federalism between Globalization and Regionalization', *Journal of European Public Policy* 12 (3), 432– 47.

Beyme, K. von (2007), *Föderalismus und regionales Bewusstsein: Ein internationaler Vergleich*. Munich: Beck.

Bicchi, F. and Lovato, M. (2023), 'Diplomats as Skilful Bricoleurs of the Digital Age: EU Foreign Policy Communications from the COREU to WhatsApp', *The Hague Journal of Diplomacy* 19 (1), 184–223.

Biermann, F., Hickmann, T. and Sénit, C.-A. (2022), *The Political Impact of the Sustainable Development Goals*. Cambridge UK: Cambridge University Press.

Biermann, F. and Siebenhühner, B. (eds) (2009), *Managers of Global Change. The Influence of International Environmental Bureaucracies*. Cambridge MA: MIT Press.

Bird, R. M. and Ebel, R. D. (2006), 'Fiscal Federalism and National Unity', in E. Ahmad and G. Brosio (eds) *Handbook of Fiscal Federalism*. Cheltenham UK, Northampton MA: Edward Elgar Publishing, pp. 499–520.

Bird, R. M. and Ebel, R. D. (eds) (2007), *Fiscal Fragmentation in Decentralized Countries*. Cheltenham UK, Northampton MA: Edward Elgar Publishing.

Blöchliger, H. et al. (2007), 'Fiscal Equalisation in OECD Countries', *OECD Working Papers on Fiscal Federalism*, No. 4. Paris: OECD Publishing. doi: https://doi.org/10.1787/5k97b11n2gxx-en.

Boadway, R. and Shah, A. (eds) (2007), *Intergovernmental Fiscal Transfers: Principles and Practices*. Washington DC: The World Bank.

Bohman, J. (2007), *Democracy Across Borders: From Dêmos to Dêmoi*. Cambridge MA: MIT Press.

Bolleyer, N. (2009), *Intergovernmental Cooperation. Rational Choices in Federal Systems and Beyond*. Oxford: Oxford University Press.

Bolleyer, N. (2010), 'Why Legislatures Organise. Inter-Parliamentary Activism in Federal Systems and its Consequences', *Journal of Legislative Studies* 16 (4), 411–37.

Borràs, S. (2009), 'The Politics of the Lisbon Strategy. The Changing Role of the Commission', *West European Politics* 32 (1), 97–118.

Börzel, T. A. and Risse, T. (eds) (2016), *The Oxford Handbook of Comparative Regionalism*. Oxford: Oxford University Press.

Börzel, T. A., and Risse, T. (2020), 'Identity Politics, Core State Powers and Regional Integration: Europe and beyond', *Journal of Common Market Studies* 58 (1), 21–40.

Börzel, T. A. and Risse, T. (2021), *Effective Governance Under Anarchy: Institutions, Legitimacy, and Social Trust in Areas of Limited Statehood*. Cambridge UK: Cambridge University Press.

Bouteligier, S. (2012), *Global Cities and Networks for Global Environmental Governance*. Hoboken: Taylor and Francis.

Braun, D., Ruiz-Palermo, C. and Schnabel, J. (2017), *Consolidation Policies in Federal States. Conflicts and Solutions*. London, New York: Routledge.

Breda, V. (2023), *Constitutional Crises and Regionalism*. Cheltenham UK, Northampton MA: Edward Elgar Publishing.

Brenner, N. (2004), *New State Spaces*. Oxford: Oxford University Press.

Breton, A. (1996), *Competitive Governments. An Economic Theory of Politics and Public Finance*. Cambridge UK: Cambridge University Press.

Brooker, P. (2009), *Non-democratic Regimes*. 2nd edn. New York: Palgrave Macmillan.

Brubaker, R. (2020), 'Populism and Nationalism', *Nations and Nationalism* 26 (1), 44–66.

Buchanan, J. M. (1950), 'Federalism and Fiscal Equity', *The American Economic Review* 40 (4), 583–99.

Buchanan, J. M. (1995), 'Federalism as an Ideal Political Order and an Objective for Constitutional Reform', *Publius: The Journal of Federalism* 25 (1), 19–27.

Büchs, M. (2007), *New Governance in European Social Policy*. New York: Palgrave Macmillan.

Buhi, J. (2019), 'Constitutional Asymmetry in the People's Republic of China. Struggles for Autonomy under a Communist Party State', in P. Popelier and M.

Sahadžić (eds) *Constitutional Asymmetry in Multinational Federalism. Managing Multinationalism in Multi-tiered Systems*. London: Palgrave Macmillan, pp. 105–35.

Bulmer, J., Doelle, M. and Klein, D. (2017), 'Negotiating History of the Paris Agreement', in D. Klein et al. (eds) *The Paris Agreement on Climate Change. Analysis and Commentary*. Oxford, New York: Oxford University Press, pp. 50–73.

Burgess, M. (2006), *Comparative Federalism. Theory and Practice*. London, New York: Routledge.

Busch, P.-O. and Liese, A. (2017), 'The Authority of International Public Administrations', in M. W. Bauer, S. Eckhard and C. Knill (eds.) *International Bureaucracy. Challenges and Lessons for Public Administration Research*. Basingstoke: Palgrave Macmillan, pp. 97–121.

Büthe, T. and Mattli, W. (2010), 'Standards for Global Markets: Domestic and International Institutions', in H. Enderlein, S. Wälti and M. Zürn, (eds), *Handbook on Multi-Level Governance*. Cheltenham UK, Northampton MA: Edward Elgar Publishing, pp. 455–76.

Cairney, P. (2006), 'Venue Shift Following Devolution: When Reserved Meets Devolved in Scotland', *Regional & Federal Studies* 16 (4), 429–45.

Cairney, P. (2019), *Understanding Public Policy: Theories and Issues*. London, New York, Dublin: Bloomsbury Publishing.

Capano, G., Howlett, M. and Ramesh, M. (2015), 'Re-Thinking Governance in Public Policy. Dynamics, Strategy and Capacities', in G. Capano, M. Howlett and M. Ramesh (eds) *Varieties of Governance. Dynamics, Strategies and Capacities*. Houndmills, Basingstoke, New York: Palgrave Macmillan, pp. 3–24.

Cappelletti, M., Seccombe, M. and Weiler, J. H. H. (eds) (1986), *Integration Through Law: Europe and the American Federal Experience*. Berlin, New York: De Gruyter.

Caramani, D. (2017), 'Will vs. Reason: The Populist and Technocratic Forms of Political Representation and Their Critique to Party Government', *American Political Science Review* 111 (1), 54–67.

Castells, M. (2009a), *The Rise of the Network Society (The Information Age: Economy, Society and Culture Vol. I)*. 2nd edn. Malden MA, Oxford: Blackwell.

Castells, M. (2009b), The Power of Identity *(The Information Age: Economy, Society and Culture Vol. II)*. 2nd edn. Cambridge MA, Oxford: Blackwell.

Chancel, L. et al. (2022), World Inequality Report. *World Inequality Lab*. Available at: https://wir2022.wid.world/download/ (Accessed 1 May 2024).

Chandler, D. (2014), *Resilience: The Governance of Complexity*. New York: Routledge.

Checkel, J. T. (2016), 'Regional Identities and Communities', in T. A. Börzel and T. Risse (eds) *The Oxford Handbook of Comparative Regionalism*. Oxford: Oxford University Press, pp. 559–78.

Christiansen, T. and Reh, C. (2009), *Constitutionalizing the European Union*. London: Palgrave Macmillan.

Costa, O., Dri, C. and Stavridis, S. (2013), *Parliamentary Dimensions of Regionalization and Globalization*. London: Palgrave Macmillan UK.

Costa Buranelli, F. and Tskhay, A. (2019) 'Regionalism', in *Oxford Research Encyclopedia of International Studies*. Oxford: Oxford University Press. doi: https://doi.org/10.1093/acrefore/9780190846626.013.517

Cotta, M. and Isernia, P. (2021), 'Introduction. The Challenges to the European Representation System – Away from the "Old Normal"?', in M. Cotta and P. Isernia (eds) *The EU through Multiple Crises: Representation and Cohesion Dilemmas for a 'sui generis' Polity*. Abingdon: Routledge, pp. 1–19.

Crouch, C. et al. (2001), *Local Production Systems in Europe: Rise or Demise?* Oxford: Oxford University Press.

Crum, B. and Fossum, J. E. (eds) (2013), *Practices of Inter-Parliamentary Coordination in International Politics – The European Union and Beyond*. Colchester: ECPR Press.

Cutler, A. C. and Dietz, T. (eds) (2017), *The Politics of Private Transnational Governance by Contract*. London, New York: Routledge.

da Conceição-Heldt, E. (2017), 'Multiple Principals' Preferences, Types of Control Mechanisms and Agent's Discretion in Trade Negotiations', in T. Delreux and J. Adriaensen (eds) *The Principal Agent Model and the European Union*. Cham CH: Palgrave Macmillan.

da Conceição-Heldt, E. and Mello, P. A. (2017), 'Two-Level Games in Foreign Policy Analysis', in *Oxford Research Encyclopedia of Politics*. Oxford: Oxford University Press. doi: http://dx.doi.org/ 10.1093/acrefore/9780190228637.013.496.

d'Aiglepierre, R. et al. (2020), 'A Global Profile of Emigrants to OECD Countries: Younger and More Skilled Migrants from more Diverse Countries', *OECD Social, Employment and Migration Working Papers*, No. 239. Paris: OECD Publishing. doi: https://doi.org/10.1787/0cb305d3-en.

Dahl, R. A. (1994), 'A Democratic Dilemma: System Effectiveness versus Citizen Participation', *Political Science Quarterly* 109 (1), 23–34.

Dardanelli, P. and Kincaid, J. (eds) (2019), *Dynamic De/Centralization in Federations* (Special Issue of *Publius: The Journal of Federalism* 49 [1]). Oxford: Oxford University Press.

De Vries, C. E., Leuffen, D. and Schimmelfennig, F. (eds) (2023), *Differentiated Integration in the European Union: Institutional Effects, Public Opinion, and Alternative Flexibility Arrangements* (Special issue of *European Union Politics* 24 [1]). Los Angeles: Sage Publications.

DeBardeleben, J. and Hurrelmann, A. (eds) (2007), *Democratic Dilemmas of Multilevel Governance*. Basingstoke: Palgrave Macmillan.

Deeg, R. (2006), 'Governance and the Nation-State in a Global Era', in S. Lütz (ed), *Governance in der politischen Ökonomie. Struktur und Wandel des modernen Kapitalismus*. Wiesbaden: Verlag für Sozialwissenschaften, pp. 57–106.

Denters, B. et al. (2014), *Size and Local Democracy*. Cheltenham UK, Northampton MA: Edward Elgar Publishing.

Dermine, P. (2018), 'European Economic Governance in a Post-crisis Era – A Conceptual Appraisal', *European Papers – A Journal on Law and Integration* 3 (1), 281–306.

Deters, H. (2018), *The EU's Green Dynamism. Deadlock and Change in Energy and Environmental Policy*. Essex: ECPR Press.

Detterbeck, K. and Hepburn, E. (2018), 'Statewide Parties in Western and Eastern Europe: Territorial Patterns of Party Organizations', in K. Detterbeck and E. Hepburn (eds) *Handbook of Territorial Politics*. Cheltenham UK, Northampton MA: Edward Elgar Publishing, pp. 120–38.

Deutsche Bundesbank (2022), 'Member States' Financial Relationships with the EU Budget and the Next Generation EU Off-budget Entity in 2021', *Monthly Report*, October, 35–46. Available at: https://www.bundesbank.de/resource/blob/900052/25d7e548dc40213940247c230435a901/mL/2022-10-finanzbeziehungen-data.pdf (Accessed 1 May 2024).

Dougherty, S. and Forman, K. (2021), 'Evaluating Fiscal Equalisation: Finding the Right Balance', *OECD Working Papers on Fiscal Federalism*, No. 36. Paris: OECD Publishing. doi: https://doi.org/10.1787/253da2b8-en.

Dowding, K. (2019), *Rational Choice and Political Power*. Bristol: Bristol University Press.

Dowding, K. (2021), 'Power: Ambiguous not Vague', *Journal of Political Power* 14 (1), 11–26.

Duina, F. and Raunio, T. (2007), 'The Open Method of Co-ordination and National Parliaments: Further Marginalization or New Opportunities?', *Journal of European Public Policy* 14 (4), 489–506.

Dür, A. and Elsig, M. (eds) (2012), *Principals, Agents, and the European Union's Foreign Economic Policies*. Abingdon, New York: Routledge.

Duttle, T. et al. (2017), 'Opting out from European Union Legislation: The Differentiation of Secondary Law', *Journal of European Public Policy* 24 (3), 406–28.

Dylan, H., Gioe, D. V. and Grossfeld, E. (2022), 'The Autocrat's Intelligence Paradox: Vladimir Putin's (Mis)management of Russian Strategic Assessment in the Ukraine War', *The British Journal of Politics and International Relations* 25 (3), 385–404.

Eckstein, H. (1969), 'Authority Relations and Governmental Performance: A Theoretical Framework', *Comparative Political Studies* 2 (3), 269–325.

Eilstrup-Sangiovanni, M. (2020), 'Death of International Organizations. The Organizational Ecology of Intergovernmental Organizations, 1815–2015', *The Review of International Organizations* 15 (2), 339–70.

Elazar, D. J. (1987), *Exploring Federalism*. Tuscaloosa AL: University of Alabama Press.

Elster, J. (1979), *Ulysses and the Sirens: Studies in Rationality and Irrationality*. Cambridge UK: Cambridge University Press.

Enderlein, H., Wälti, S. and Zürn, M. (eds) (2010), *Handbook on Multi-Level Governance*. Cheltenham UK, Northampton MA: Edward Elgar Publishing.

Esping-Andersen, G. (1990), *The Three Worlds of Welfare Capitalism*. Cambridge MA: Princeton University Press.

Evans, P. (1993), 'Building an Integrative Approach to International and Domestic Politics: Reflections and Projections', in P. Evans, H. Jacobson and R. Putnam (eds) *Double-Edged Diplomacy: Interactive Games in International Affairs*. Berkeley CA: University of California Press, pp 397–430.

Evans, P., Jacobson, H. and Putnam, R. (eds) (1993), *Double-Edged Diplomacy: Interactive Games in International Affairs*. Berkeley CA: University of California Press.

Falkner, G. (ed) (2011), *The EU's Decision Traps: Comparing Policies*. Oxford: Oxford University Press.

Fichte, J. G. ([1800] 1979), *Der geschlossne Handelsstaat*. 3rd edn. Hamburg: Meiner.

Filippov, M., Ordeshook, P. C. and Shvetsova O. (2004), *Designing Federalism: A Theory of Self-sustainable Federal Institutions*. New York: Cambridge University Press.

Filippov, M. and Shvetsova, O. (2013), 'Federalism, Democracy, and Democratization', in A. Benz and J. Broschek (eds) *Federal Dynamics. Continuity, Change, and the Varieties of Federalism*. Oxford: Oxford University Press, pp. 167–84.

Fischlin, A. (2017), 'Background and Role of Science', in D. Klein et al. (eds) *The Paris Agreement on Climate Change. Analysis and Commentary*. Oxford, New York: Oxford University Press, pp. 3–16.

Fossum, J. E. and Laycock, D. (2021), 'Out of Balance. Executive Dominance in Federal Settings', in A. Benz and J. Sonnicksen (eds) *Federal Democracies at Work. Varieties of Complex Governments*. Toronto: University of Toronto Press, 58–77.

Frantz, E. (2018), *Authoritarianism. What Everyone Needs to Know*. Oxford: Oxford University Press.

Frye, T. (2021), *Weak Strongman. The Limits of Power in Putin's Russia*. Princeton NJ: Princeton University Press.

Fujita, M. (2010), 'The Evolution of Spatial Economics: From Thünen to the New Economic Geography', *The Japanese Economic Review* 61 (1), 1–32.

Fujita, M., Krugman, P. and Venables, A. J. (1999), *The Spatial Economy: Cities, Regions, and International Trade*. Cambridge MA: MIT Press.

Fukuyama, F. (2013), 'What Is Governance?', *Governance* 26 (3), 347–68.

Fukuyama, F. (2018), *Identity: The Demand for Dignity and the Politics of Resentment*. New York: Farrar, Straus and Giroux.

Gallarotti, G. M. (ed) (2021), *The Changing Faces of Power 1979–2019* (Special Issue of *Journal of Political Power* 14 [1]). London: Taylor and Francis.

Gamper, A. (2021), 'Suum Cuique Tribuere – A Common Narrative of Federalism and Equality?', in E. M. Belser et al. (eds) T*he Principle of Equality in Diverse States: Reconciling Autonomy with Equal Rights and Opportunities*. Leiden: Brill, pp. 13–35.

Gandhi, J. and Przeworski, A. (2007), 'Authoritarian Institutions and the Survival of Autocrats', *Comparative Political Studies* 40 (11), 1279–301.

Gänzle, S., Leruth, B. and Trondal, J. (2020a), 'Introduction. Differentiation in the European Union as a Field of Study', in S. Gänzle, B. Leruth and J. Trondal (eds) *Differentiated Integration and Disintegration in a Post-Brexit Era*. Abingdon: Routledge, pp. 1–16.

Gänzle, S., Leruth, B. and Trondal, J. (eds) (2020b), *Differentiated Integration and Disintegration in a Post-Brexit Era*. Abingdon: Routledge.

Gauvin, J.-P. and Papillon, M. (2017), 'Intergovernmental Relations in Canada: Still and Executive Club', in A.-G. Gagnon and J. Poirier (eds) *Canadian Federalism and its Future. Actors and Institutions*. Montreal, Kingston: McGill-Queen's University Press, pp. 336–64.

Gerber, E. and Kollman, K. (2004), 'Introduction – Authority Migration: Defining an Emerging Research Agenda', *PS: Political Science and Politics* 37 (3), 397–400.

Gerschewski, J. (2013), 'The Three Pillars of Stability: Legitimation, Repression, and Co-optation in Autocratic Regimes', *Democratization* 20 (1), 13–38.

Gibson, E. L. (ed) (2004), *Federalism and Democracy in Latin America*. Baltimore: J. Hopkins University Press.

Gibson, E. L. (2012), *Boundary Control. Subnational Authoritarianism in Federal Democracies*. Cambridge UK: Cambridge University Press.

Giraudy, A. (2015), *Democrats and Autocrats. Pathways of Subnational Undemocratic Regime Continuity within Democratic Countries*. Oxford: Oxford University Press.

Goetz, K. H. and Patz, R. (2017), 'Resourcing International Organizations: Resource Diversification, Organizational Differentiation, and Administrative Governance', *Global Policy* 8 (S 5), 5–14.

Goodin, R. E. and Spiekermann, K. (2018), *An Epistemic Theory of Democracy*. Oxford: Oxford University Press.

Gornitzka, Å. (2018), 'Organising Soft Governance in Hard Times – The Unlikely Survival of the Open Method of Coordination in EU Education Policy', *European Papers – A Journal on Law and Integration* 3 (1), 235–55.

Gould, A., Barry, M. and Wilkinson, A. (2015), 'Varieties of Capitalism Revisited: Current Debates and Possible Directions', *Relations Industrielles/ Industrial Relations* 70 (4), 587–602.

Graham, E. R. (2017), 'Follow the Money: How Trends in Financing Are Changing Governance at International Organizations', *Global Policy* 8 (S 5), 15–25.

Grande, E. (1996), 'The State and Interest Groups in a Framework of Multi-level Decision Making. The Case of the European Union', *Journal of European Public Policy* 3 (3), 318–38.

Granovetter, M. (1985), 'Economic Action and Social Structure. The Problem of Embeddedness', *American Journal of Sociology* 91 (3), 481–510.

Gray, I. and Cointet, J.-P. (2023), 'Multilateralism of the Marginal: How the Least Developed Countries Find Their Voice in International Political Deliberations', *American Journal of Sociology* 129 (3), 796–855.

Grote, J. R. and Gbikpi, B. (eds) (2002), *Participatory Governance. Political and Societal Implications*. Opladen: Leske + Budrich.

Groussot, X. (2012), 'Constitutional Dialogues, Pluralism and Conflicting Identities', in M. Avbelj and J. Komárek (eds) *Constitutional Pluralism in the European Union and Beyond.* New York: Hart Publishing, pp. 319–42.

Haas, P. M. (1992), 'Introduction. Epistemic Communities and International Policy Coordination', *International Organization* 46 (1), 1–37.

Habermas, J. (1981), *Theorie des kommunikativen Handelns. Band 1: Handlungsrationalität und gesellschaftliche Rationalisierung*. Frankfurt: Suhrkamp.

Hall, P. and Soskice, D. (2001), *Varieties of Capitalism: The Institutional Foundations of Comparative Advantage*. Oxford: Oxford University Press.

Hanrieder, W. F. (1978), 'Dissolving International Politics: Reflections on the Nation-State', *The American Political Science Review* 72 (4), 1276–87.

Harguindéguy, J.-B., Cole, A. and Pasquier, R. (2021), 'The Variety of Decentralization Indexes: A Review of the Literature', *Regional & Federal Studies* 31 (2), 185–208.

Harmes, A. (2019), *The Politics of Fiscal Federalism: Neoliberalism versus Social Democracy in Multilevel Governance*. Montreal, Kingston: McGill-Queen's University Press.

Hassel, A. (2010), 'Multi-level Governance and Organized Interests', in H. Enderlein, S. Wälti and M. Zürn, (eds), *Handbook on Multi-Level Governance*. Cheltenham UK, Northampton MA: Edward Elgar Publishing, pp. 153–67.

Haugaard, M. (2022), 'Power', in C. Ansell and J. Torfing (eds) *Handbook on Theories of Governance*. 2nd edn. Cheltenham UK, Northampton MA: Edward Elgar Publishing, pp. 187–95.

Hearson, M. (2021), *Imposing Standards. The North-South Dimension to Global Tax Politics*. Ithaca NY, London: Cornell University Press.

Heinelt, H. and Niederhafner, S. (2008), 'Cities and Organized Interest Intermediation in the EU Multi-Level System', *European Urban and Regional Studies* 15 (2), 173–87.

Heinkelmann-Wild, T. et al. (2023), 'Blame Shifting and Blame Obfuscation: The Blame Avoidance Effects of Delegation in the European Union', *European Journal of Political Research* 62 (1), 221–38.

Hendriks, F., Loughlin, J. and Lidström, A. (2011), 'European Subnational Democracy: Comparative Reflections and Conclusions', in J. Loughlin, F. Hendriks and A. Lidström (eds) *The Oxford Handbook of Local and Regional Democracy in Europe*. Oxford: Oxford University Press, pp. 715–42.

Héritier, A. (1999), *Policy-Making and Diversity in Europe. Escaping Deadlock*. Cambridge UK: Cambridge University Press.

Héritier, A. (2007), *Explaining Institutional Change in Europe*. Oxford: Oxford University Press.

Heyes, C. (2020), 'Identity Politics', in E. N. Zalta (ed) *The Stanford Encyclopedia of Philosophy*. Fall 2020 edn. Stanford CA: Philosophy Department, Stanford University. Available at: https://plato.stanford.edu/archives/fall2020/entries/identity-politics/ (Accessed 1 May 2024).

Higashijima, M. (2022), *The Dictator's Dilemma at the Ballot Box: Electoral Manipulation, Economic Maneuvering, and Political Order in Autocracies*. Ann Arbor MI: University of Michigan Press.

Hirschl, R. (2008), 'The Judicialization of Mega-Politics and the Rise of Political Courts', *Annual Review of Political Science* 11 (1), 93–118.

Holzinger, K. (2008), *Transnational Common Goods. Strategic Constellations, Collective Action Problems, and Multi-level Provision*. New York: Palgrave Macmillan.

Hombrado, A. (2011), 'Learning to Catch the Wave? Regional Demands for Constitutional Change in Contexts of Asymmetrical Arrangements', *Regional & Federal Studies* 21 (4–5), 479–501.

Hooghe, L. et al. (2016), *Measuring Regional Authority. A Postfunctionalist Theory of Governance*. Vol. I. Oxford: Oxford University Press.

Hooghe, L. et al. (2017), *Measuring International Authority. A Postfunctionalist Theory of Governance*. Vol. III. Oxford: Oxford University Press.

Hooghe, L., Lenz, T. and Marks, G. (2019), *A Theory of International Organization. A Postfunctionalist Theory of Governance*. Vol. IV. Oxford: Oxford University Press.

Hooghe, L. and Marks, G. (2001), *Multilevel Governance and European Integration*. Lanham MD: Rowman & Littlefield Publishers.

Hooghe, L. and Marks, G. (2003), 'Unraveling the Central State, but How? Types of Multi-level Governance', *American Political Science Review* 97 (2), 233–43.

Hooghe, L. and Marks, G. (2009), 'A Postfunctionalist Theory of European Integration. From Permissive Consensus to Constraining Dissensus', *British Journal of Political Science* 39 (1), 1–23.

Hooghe, L., and Marks, G. (2012), 'Politicization', in E. Jones, A. Menon, and S. Weatherill (eds) *The Oxford Handbook of the European Union*. Oxford: Oxford University Press, pp. 840–54.

Hooghe, L. and Marks, G. (2016), *Community, Scale and Regional Governance. A Postfunctionalist Theory of Governance*. Vol. II. Oxford: Oxford University Press.

Hooghe, L. and Marks, G. (2018), 'Cleavage Theory Meets Europe's Crises. Lipset, Rokkan, and the Transnational Cleavage', *Journal of European Public Policy* 25 (1), 109–35.

Hooghe, L. and Marks, G. (2020), 'A Postfunctionalist Theory of Multilevel Governance', *The British Journal of Politics and International Relations* 22 (4), 820–26.

Hooghe, L. and Marks, G. (2021), 'Multilevel Governance and the Coordination Dilemma', in A. Benz, J. Broschek and M. Lederer (eds) *A Research Agenda for Multilevel Governance*. Cheltenham UK, Northampton MA: Edward Elgar Publishing, pp. 19–37.

Hooghe, L. and Marks, G. (2023), 'Differentiation in the European Union and Beyond', *European Union Politics* 24 (1), 225–35.

Hooghe, L., Marks, G. and Schakel, A. H. (2010), *The Rise of Regional Authority*. New York: Routledge Chapman & Hall.

Hueglin, T. O. (1986), 'Regionalism in Western Europe. Conceptual Problems and New Political Perspectives', *Comparative Politics* 18 (4), 439–58.

Hueglin, T. O. (2021), *Federalism in Canada: Contested Concepts and Uneasy Balances*. Toronto: University of Toronto Press.

Hueglin, T. O. and Fenna, A. (2015), *Comparative Federalism. A Systematic Inquiry*. Toronto: University of Toronto Press.

Hurrelmann, A. (2023), 'Constitutional Abeyances: Reflecting on EU Treaty Development in Light of the Canadian Experience', *Politics and Governance* 11 (3), 241–50.

Hurrelmann, A. and DeBardeleben, J. (2009), 'Democratic Dilemmas in EU Multilevel Governance. Untangling the Gordian Knot', *European Political Science Review* 1 (2), 229–47.

Inman, R. P. and Rubinfeld, D. L. (2020), *Democratic Federalism*. Princeton NJ, Oxford: Princeton University Press.

Jachtenfuchs, M. and Kasack, C. (2017), 'Balancing Sub-unit Autonomy and Collective Problem-solving by Varying Exit and Voice. An Analytical Framework', *Journal of European Public Policy* 24 (4), 598–614.

Jeffery, C. and Peterson, J. (2020), '"Breakthrough" Political Science: Multi-level Governance – Reconceptualising Europe's Modernised Polity', *The British Journal of Politics and International Relations* 22 (4), 753–66.

Jessop, B. (2002), *The Future of the Capitalist State*. London: Polity Press.

Jessop, B. (2015), 'From Governance to Governance Failure and from Multi-Level Governance to Multi-Scalar Meta-Governance', in I. Bache and M. Flinders (eds) *Multi-Level Governance: Essential Readings*. Vol. I. Cheltenham UK, Northampton MA: Edward Elgar Publishing, pp. 625–46.

Johnson, T. (2014), *Organizational Progeny. Why Governments are Losing Control over the Proliferating Structures of Global Governance*. Oxford: Oxford University Press.

Jordan, A. et al. (eds) (2018), *Governing Climate Change: Polycentricity in Action?* Cambridge UK: Cambridge University Press.

Jordan, A. and Schout, A. (eds) (2006), *The Coordination of the European Union. Exploring the Capacities of Networked Governance*. Oxford: Oxford University Press.

Jörke, D. (2019), *Die Größe der Demokratie. Über die räumliche Dimension von Herrschaft und Partizipation*. Frankfurt: Suhrkamp.

Juergensmeyer, M. (2019), 'Religious Nationalism in a Global World', *Religions* 10 (2), 97, 1–8.

Kailitz, S. (2013), 'Classifying Political Regimes Revisited: Legitimation and Durability', *Democratization* 20 (1), 39–60.

Kaldor, M. (2004), 'Nationalism and Globalisation', *Nations and Nationalism* 10 (1–2), 161–77.

Karch, A. (2010), *Democratic Laboratories. Policy Diffusion among the American States*. Ann Arbor MI: University of Michigan Press.

Kassim, H., Saurugger, S. and Puetter, U. (2020), 'The Study of National Preference Formation in Times of the Euro Crisis and Beyond', *Political Studies Review* 18 (4), 463–74.

Katz Cogan, J. (2016), 'Financing and Budgets', in J. Katz Cogan, I. Hurd and I. Johnstone (eds) *The Oxford Handbook of International Organizations*. Oxford: Oxford University Press, pp. 903–19.

Katzenstein P. J. (1996), 'Regionalism in Comparative Perspective,' *Cooperation and Conflict* 31 (2), 123–59.

Katzenstein P. J. (2005), *A World of Regions: Asia and Europe in the American Imperium*. Ithaca NY: Cornell University Press.

Keating, M. (1998), *The New Regionalism in Western Europe: Territorial Restructuring and Political Change*. Cheltenham UK, Northampton MA: Edward Elgar Publishing.

Keating, M. (1999), 'Asymmetrical Government: Multinational States in an Integrating Europe', *Publius: The Journal of Federalism* 29 (1), 77–82.

Keating, M. (2013), *Rescaling the European State. The Making of Territory and the Rise of the Meso*. Oxford: Oxford University Press.

Keating, M. (2015), 'Plurinational States', in S. Leibfried et al. (eds) *The Oxford Handbook of Transformation of the State*. Oxford: Oxford University Press, pp. 532–46.

Keating, M., Hooghe, L. and Tatham, M. (2015), 'By-passing the Nation State? Regions and the EU Policy Process', in J. Richardson and S. Mazey (eds*) European Union. Power and Policy-making*. 4th edn. London, New York: Routledge, pp. 445–66.

Keil, S. (2019), 'Federalism as a Tool of Conflict Resolution', in J. Kincaid (ed) *A Research Agenda for Federalism Studies*. Cheltenham UK, Northampton MA: Edward Elgar Publishing, pp. 151–61.

Keil, S. and Kropp, S. (2022a), 'The Emergence and Regression of Federal Structures: Theoretical Lenses and Analytical Dimensions', in S. Keil and S. Kropp (eds) *Emerging Federal Structures in the Post-Cold War Era*. Cham CH: Springer International Publishing, pp. 3–30.

Keil, S. and Kropp, S. (eds) (2022b), *Emerging Federal Structures in the Post-Cold War Era*. Cham CH: Springer International Publishing.

Kelemen, R. D. and McNamara, K. R. (2022), 'State-building and the European Union: Markets, War, and Europe's Uneven Political Development', *Comparative Political Studies* 55 (6), 963–91.

Kemp, L. (2016), 'Framework for the Future? Exploring the Possibility of Majority Voting in the Climate Negotiations', *International Environment Agreements: Politics, Law and Economics* 16 (5), 757–79.

Keohane, R. (2004), Global Governance and Democratic Accountability, in D. Held and M. Koenig-Archibugi (eds) *Taming Globalization: Frontiers of Governance*. London: Polity Press, pp. 130–59.

Kern, K. (2019), 'Cities as Leaders in EU Multilevel Climate Governance: Embedded Upscaling of Local Experiments in Europe', *Environmental Politics* 28 (1), 125–45.

Kern, K. and Bulkeley, H. (2009), 'Cities, Europeanization and Multi-level Governance: Governing Climate Change through Transnational Municipal Networks', *Journal of Common Market Studies* 47 (2), 309–32.

Kettl, D. F. (2020), *The Divided States of America: Why Federalism Doesn't Work*. Princeton NJ: Princeton University Press.

Kincaid, J. and Jedwab, J. (eds) (2019), *Identities, Trust, and Cohesion in Federal Systems. Public Perspectives*. Montreal, Kingston: McGill-Queen's University Press.

Kirton, J. J., Kokotsis, E. and Warren, B. (2022), *Reconfiguring the Global Governance of Climate Change*. Abingdon: Routledge.

Kleider, H. (2020), 'Multilevel Governance: Identity, Political Contestation, and Policy', *The British Journal of Politics and International Relations* 22 (4), 792–99.

Kleider, H. and Stoeckel, F. (2019), 'The Politics of International Redistribution: Explaining Public Support for Fiscal Transfers in the EU', *European Journal of Political Research* 58 (1), 4–29.

Knill, C. and Steinebach, Y. (eds) (2023), *International Public Administrations in Global Public Policy: Sources and Effects of Bureaucratic Influence*. London: Routledge.

Kohler-Koch, B. and Quittkat, C. (2013), *De-Mystification of Participatory Democracy. EU-Governance and Civil Society*. Oxford: Oxford University Press.

Kohler-Koch, B. and Rittberger, B. (2007), 'Charting Crowded Territory: Debating the Democratic Legitimacy of the European Union', in B. Kohler-Koch and B. Rittberger (eds) *Debating the Democratic Legitimacy of the European Union*. Plymoth: Rowman & Littlefield, pp. 1–29.

König, T., Tsebelis, G. and Debus, M. (eds) (2010), *Reform Processes and Policy Change. Veto Players and Decision-making in Modern Democracies*. New York, Heidelberg: Springer.

Kooiman, J. (2003), *Governing as Governance*. London: Sage.

Kramer, L. D. (2000), 'Putting the Politics Back into the Political Safeguards of Federalism', *Columbia Law Review* 100 (1), 215–93.

Kriesi, H.-P. et al. (2006), 'Globalization and the Transformation of the National Political Space: Six European Countries Compared', *European Journal of Political Research* 45 (6), 921–56.

Kropp, S. (2015), 'Federalism and Subnational Parliaments—A Delicate Relationship', in G. Abels and A. Eppler (eds) *Subnational Parliaments in an EU Multi-level Parliamentary System: Taking Stock of the Post-Lisbon Era*. Innsbruck: StudienVerlag, pp. 91–126.

Krugman, P. R. (1991), 'Increasing Returns and Economic Geography', *Journal of Political Economy* 99 (3), 483–99.

Kymlicka, W. (2005), 'Federalism, Nationalism and Multiculturalism', in D. Karmis and W. Norman (eds) *Theories of Federalism: A Reader*. New York: Palgrave Macmillan, pp. 269–92.

Ladner, A., Keuffer, N. and Bastianen, A. (2021), *Self-rule Index for Local Authorities in the EU, Council of Europe and OECD Countries, 1990-2020*. Luxembourg: Publications Office of the European Union. Available at: https:// ec .europa .eu/ regional_policy/sources/policy/analysis/KN-07-22-144-EN-N.pdf (Accessed 1 May 2024).

Laffan B. (2023), 'Collective Power Europe? (The Government and Opposition/ Leonard Schapiro Lecture 2022)', *Government and Opposition* 58 (4), 623–40.

Lafont, C. (2020), *Democracy Without Shortcuts. A Participatory Conception of Deliberative Democracy*. New York: Oxford University Press.

Lake, D., Martin, L. and Risse, T. (2021), 'Challenges to the Liberal Order: Reflections on International Organization', *International Organization* 75 (2), 225–57.

Landau, M. (1969), 'Redundancy, Rationality and the Problem of Duplication and Overlap', *Public Administration Review* 29 (4), 348–58.

Landau, M. (1973), 'Federalism, Redundancy and System Reliability', *Publius: The Journal of Federalism* 3 (2), 173–96.

Lasswell, H. D. (1936), *Politics: Who Gets What, When, How*. New York: McGraw-Hill.

Law, D. S. and Tushnet, M. V. (2023), 'The Politics of Judicial Dialogue', in M. V. Tushnet and D. Kochenov (eds) *Research Handbook on the Politics of Constitutional Law*. Cheltenham UK, Northampton MA: Edward Elgar Publishing, pp. 286–308.

Lecours, A. (2021), *Nationalism, Secessionism, and Autonomy*. Oxford: Oxford University Press.

Lecours, A. and Béland, D. (2019), 'From Secessionism to Regionalism: The Changing Nature of Territorial Politics in Western Australia', *Regional & Federal Studies* 29 (1), 25–44.

Lehmbruch, G. (1978), 'Party and Federation in Germany: A Developmental Dilemma', *Government and Opposition* 13 (2), 151–77.

Leslie, P. (1987), *Federal State, National Economy*. Toronto: University of Toronto Press.

Leuffen, D., Rittberger, B. and Schimmelfennig, F. (2013), *Differentiated Integration. Explaining Variation in the European Union*. Basingstoke: Palgrave Macmillan.

Levi-Faur, D. (2012), 'From "Big Government" to "Big Governance"', in D. Levi-Faur (ed) *The Oxford Handbook of Governance*. Oxford: Oxford University Press, pp. 3–18.

Liese, A. et al. (2021), 'The Heart of Bureaucratic Power: Explaining International Bureaucracies' Expert Authority', *Review of International Studies*, 47 (3), 353–76.

Lijphart, A. (1977), *Democracy in Plural Societies: A Comparative Exploration*. New Haven: Yale University Press.

Linz, J. J. (2000), *Totalitarian and Authoritarian Regimes*. Boulder CO: Lynne Rienner Publishers.

Littoz-Monnet, A. (ed) (2017), *The Politics of Expertise in International Organizations: How International Bureaucracies Produce and Mobilize Knowledge*. London: Routledge.

Livingston, W. S. (1952), 'A Note on the Nature of Federalism', *Political Science Quarterly* 67 (1), 81–95.

Loughlin, J. (2000), 'Regional Autonomy and State Paradigm Shifts in Western Europe', *Regional & Federal Studies* 10 (2), 10–34.

Lowi, T. J. (1964), 'American Business, Public Policy, Case Studies, and Political Theory', *World Politics* 16 (4), 677–715.

Lowi, T. J. (1972), 'Four Systems of Policy, Politics and Choice', *Public Administration Review* 32 (4), 298–310.

Maas, W. (2017), 'Multilevel Citizenship', in A. Shachar et al. (eds) *The Oxford Handbook of Citizenship*. Oxford: Oxford University Press, pp. 644–68.

Mahoney, J. and Thelen, K. (2010), 'A Theory of Gradual Institutional Change', in J. Mahoney and K. Thelen (eds) *Explaining Institutional Change. Ambiguity, Agency, and Power*. Cambridge UK: Cambridge University Press, pp. 1–37.

Marcussen, M. and Torfing, J. (2007), *Democratic Network Governance in Europe*. Houndmills, New York: Palgrave Macmillan.

Marks, G. (1993), 'Structural Policy and Multilevel Governance in the EC', in A. W. Cafruny and G. G. Rosenthal (eds) *The State of the European Community. Vol. 2: The Maastricht Debates and Beyond*. Boulder CO: Lynne Rienner, pp. 391–410.

Marks, G. (1996), 'An Actor-Centred Approach to Multi-Level Governance', *Regional & Federal Studies* 6 (2), 20–38.

Marquardt, J. and Lederer, M. (eds) (2022), *Operating at the Frontiers of Democracy? Mitigating Climate Change in Times of Populism* (Special Issue of *Environmental Politics* 31 [5]). Abingdon, New York: Routledge.

Marshall, A. (1890), *Principles of Economics*. London: Macmillan and Co.

Massetti, E. and Schakel, A. H. (2020), 'Regionalist Parties and the European Union', in *Oxford Research Encyclopedia of Politics*. Oxford: Oxford University Press. doi: https://doi.org/10.1093/acrefore/9780190228637.013.1983

Mavrot, C. and Sager, F. (2018), 'Vertical Epistemic Communities in Multilevel Governance', *Policy & Politics* 46 (3), 391–407.

Mayer, F. C. (2020), 'The Ultra Vires Ruling: Deconstructing the German Federal Constitutional Court's PSPP decision of 5 May 2020', *European Constitutional Law Review* 16 (4), 733–69.

Mayntz, R. (ed) (2015), *Negotiated Reform: The Multilevel Governance of Financial Regulation*. Frankfurt, New York: Campus.

Mayntz, R. and Scharpf, F. W. (1995), 'Der Ansatz des akteurszentrierten Institutionalismus', in R. Mayntz and F. W. Scharpf (eds), *Gesellschaftliche Selbstregelung und politische Steuerung*. Frankfurt, New York: Campus, pp. 39–72.

McCoy, J., Rahman, T., and Somer, M. (2018), 'Polarization and the Global Crisis of Democracy: Common Patterns, Dynamics, and Pernicious Consequences for Democratic Polities', *American Behavioral Scientist* 62 (1), 16–42.

McRoberts, K. (2023), 'Political Asymmetries. "Opting In and Opting Out" Decision-Making Procedures in Canada', in F. Requejo and M. Sanjaume-Calvet (eds) *Defensive Federalism: Protecting Territorial Minorities from the 'Tyranny of the Majority'*. London: Routledge, pp. 105–30.

Meckling, J. and Allan, B. B. (2020) 'The Evolution of Ideas in Global Climate Policy'. *Nature Climate Change* 10 (5), 434–38.

Mende, J. (2021), 'Private Actors, NGOs and Civil Society in Multilevel Governance', in A. Benz, J. Broschek and M. Lederer (eds) *A Research Agenda for Multilevel Governance*. Cheltenham UK, Northampton MA: Edward Elgar Publishing, pp. 171–89.

Merkel, W. (2004), 'Embedded and Defective Democracies', *Democratization* 11 (5), 33–58.

Milanocvić, B. (2011), *The Haves and the Have-Nots: A Brief and Idiosyncratic History of Global Inequality*. New York: Basic Books.

Milanocvić, B. (2012), 'Global Inequality: From Class to Location, from Proletarians to Migrants', *Global Policy* 3 (2), 125–34.

Milkoreit, M. (2019), 'The Paris Agreement on Climate Change – Made in USA?', *Perspectives on Politics* 17 (4), 1019–37.

Miller, D. (1995), *On Nationality*. Oxford: Clarendon Press.

Miller, D. (2000), *Citizenship and National Identity*. Cambridge MA: Polity Press.

Moore, C. (2008), 'A Europe of the Regions vs. the Regions in Europe. Reflections on Regional Engagement in Brussels', *Regional & Federal Studies* 18 (5), 517–35.

Moore, M. (2015), *A Political Theory of Territory*. Oxford: Oxford University Press.

Moravcsik, A. (1993), 'Integrating International and Domestic Theories of International Bargaining', in P. Evans, H. Jacobson and R. Putnam (eds) *Double-Edged Diplomacy: Interactive Games in International Affairs*. Berkeley CA: University of California Press, pp. 3–42.

Mueller, S. (2024), S*hared Rule in Federal Theory and Practice: Concept, Causes, Consequences*. Oxford: Oxford University Press.

Mudde, C. (2004), 'The Populist Zeitgeist', *Government and Opposition* 39 (4), 542–63.

Nordhaus, W. (2015), 'Climate Clubs: Overcoming Free-riding in International Climate Policy', *American Economic Review* 105 (4), 1339–70.

Oates, W. E. (1972), *Fiscal Federalism*. New York: Harcourt Brace Jonavich.

Oates, W. E. (2005), 'Towards a Second-Generation Theory of Fiscal Federalism', *International Tax and Public Finance* 12 (4), 349–73.

Oelsner, A. (2013), 'The Institutional Identity of Regional Organizations, Or Mercosur's Identity Crisis', *International Studies Quarterly* 57 (1), 115–27.

O'Leary, B. (2001), 'The Elements of Right-Sizing and Right-Peopling the State', in B. O'Leary, I. S. Lustick and T. Callaghy (eds) *Right-sizing the State*. Oxford: Oxford University Press, pp. 15–73.

O'Leary, B. (2013), 'Power Sharing in Deeply Divided Places. An Advocate's Introduction', in J. McEvoy and B. O'Leary (eds) *Power Sharing in Deeply Divided Places*. Philadelphia PA: University of Pennsylvania Press, pp. 1–64.

Ordóñez, A. and Raven, R. (2022), 'Implementation at Multiple Levels', F. Biermann, T. Hickmann, and C.-A. Sénit (eds), *The Political Impact of the Sustainable Development Goals*. Cambridge UK: Cambridge University Press, pp. 59–91.

Ostrom, E. (2005), *Understanding Institutional Diversity*. Princeton NJ: Princeton University Press.

Ostrom, E. (2010), 'Beyond Markets and States: Polycentric Governance of Complex Economic Systems', *The American Economic Review* 100 (3), 641–72.

Orton, J. D. and Weick, K. E. (1990), 'Loosely Coupled Systems: A Reconceptualization', *Academy of Management Review* 15 (2), 203–23.

Page, S. E. (2011), *Diversity and Complexity*. Princeton NJ: Princeton University Press.

Painter, M. (1991), 'Intergovernmental Relations in Canada: An Institutional Analysis', *Canadian Journal of Political Science* 24 (2), 269–88.

Painter, M. (1998), *Collaborative Federalism. Economic Reform in Australia in the 1990s*. Cambridge UK: Cambridge University Press.

Pansardi, P. and Bindi, M. (2021), 'The New Concepts of Power? Power-over, Power-to and Power-with', *Journal of Political Power* 14 (1), 51–71.

Papadopoulos, Y. (2010), 'Accountability and Multi-level Governance. More Accountability, Less Democracy?', *West European Politics* 33 (5), 1030–49.

Papadopoulos, Y., Tortola, P. D. and Geyer, N. (2024), 'Taking Stock of the Multilevel Governance Research Programme: A Systematic Literature Review'; *Regional & Federal Studies*, DOI: 10.1080/13597566.2024.2334470.

Peck, J. (2002), 'Political Economies of Scale: Fast Policy, Interscalar Relations, and Neoliberal Workfare', *Economic Geography* 78 (3), 331–60.

Peet, R. (2011), 'Inequality, Crisis and Austerity in Finance Capitalism', *Cambridge Journal of Regions, Economy and Society* 4 (3), 383–99.

Peters, B. G. (2023), 'Public Administration in Authoritarian Regimes', *Asia Pacific Journal of Public Administration* 45 (1), 7–15.

Peters, B. G. and Pierre, J. (2004), 'Multi-level Governance and Democracy. A Faustian Bargain?', in I. Bache and M. Flinders (eds) *Multi-level Governance*. Oxford: Oxford University Press, pp. 75–89.

Piattoni, S. (2010), *The Theory of Multi-Level Governance*. Oxford: Oxford University Press.

Piattoni, S. (2015), 'Multi-Level Governance: Underplayed Features, Overblown Expectation and Missing Linkages', in E. Ongaro (ed) *Multi-Level Governance. The Missing Linkages*. Bradford: Emerald Group Publishing Limited, pp. 321–42.

Piattoni, S. and Polverari, L. (eds) (2016), *Handbook on Cohesion Policy in the EU*. Cheltenham UK, Northampton MA: Edward Elgar Publishing.

Pierre, J. (2000a), 'Introduction: Understanding Governance', in J. Pierre (eds) *Debating Governance. Authority, Steering, and Democracy*. Oxford: Oxford University Press, pp. 1–11.

Pierre, J. (ed.) (2000b), *Debating Governance. Authority, Steering, and Democracy*. Oxford: Oxford University Press.

Piketty, T. (2020), *Capital and Ideology*. Cambridge MA: The Belknap Press of Harvard University Press.

Pistor, K. (2019), *The Code of Capital. How the Law Creates Wealth and Inequality*. Princeton NJ, Oxford: Princeton University Press.

Poirier, J. and Saunders, C. (2015), 'Conclusion: Comparative Experiences of Intergovernmental Relations in Federal Systems', in J. Poirier, C. Saunders and J. Kincaid (eds) *Intergovernmental Relations in Federal Systems*. Oxford: Oxford University Press, pp. 440–98.

Pontusson, H. J. and Rueda, D. (2008), 'Inequality as a Source of Political Polarization: A Comparative Analysis of Twelve OECD Countries', in P. Beramendi and C. J. Anderson (eds) *Democracy, Inequality, and Representation in Comparative Perspective*. New York: Russell Sage Foundation, pp. 312–53.

Popelier, P. and Sahadžić, M. (2019a), 'Linking Constitutional Symmetry with Multinationalism. An Attempt to Crack the Code in Five Hypotheses', in P. Popelier and M. Sahadžić, (eds) *Constitutional Asymmetry in Multinational Federalism. Managing Multinationalism in Multi-tiered Systems*. London: Palgrave Macmillan, pp. 1–16.

Popelier, P. and Sahadžić, M. (eds) (2019b), *Constitutional Asymmetry in Multinational Federalism. Managing Multinationalism in Multi-tiered Systems*. London: Palgrave Macmillan.

Porter, M. E. (1998), 'Clusters and the New Economics of Competition', *Harvard Business Review* 76 (6), 77–90.

Provan, K. G. and Kenis, P. (2008), 'Modes of Network Governance: Structure, Management, and Effectiveness', *Journal of Public Administration Research and Theory* 18 (2), 229–52.

Psychogiopoulou, E. (2018), 'The Cultural Open Method of Coordination: A New but Different OMC?', *European Papers – A Journal on Law and Integration* 3 (1), 257–79.

Putnam, R. D. (1988), 'Diplomacy and Domestic Politics: The Logic of Two-level Games', *International Organization*, 42 (3), 427–60.

Putnam, R. D. (1993), *Making Democracy Work. Civic Traditions in Modern Italy*. Princeton NJ: Princeton University Press.

Rawls, J. (1999), *A Theory of Justice*. Revised edn. Cambridge MA: Harvard University Press.

Reckwitz, A. (2020), *The Society of Singularities*. Cambridge UK, Medford MA: Polity Press.

Riker, W. H. (1964), *Federalism. Origins, Operation, Significance*. Boston: Little Brown & Co.

Risse, T. (2000), '"Let's Argue". Communicative Action in World Politics', *International Organization* 54 (1), 1–39.

Rittberger, V. and Zangl, B. (2007), *International Organisations. Polity, Politics and Policies*. Basingstoke, Hampshire: Palgrave Macmillan.

Robertson, D. B. (2012), *Federalism and the Making of America*. New York, London: Routledge.

Rosenau, J. (2004), 'Strong Demand, Huge Supply: Governance in an Emerging Epoch', in I. Bache and M. Flinders (eds) *Multi-level Governance*. Oxford: Oxford University Press: 31–48.

Roy, J. (2021), 'Digitalization and Multilevel Governance', in A. Benz, J. Broschek and M. Lederer (eds) *A Research Agenda for Multilevel Governance*. Cheltenham UK, Northampton MA: Edward Elgar Publishing, pp. 95–113.

Sabel, C. F. and Zeitlin, J. (2008), 'Learning from Difference. The New Architecture of Experimentalist Governance in the EU', *European Law Journal* 14 (2), 271–327.

Sahadžić, M. (2021), *Asymmetry, Multinationalism and Constitutional Law. Managing Legitimacy and Stability in Federalist States*. Abingdon: Routledge.

Salmon, P. (2019), *Yardstick Competition among Governments. Accountability and Policymaking when Citizens Look Across Borders*. Oxford: Oxford University Press.

Sambanis, N. (2000), 'Partition as a Solution to Ethnic War: An Empirical Critique of the Theoretical Literature', *World Politics* 52 (4), 437–83.

Sandholtz, W. (2021), 'Human Rights Courts and Global Constitutionalism: Coordination through Judicial Dialogue', *Global Constitutionalism* 10 (3), 439–64.

Sassen, S. (2018), *Cities in a World Economy*. 5th edn. Los Angeles CA: Sage Publications.

Schäfer, A. (2006), 'A New Form of Governance? Comparing the Open Method of Coordination to Multilateral Surveillance by the IMF and the OECD', *Journal of European Public Policy* 13 (1), 70–88.

Scharpf, F. W. (1970), *Demokratietheorie zwischen Utopie und Anpassung*. Konstanz: Universitätsverlag.

Scharpf, F. W. (1976), 'Theorie der Politikverflechtung', in F. W. Scharpf, B. Reissert and F. Schnabel (eds) *Politikverflechtung. Theorie und Empirie des kooperativen Föderalismus in der Bundesrepublik*. Kronberg: Scriptor, pp. 13–70.

Scharpf, F. W. (1988), 'The Joint-Decision Trap. Lessons from German Federalism and European Integration', *Public Administration* 66 (3), 239–78.

Scharpf, F. W. (1991), 'Games Real Actors Could Play. The Challenge of Complexity', *Journal of Theoretical Politics* 3 (3), 277–304.

Scharpf, F. W. (1997), *Games Real Actors Play. Actor-Centered Institutionalism in Policy Research*. Boulder CO: Westview Press.

Scharpf, F. W. (1999), *Governing in Europe. Effective and Democratic?* Oxford, New York: Oxford University Press.

Scharpf, F. W. (2000), 'Interdependence and Democratic Legitimation', in S. J. Pharr and R. D. Putnam (eds) *Disaffected Democracies: What's Troubling the Trilateral Countries?* Princeton NJ: Princeton University Press, pp. 101–20.

Scharpf, F. W. (2001), 'Notes Toward a Theory of Multilevel Governing in Europe', *Scandinavian Political Studies* 24 (1), 1–26.

Scharpf, F. W. (2006), 'The Joint-Decision Trap Revisited', *Journal of Common Market Studies* 44 (4), 845–64.

Scharpf, F. W. (2009), 'Legitimacy in the Multilevel European Polity', *European Political Science Review* 1 (2), 173–204.

Scharpf, F. W. (2017), 'De-Constitutionalisation and Majority Rule: A Democratic Vision for Europe', *European Law Journal* 23 (5), 315–34.

Schelling, T. (1960), *The Strategy of Conflict*. Cambridge MA: Harvard University Press.

Schimmelfennig, F. and Winzen, T. (2019), 'Grand Theories, Differentiated Integration', *Journal of European Public Policy* 26 (8), 1172–92.

Schimmelfennig, F. and Winzen, T. (2020), *Ever Looser Union? Differentiated European Integration*. Oxford: Oxford University Press.

Schlumberger, O. (2017), 'Authoritarian Regimes', in *Oxford Handbooks Online: Political Science*. Oxford: Oxford University Press, doi: https://doi.org/10.1093/oxfordhb/9780199935307.013.18.

Schmidt, S. K. (2018), *The European Court of Justice and the Policy Process. The Shadow of Case Law*. Oxford: Oxford University Press.

Schmidt, V. A. (2006), *Democracy in Europe: The EU and National Polities*. Oxford: Oxford University Press.

Schmidt, V. A. (2009), 'Re-Envisioning the European Union: Identity, Democracy, Economy', *Journal of Common Market Studies*, 47 (SI), 17–42.

Schmidt, V. A. (2010), 'Taking Ideas and Discourse Seriously: Explaining Change through Discursive Institutionalism as the Fourth "New Institutionalism"', *European Journal of Political Research* 2 (1), 1–25.

Schmidt, V. A. (2020), *Europe's Crisis of Legitimacy*. Oxford: Oxford University Press.

Schmitter, P. C. (2004), 'Neo-functionalism', in A. Wiener and T. Diez (eds) *European Integration Theory*. Oxford: Oxford University Press, pp. 45–74.

Schmitter, P. C. (2006), 'Governance in the European Union. A Viable Mechanism for Future Legitimation?', in A. Benz and Y. Papadopoulos (eds) *Governance and Democracy*. London: Routledge, pp. 158–75.

Schnabel, J. (2020), *Managing Interdependencies in Federal Systems. Intergovernmental Councils and the Making of Public Policy*. London: Palgrave Macmillan.

Schütze, R. (2009), *From Dual to Cooperative Federalism. The Changing Structure of the European Law*. Oxford: Oxford University Press.

Seckelmann, M. (2011), 'Durch Kooperation zum Wettbewerb? Leistungsvergleiche nach Art. 91d GG', in B. Blanke et al. (eds) *Handbuch zur Verwaltungsreform*. 4th edn. Wiesbaden: Springer VS, pp. 571–81.

Selin H. and VanDeveer, S. D. (2020), 'Climate Change Politics and Policy in the United States. Forward, Reverse and through the Looking Glass' in R. K. W. Wurzel, M. S. Andersen and P. Tobin (eds), *Climate Governance across the Globe: Pioneers, Leaders and Followers*. Abingdon, New York: Routledge, pp. 123–41.

Sendling, O. J. (2017), *The Politics of Expertise. Competition for Authority in Global Governance*. Ann Arbor MI: University of Michigan Press.

Seybert, L. A. and Katzenstein, P. J. (eds) (2018), *Protean Power. Exploring the Uncertain and Unexpected in World Politics*. Cambridge UK: Cambridge University Press.

Shah, A. (2007), 'Institutional Arrangements for Intergovernmental Fiscal Transfers and a Framework for Evaluation', in R. Boadway and A. Shah (eds) *Intergovernmental Fiscal Transfers: Principles and Practices*. Washington DC: The World Bank, pp. 293–317.

Sharman, C. (1990), 'Parliamentary Federations and Limited Government. Constitutional Design and Redesign in Australia and Canada', *Journal of Theoretical Politics* 2 (2), 205–30.

Shaw, C. (2011), 'Classifying and Mapping the OMC in Different Policy Areas', in U. Diedrichs, W. Reiners and W. Wessels (eds) *The Dynamics of Change in EU Governance*. Cheltenham UK, Northampton MA: Edward Elgar Publishing, pp. 52–79.

Simmons, J. (2017), 'Canadian Multilateral Intergovernmental Institutions and the Limits of Institutional Innovation', *Regional & Federal Studies*, 27 (5), 573–96.

Simon, H. (1962), 'The Architecture of Complexity', *Proceedings of the American Philosophical Society* 106 (6), 467–82.

Smart, M. (2007), 'The Incentive Effects of Grants', in R. Boadway and A. Shah (eds) *Intergovernmental Fiscal Transfers: Principles and Practices*. Washington, DC: The World Bank, pp. 203–22.

Smith, A. ([1776] 1993), *An Inquiry into the Nature and Causes of the Wealth of Nations*, K. Sutherland (ed). Oxford: Oxford University Press.

Somer, M. and McCoy, J. (2018), 'Déjà vu? Polarization and Endangered Democracies in the 21st Century', *American Behavioral Scientist* 62 (1), 3–15.

Sørensen, G. (2004), *The Transformation of the State. Beyond the Myth of Retreat*. New York: Palgrave Macmillan.

Spencer, P. and Wollman, H. (2002), *Nationalism: A Critical Introduction*. London: Sage.

Steffek, J. (2023), 'Triangulating the Legitimacy of International Organizations: Beliefs, Discourses, and Actions', *International Studies Review* 25 (4), viad054. doi: https://doi.org/10.1093/isr/viad054

Stephenson, P. (2013), 'Twenty Years of Multi-level Governance. Where Does it Come from? What Is it? Where Is it Going?', *Journal of European Public Policy* 20 (6), 817–37.

Stilwell, F. (2019), *The Political Economy of Inequality*. Cambridge UK: Polity Press.

Stimson, R., Stough, R. R. and Nijkamp, P. (2011), 'Endogenous Regional Development', in R. Stimson, R. R. Stough and P. Nijkamp (eds) *Endogenous Regional Development*. Cheltenham UK, Northampton MA: Edward Elgar Publishing, pp. 1–19.

Stoker, G. (1998), 'Governance as Theory: Five Propositions', *International Social Science Journal* 50 (155), 17–28.

Stone, C. N. (1993), 'Urban Regimes and the Capacity to Govern: A Political Economy Approach', *Journal of Urban Affairs* 15 (1), 1–28.

Stone, D. and Ladi, S. (2015), 'Global Public Policy and Transnational Administration', *Public Administration* 93 (4), 839–55.

Stone, D. and Moloney, K. (ed) (2019), *The Oxford Handbook of Global Policy and Transnational Administration*. Oxford: Oxford University Press.

Streeck, W. (2014), *Buying Time: The Delayed Crisis of Democratic Capitalism*. New York: Verso Books.

Stubb, A. C.-G. (1996), 'A Categorization of Differentiated Integration', *Journal of Common Market Studies* 34 (2), 283–95.

Swenden, W. (2006), *Federalism and Regionalism in Western Europe. A Comparative and Thematic Analysis*. Basingstoke: Palgrave.

Swenden, W. and Toubeau, S. (2013), 'Mainstream Parties and Territorial Dynamics in the UK, Spain, and India', in A. Benz and J. Broschek (eds) *Federal Dynamics: Continuity, Change, and the Varieties of Federalism*. Oxford: Oxford University Press, pp. 249–73.

Tannenberg, M. et al. (2021), 'Claiming the Right to Rule: Regime Legitimation Strategies from 1900 to 2019', *European Political Science Review* 13 (1), 77–94.

Tapscott, R. (2021), *Arbitrary States: Social Control and Modern Authoritarianism in Museveni's Uganda*. Oxford: Oxford University Press.

Tarlton, C. D. (1965), 'Symmetry and Asymmetry as Elements of Federalism', *Journal of Politics* 27 (4), 861–74.

Tavares, A. F. (2018), 'Municipal Amalgamations and their Effects: A Literature Review', *Miscellanea Geographica* 22 (1), 5–15.

Tavares, R. (2016), *Paradiplomacy: Cities and States as Global Players*. Oxford: Oxford University Press.

Télo, M. (2014), 'Introduction: Globalization, New Regionalism and the Role of the European Union', in M. Télo (ed) *European Union and New Regionalism: Competing Regionalism and Global Governance in a Post-Hegemonic Era*. Farnham UK, Burlington VT: Ashgate, pp. 1–22.

Thiel, A., Blomquist, W. and Garrick, D. E. (eds) (2019), *Governing Complexity. Analyzing and Applying Polycentricity*. Cambridge UK: Cambridge University Press.

Tholoniat, L. (2010), 'The Career of the Open Method of Coordination: Lessons from a "Soft" EU Instrument', *West European Politics* 33 (1), 93–117.

Thorlakson, L. (2006), 'Building Firewalls or Floodgates? Constitutional Design for the European Union', *Journal of Common Market Studies* 44 (1), 139–59.

Thorlakson, L. (2020), *Multi-Level Democracy. Integration and Independence Among Party System, Parties, and Voters in Seven Federal Systems*. Oxford: Oxford University Press.

Tiebout, C. M. (1956), 'A Pure Theory of Local Expenditures', *Journal of Political Economy* 65 (5), 416–24.

Timmermans, A. (2001), 'Arenas as Institutional Sites for Policymaking: Patterns and Effects in Comparative Perspective', *Journal of Comparative Policy Analysis* 3 (3), 311–37.

Tömmel, I. and Verdun, A. (eds) (2009), *Innovative Governance in the European Union. The Politics of Multilevel Policymaking*. Boulder CO: Lynne Rienner.

Torfing, J. (2022), 'Metagovernance', in C. Ansell and J. Torfing (eds) *Handbook on Theories of Governance*. 2nd edn. Cheltenham UK, Northampton MA: Edward Elgar Publishing, pp. 567–79.

Tortola, P. D. (2017), 'Clarifying Multilevel Governance', *European Journal of Political Research* 56 (2), 234–50.

Towmey, A. and Withers, G. (2007), *Federalist Paper I: Australia's Federal Future*. A Report for the Council for the Australian Federation. Canberra: Council for the Australian Federation. Available at: https://crawford.anu.edu.au/pdf/staff/glenn_withers/federalist_paper.pdf (Accessed 1 May 2024).

Trein, P. (2022), 'Multilevel Governance', in P. Graziano and J. Tosun (eds) *Elgar Encyclopedia of European Union Public Policy*. Cheltenham UK, Northampton MA: Edward Elgar Publishing, pp. 62–70.

Treisman, D. (2007), *The Architecture of Government: Rethinking Political Decentralization*. Cambridge UK, New York: Cambridge University Press.

Tridico, P. (2017), *Inequality in Financial Capitalism*. Abingdon, New York: Routledge.

Trondal, J. (2013), 'International Bureaucracy. Organizational Structure and Behavioural Implications', in B. Reinalda (ed), *Routledge Handbook of International Organization*. London: Routledge, 162–75.

Trondal, J. et al. (eds) (2022), *Governing Complexity in Times of Turbulence*. Cheltenham UK, Northampton MA: Edward Elgar Publishing.

Tsebelis, G. (2002), *Veto Players. How Political Institutions Work*. Princeton NJ: Princeton University Press.

Tully, J. (2003), 'Identity Politics', in T. Ball and R. Bellamy (eds) *The Cambridge History of Twentieth-Century Political Thought*. Cambridge UK: Cambridge University Press, pp. 517–33.

Tushnet, M. V. (2015), *The Constitution of the United States of America. A Contextual Analysis*. Oxford, Portland: Hart.

Vampa, D. (2021), 'COVID-19 and Territorial Policy Dynamics in Western Europe: Comparing France, Spain, Italy, Germany, and the United Kingdom', *Publius: The Journal of Federalism* 51 (4), 601–26.

VanNijnhatten, D. L. (2021), 'From Sustainability to Resilience: Multilevel Governance as Adaptive Governance', in A. Benz, J. Broschek and M. Lederer (eds) *A Research Agenda for Multilevel Governance*. Cheltenham UK, Northampton MA: Edward Elgar Publishing, pp. 243–59.

Voigt, S. (1999), *Explaining Constitutional Change: A Positive Economics Approach*. Cheltenham UK, Northampton MA: Edward Elgar Publishing.

Volden, C. and Shipan, C. R. (2008), 'The Mechanisms of Policy Diffusion', *American Journal of Political Science* 52 (4), 840–57.

Vosskuhle, A. (2010), 'Multilevel Cooperation of the European Constitutional Courts. Der Europäische Verfassungsgerichtsverbund', *European Constitutional Law Review* 6 (2), 175–98.

Wannop, U. (1997), 'Regional Planning and Urban Governance in Europe and the USA', in M. Keating and J. Loughlin (eds), *The Political Economy of Regionalism.* London, Portland OR: Frank Cass, pp. 139–70.

Watts, R. L. (2005), *A Comparative Perspective on Asymmetry in Federations.* Asymmetry Series 2005 (4). Kingston: IIGR, Queen's University. Available at: https://www.queensu.ca/iigr/sites/iirwww/files/uploaded_files/Watts2005.pdf (Accessed 1 May 2024).

Weaver, R. K. (1986), 'The Politics of Blame Avoidance', *Journal of Public Policy* 6 (4), 371–98.

Webber, J. (2015), *The Constitution of Canada. A Contextual Analysis.* Oxford: Hart Publishing.

Wechsler, H. (1954), 'The Political Safeguards of Federalism: The Role of the States in the Composition and Selection of the National Government', *Columbia Law Review* 54 (4), 543–60.

Weible, C. M. (ed) (2023), *Theories of the Policy Process.* 5th edn. London: Routledge.

Weingast, B. R. (1995), 'The Economic Role of Political Institutions: Market-Preserving Federalism and Economic Development', *Journal of Law, Economics, and Organization* 11 (1), 1–31.

Wellisch, D. (2000), *Theory of Public Finance in a Federal State.* Cambridge UK, New York: Cambridge University Press.

White, J. (2019), *Politics of Last Resort: Governing by Emergency in the European Union.* Oxford: Oxford University Press.

Wibbels, E. (2005), *Federalism and the Market. Intergovernmental Conflict and Economic Reform in the Developing World.* Cambridge UK: Cambridge University Press.

Wilson, C. A. (2000), 'Policy Regimes and Policy Change', *Journal of Public Policy* 20 (3), 247–74.

Winkler, H. (2019), 'The Effect of Income Inequality on Political Polarization: Evidence from European Regions, 2002–2014', *Economics & Politics* 31 (2), 137–62.

Wolf, K. D. (1999), 'The New Raison d'Etat as a Problem for Democracy in World Society', *European Journal of International Relations* 5 (3), 333–63.

Wolf, K. D. (2006), 'Private Actors and the Legitimacy of Governance Beyond the State. Conceptional Outlines and Empirical Explorations', in A. Benz and Y. Papadopoulos (eds) *Governance and Democracy – Comparing National, European and Transnational Experiences.* London: Routledge, pp. 200–27.

Younge, G. (2019), 'The Politics of Identity: From Potential to Pitfalls, and Symbols to Substance', *Identities* 26 (1), 1–11.

Zartman, I. W. (2002), 'The Structure of Negotiation', in V. A. Kremenyuk (ed*) International Negotiation. Analysis, Approaches, Issues.* 2nd edn. San Francisco: Jossey-Bass, pp. 71–84.

Zartman, I. W. (2007), 'Introduction. Towards the Resolution of International Conflicts', in I. W. Zartman (ed) *Peacemaking in International Conflicts. Methods and Techniques.* Revised edn. Washington DC: United States Institute of Peace, pp. 3–23.

Zuber, C. I. (2011), 'Understanding the Multinational Game: Toward a Theory of Asymmetrical Federalism', *Comparative Political Studies* 44 (5), 546–71.

Zumbansen, P. (2012), 'Governance: An Interdisciplinary Perspective', in D. Levi-Faur (ed) *The Oxford Handbook of Governance*. Oxford: Oxford University Press, 83–96.

Zürn, M. (2010), 'Global Governance as Multi-level Governance', in H. Enderlein, S. Wälti and M. Zürn (eds), *Handbook on Multi-level Governance*. Cheltenham UK, Northampton MA: Edward Elgar Publishing, pp. 80–99.

Zürn, M. (2018), *A Theory of Global Governance. Authority, Legitimacy, and Contestation*. Oxford: Oxford University Press.

Zürn, M., Tokhi, A. and Binder, M. (2021), 'The International Authority Database', *Global Policy* 12 (4), 430–42.

Zürn, M., Wälti, S. and Enderlein, H. (2010), 'Introduction', in H. Enderlein, S. Wälti and M. Zürn, (eds) *Handbook on Multi-Level Governance*. Cheltenham UK, Northampton MA: Edward Elgar Publishing, pp. 1–13.

Index